W9-COJ-125

HUMAN VALUES
AND
ECONOMIC POLICY

A SYMPOSIUM

Edited by Sidney Hook

New York University Press   1967

© 1967 BY NEW YORK UNIVERSITY
LIBRARY OF CONGRESS CATALOG CARD NUMBER: 67–25040
MANUFACTURED IN THE UNITED STATES OF AMERICA

The contents of this volume comprise the proceedings of the eighth annual New York University Institute of Philosophy, held at Washington Square, New York, May 13–14, 1966. Previous volumes in the series, also edited by Sidney Hook, are:

Determinism and Freedom in the Age of Modern Science
Psychoanalysis, Scientific Method, and Philosophy
Dimensions of Mind
Religious Experience and Truth
Philosophy and History
Law and Philosophy
Art and Philosophy

HUMAN VALUES AND ECONOMIC POLICY

Contents

Preface

IN THE LIGHT of the continuing program of the New York University Institute of Philosophy it was to be expected that we would take as one of our themes problems apparently common to the disciplines of economics and philosophy. American philosophers, in the course of their professional associations, have met in occasional joint sessions with physical scientists, biologists, psychologists, jurists, historians, and other practitioners of the arts and sciences. I do not recall, however, any meeting between economists and philosophers, although from time to time individual philosophers and economists of distinction have been invited to appear on the programs organized by one group or the other.

This relative indifference to one another's intellectual interests is strange for two reasons. However economies be defined, it has always been concerned with problems of wealth and welfare— which are conspicuously problems of value—and however philosophy be defined, it has traditionally been concerned with a *normative* approach to judgments of value. To the extent that philosophy is more than a method of conceptual analysis, its continuing subject matter has been the nature of good and evil in man and society, and the cosmic and epistemic issues presumably related to the question of the good life in the good society. Until recently the philosopher has always been a moralist, although few moralists have been distinguished philosophers.

Secondly, the great philosophers have concerned themselves with economic questions to a point where the history of philosophic thought and the history of economic thought are to some extent overlapping. Adam Smith, John Stuart Mill, and John Maynard Keynes were philosophers. Aristotle wrote on the problems of household economy. Although it would be somewhat farfetched to assert that his influence has stretched to those today who naively take the model of household economy as a model for our social or public economy, and wonder how we can live with a permanently unbalanced budget, it does testify to the fact that the intelligent quest for desirable ends in a world of limited resources requires reflective consideration of economic means. On the other hand, some academic economists have been drawn to their discipline by the strength of their interest in moral problems. Thus Alfred Marshall relates that his desire to answer troubling questions in the "Moral Sciences" led to his resolution to study Political Economy.

The reasons for the estrangement between philosophy and economics in recent times are many and complex. And although there are signs of convergence of interest in the methodological questions involved in the theory of rational decision, philosophers and economists seem to be still far apart, often talking past each other when talking with each other, even when they talk about the nature and problems of social and individual welfare. The Conference was in the nature of an intellectual experiment to determine the relevance of the theoretical and practical approach of economists today to the normative questions of value that have been the continuing concern of philosophers.

The assessment of the upshot of the confrontation must be made by the reader. Most of the participants agreed that it was a rewarding experience although they would be hard put to it to justify their judgment in purely economic terms.

The New York University Institute of Philosophy is grateful to the Committee for Economic Development for helping to underwrite the costs of the sessions, and to Mr. Lawrence R. Kegan, Director of Special Studies, for his invaluable assistance in organizing the program of the Eighth Annual Conference.

Sidney Hook

HUMAN VALUES AND ECONOMIC POLICY

PART I
Public and Private Values

A

Public and Private Values

KENNETH J. ARROW
Stanford University

I. VALUES OF A SINGLE INDIVIDUAL

AS AN EXERCISE in clarifying terminology, let us consider what can be said about the values of an imaginary, completely isolated individual. His personal skills and qualities and the physical world available to him jointly delimit a range of *actions* possible to him. To be precise, I shall so define the concept of action that alternative actions are mutually exclusive. An action, then, means a complete description of all the activities that an individual carries on, and two alternative actions are any two descriptions that differ in any relevant way. For example, an individual may describe his activities by indicating the amount of time he spends on each of the alternative modalities of performance available to him; thus, three hours at farming, three hours at hunting, four hours of violin playing, etc. A change in any one of these time allocations would represent a change in action. This particular definition is truly a formal choice of language, and does not by itself change the nature of the problem. It simply brings out formally that the basic question of the individual is a choice of actions.

1. *Values, Tastes, and Hypothetical Imperatives*

To an economist, and I suppose to most philosophers, a value system would, in these terms, be simply the rule an individual uses to choose which of the mutually exclusive actions he will undertake. If an individual is facing a given set of al-

3

ternative actions, he will choose one, and there seems to be
little of interest to talk about. However, the problem, at least
to the economist, is put in slightly different form. Consider an
individual who does not yet know which actions will be available and which will not. Let us term the set of available actions
the *environment*. One might ask him what action he *would
choose* if offered some particular environment. By repeating
this question for many alternative environments, we have ob-
tained a description of his value system in the sense of a rule
giving his hypothetical choice for many or all possible environments.[1]

One might want to reserve the term "values" for a specially
elevated or noble set of choices. Perhaps choices in general
might be referred to as "tastes." We do not ordinarily think of
the preference for additional bread over additional beer as
being a value worthy of philosophic inquiry. I believe, though,
that the distinction cannot be made logically, and certainly not
in dealing with the single isolated individual. If there is any
distinction between values and tastes, it must lie in the realm of
interpersonal relations.

2. *The Assumptions of Ordering*

The description of a value system as a correlation between
possible environments and the hypothetical choices to be made
from them is not by itself a very informative procedure. Economists have been accustomed to adding considerable strength
(empirical restrictiveness) by specifying that the value system
shall have a particular structure, namely, being derivable from
an *ordering*. To define this concept, let us first consider environments consisting of just two alternative actions. For such
two-member environments we can find the one chosen, in accordance with the individual's value system, and we will speak
of it as having been preferred to the other action in the environment. We may have to admit that the individual is equally
willing to choose neither of the two actions, in which case we
speak of the two actions as being *indifferent*. The assumption

of an ordering means that certain consistency assumptions are postulated about the relations of preference and indifference, and it is further assumed that choices from any environment can be described in terms of the ordering, which relates to choices in two-member environments.

The first assumption is that of *connexity* (or connectedness, or completeness, or comparability). It is assumed that for each pair of alternatives, either one is preferred to the other or the two are indifferent. The second assumption is that of transitivity. Consider three alternatives, to be designated by A, B, and C. Then if A is preferred to B, and B is preferred to C, we assume that A is preferred to C. We can and must also include in the definition cases where some of the choices are indifferent; for example, if A is indifferent to B, and B is indifferent to C, then A is indifferent to C.

Finally, and perhaps most important, it is assumed that the choice from any environment is determined by the ordering, in the sense that if there is an alternative that is preferred to every other alternative in the environment, then it is the chosen element. This is an additional assumption not logically implied by the existence of an ordering itself.

Obviously, the assumption of ordering is by no means unreasonable. The notion of connexity carries the idea that choices have to be made, whether we will or no. The idea of transitivity clearly corresponds to some strong feeling of the meaning of consistency in our choice. Economists have typically identified the concept of rationality with the notion of choices derivable from an ordering.

It may be worthwhile to dwell on the meaning of these two assumptions a little more, in view of their importance. It is not at all uncommon to find denials of the connexity assumption. Sufficiently remote alternatives are held to be incomparable. But I must say I do not find this line of argument at all convincing. If a choice has to be made, it has to be made. In most practical choice situations there is some *null* alternative, which will be chosen in the absence of what might be termed a positive decision. Thus, if there is dispute about the nature of new legislation, the preexisting legislation remains in force. But this does not mean that no choice is made; it means rather that the system produces as its choice the null alternatives. I think what those who emphasize incomparability have in mind is rather that if one is forced to make a choice between alternatives that are difficult to compare, then the choice is not apt to satisfy the assumption of transitivity.

The possibility of regarding inaction as an always available alternative is part of the broader question of whether or not social choices should be historically conditioned. It is here that the importance of transitivity becomes clear. Transitivity implies that the final choice made from any given environment is independent of the path by which it has been derived. From any environment there will be a given chosen alternative, and in the absence of a deadlock no place for the historically given alternatives to be chosen by default.

3. *Independence of Irrelevant Alternatives*

Since the chosen element from any environment is completely defined by knowledge of the preferences as between it and any other alternative in the environment, it follows that the choice depends only on the ordering of the elements of that environment. In particular, the choice made does not depend on preferences as between alternatives that are not in fact available in the given environment, nor, and this is probably more important, on preferences as between elements in the environment and those not in the environment. It is never necessary to compare available alternatives with those that are not available at a given moment in order to arrive at a decision. It is this point that is being made when it is argued that only ordinal measures of utility or preference are relevant to decisions. Any cardinal measure, any attempt to give a numerical representation of utility, depends basically on comparisons involving alternative actions that are not, or at least may not be, available, given the environment prevailing at the moment.

4. *Omitted Considerations*

For the sake of economy of discussion, we pass by many interesting issues. Most important, probably, is the relation between hypothetical choices and real ones. It is implied in the above discussion, and below, that a preference will in fact be translated into a choice if the opportunity ever comes. But the question may be raised how we can possibly know about hypothetical choices if they are not actually made. This is not merely a problem of finding out about somebody else's values; we may not know our own values until put to the crucial test.

Even the actual preferences may not be regarded as in some sense true values. An observer looking from the outside on our isolated individual may say that his decision was wrong either in the sense that there is some other standard of values to which it does not conform or in the sense that it was made on the grounds of insufficient information or improper calculation. The latter possibility is a real one, but I will simply state that I am abstracting from it in the course of the present discussion. The former interpretation I am rejecting here. For the single isolated individual there can be no other standard than his own values. He might indeed wish to change them under criticism, but this, I take it, means basically that he hasn't fully thought through or calculated the consequences of his actions and, upon more consideration, wishes to modify them.

II. PUBLIC VALUES

1. *Interpersonal Nature of Social Action*

The fundamental fact that causes the need for discussing public values at all is that all significant actions involve joint participation of many individuals. As economic textbooks are fond of noting, even the apparently simplest act of production involves the participation of a whole society.

It is important to note that this observation tells us all nontrivial actions are essentially the property of society as a whole, not of individuals. It is quite customary in economics to think of each individual as being able to undertake actions on his own (decisions of consumption, production, and exchange). Formally, a social action is then taken to be the resultant of all individual actions. In other words, any social action is thought of as being factored into a sequence of individual actions.

I certainly do not wish to deny that such factoring takes place, but I do wish to emphasize that the partition of a social action into individual components, and the corresponding assignment of individual responsibility, is *not* a datum. Rather, the particular factoring in any given context is itself the result of a social policy and therefore already the outcome of earlier and logically more primitive social values.

In economic transactions the point is clearest when we consider what we call property. Property is clearly a creation of society through its legal structure. The actions of buying and selling through offers of property are only at a superficial level the actions of an individual. They reflect a whole series of social institutions, and with different institutions different people would be having control over any given piece of property. Furthermore, the very notion of control over one's "own" property, as is apparent upon the most casual inspection, itself acquires its meaning through the regulations of society.

These are no idle or excessively nice distinctions. When it comes to racial discrimination, notions of liability and responsibility for injury to others, or the whole concept of a corporation and its special and complex relations to the world as a whole, economic and social, we know that social values have altered considerably the terms on which property can be used in the marketplace or transmitted to others. Needless to say, the taxation system constitutes one of the strongest examples in which the state, as one aspect of society, makes clear the relative nature of ownership. Nor, in this context, should it be forgotten that the claims of society, as modifying the concept of ownership, are by no means confined to the state. Our particular culture has tended to minimize noncoercive obligations relative to the predominant role they have played elsewhere, but they are far from absent even today. There is certainly a whole complex of obligations implied in the concept of a "good neighbor." The use of one's real property is limited by more than legal conditions. As everyone knows—sometimes painfully—there are obligations of generosity and organized giving appropriate to an individual's income status and social position. In short, we argue that the facts of social life show clearly that there is no universally acceptable division of actions with regard to property into mine and thine.

To be sure, there is another category of actions, those that involve the person himself as opposed to his property. We have a stronger feeling here that there is a natural meaning to speaking of one's own actions as opposed to others. Presumably there is a meaningful sense in which we say that *I* am writing this paper—not anyone else. But of course even here the action is full of social interconnections. I am here in a conference arranged by others, using words that are a common part of the culture, expressing ideas that draw upon a wide range of concepts of others, and which embody my education.

Of course, I am using my own capacities at some point in this process. But how logically do we distinguish between the capacities that somehow define the person, and those that are the result of external actions of a society? I may see well because my vision is intrinsically good or because I have glasses. Is the vision more peculiarly *mine* in one case than in the other? One may concede that there is more of an intrinsic idea of property here in certain personal actions, but I think this whole matter needs deeper exploration than it has received thus far. In any case, there are obviously very strong social obligations on personal behavior and the use of one's personal capacities, just as there are on the use of property.

To conclude, then, we must in a general theory take as our unit a social action, that is, an action involving a large proportion or the entire domain of society. At the most basic axiomatic level, individual actions play little role. The need for a system of public values then becomes evident; actions being collective or interpersonal in nature, so must the choice be among them. A public or social value system is essentially a logical necessity.

This point is very important to emphasize because it is also true that economic analysis has supplied us with a model of factorization of social actions, that achieved through the price system. The system itself is certainly one of the most remarkable of social institutions and the analysis of its working is, in my judgment, one of the more significant intellectual achievements of mankind. But the factorization implied is a particular one made in a particular way. It is one that has turned out to be highly convenient, particularly from the point of view of economizing on the flow of information in the economic system. But at the fundamental level of discourse we are now engaged in we cannot regard the price system as a datum. On the contrary, it is to be thought of as one of the instrumentalities, possibly the major one, by which whatever social value system there may be is realized.

2. *Individual Preferences for Social Actions*

The individual plays a central role in social choice as the judge of alternative social actions according to his own standards. We presume that each individual has some way of ranking social actions according to his preferences for their consequences. These preferences constitute his value system. They are assumed to reflect already in full measure altruistic or egoistic motivations, as the case may be.

Following the discussion in Part I, we assume that the values are expressed in the form of an ordering. Thus, in effect, individuals are taken to be rational in their attitudes toward social actions.

We are face to face with an extremely difficult point. A standard liberal point of view, which has dominated formal welfare economics, asserts that an individual's preferences are, or ought to be (a distinction not usually made clear), concerned only with the effects of social actions on him. But there is no logical way to distinguish a particular class of consequences that pertain to a given individual. If I feel that my satisfaction is reduced by somebody else's poverty (or, for that matter, by somebody else's wealth), then I am injured in precisely the same sense as if my purchasing power were reduced. To parallel the observations of the preceding section, I am in effect arguing here that just as we cannot factor social actions so as to make each component pertain to a given individual, so we cannot factor the consequences of social actions in any meaningful way into separable consequences to individual members of the society. That is, let me make it clear, we cannot do it as a matter of fact. The interdependence of mankind is after all not a novel ethical doctrine. The man who questioned whether he was his brother's keeper was, according to an ancient source, not highly approved of. The general conclusion here is not one that I find myself entirely comfortable with. I do share the general liberal view that every individual should have the opportunity to find his own way to personal development and satisfaction. The question of interferences with the actions of others has been raised most acutely in recent years in legal rather than economic contexts, specifically in the English discussion on laws regulating deviant sexual behavior. Homosexual behavior between consenting adults is presumably a classic example of an action affecting no one else, and therefore should be exempt from social control. Yet many find themselves shocked and outraged. They would strongly prefer, let us say, the situation to be different. Similarly, I may be disturbed that the Negro is discriminated against and judge accordingly social actions that lead to this result.

One could of course say that the general principle of restraint in judging the affairs of others is an empirical assumption, that people in fact do not care about (or strictly have no preferences concerning) matters that would in the usual terminology be regarded as none of their business. But of course empirically we know that this is quite false. The very fact that restrictive legislation is passed or even proposed shows clearly that people are willing to sacrifice effort and time because of the satisfactions to be received from seeing others' patterns of life altered.

The only rational defense of what may be termed a liberal position, or perhaps more precisely a principle of limited social preference, is that it is itself a value judgment. In other words, an individual may have as part of his value structure precisely that he does not think it proper to influence consequences outside a limited realm. This is a perfectly coherent position, but I find it difficult to insist that this judgment is of such overriding importance that it outweighs all other considerations. Personally, my values are such that I am willing to go very far indeed in the direction of respect for the means by which others choose to derive their satisfactions.

At this stage I want to emphasize that value judgments in favor of limited social preference, just as other value judgments, emphasizing social solidarity, must be counted as part of the value systems that individuals use in the judgment of alternative social actions.

III. WELFARE JUDGMENTS AND THE AGGREGATION OF PREFERENCES

The problem of social choice is the aggregation of the multiplicity of individual preference scales about alternative social actions.

1. *Welfare Judgments and Constitutions*

Classical utilitarianism specifies that alternative social actions be judged in terms of their consequences for people. In the present terminology I take this to mean that they are to be judged in terms of the individual preference scales. This by itself does not supply a sufficient basis for action in view of the multiplicity and divergence of individual preference scales. It is therefore at least implicit in classical utilitarianism that there is a second level at which the individual judgments are themselves evaluated, and this point has been given explicit recognition in a classic paper of Abram Bergson.[2] Let us call this second-order evaluation a *welfare judgment;* it is an evaluation of the consequences to all individuals based on their evaluations. If in each individual evaluation two social actions are indifferent, then the welfare judgment as between the two must also be one of indifference.

The process of formation of welfare judgments is logically equivalent to a social decision process or *constitution.* Specifically, a constitution is a rule that associates to each possible set of individual orderings a social choice function, i.e., a rule for selecting a preferred action out of every possible environment. That a welfare judgment is a constitution indeed follows immediately from the assumption that a welfare judgment can be formed given any set of individual preference systems for social actions. The classification of welfare judgments as constitutions is at this stage a tautology, but what makes it more than that is a specification of reasonable conditions to be imposed on constitutions, and it is here that any dispute must lie.

2. *Social Decision Processes and the Notion of Social Welfare*

While I have just argued that a welfare judgment is necessarily a constitution or process of social decision, the converse need not be true, at least not without further clarification of the meaning of "welfare judgment." A welfare judgment requires that some one person is judge; a rule for arriving at social decisions may be agreed upon for reasons of convenience and necessity without its outcomes being treated as evaluations by anyone in particular.[3] Indeed, I would go further and argue that the appropriate standpoint for analyzing social decision processes is precisely that they not be welfare judgments of any particular individuals. This seems contrary to Bergson's point of view.[4] In my view, the location of welfare judgments

in any individual, while logically possible, does not appear to
be very interesting. "Social welfare" is related to social policy
in any sensible interpretation; the welfare judgments of any
single individual are unconnected with action and therefore
sterile. In a more recent paper Bergson has recognized that
there may be this alternative interpretation of the concept of
social welfare; I quote the passage at length since it displays
the issue so well: "I have been assuming that the concern of
welfare economics is to counsel individual citizens generally.
If a public official is counseled, it is on the same basis as any
other citizen. In every instance reference is made to some ethical values which are appropriate for the counseling of the individual in question. In all this I believe I am only expressing the
intent of welfare writings generally; or if this is not the intent,
I think it should be. But some may be inclined nevertheless to
a different conception, which allows still another interpretation
of Arrow's theorem. *According to this view, the problem is to
counsel not citizens generally but public officials.* [Emphasis
added.] Furthermore, the values to be taken as data are not
those which would guide the official if he were a private citizen.
The official is envisaged instead as more or less neutral ethically. His one aim in life is to implement the values of other
citizens as given by some rule of collective decision making." [5]
My interpretation of the social choice problem agrees fully
with that given by Bergson beginning with the italicized statement, though, as can be seen, this is not the view that he himself endorses.

IV. SOME CONDITIONS FOR A SOCIAL DECISION PROCESS AND THE IMPOSSIBILITY THEOREM

The fundamental problem of public value formation, then,
is the construction of constitutions. In general, of course, there
is no difficulty in constructing a rule if one is content with arbitrary ones. The problem becomes meaningful if reasonable
conditions are suggested, which every constitution should
obey.[6]

1. *Some Conditions on Constitutions*

I suggest here four conditions that seem very reasonable to impose on any constitution. More can undoubtedly be suggested, but unfortunately, as we shall see in Section 2 below, these four more than suffice.

Recall that a constitution is a rule that assigns to any set of individual preference orderings a rule for making society's choices among alternative social actions in any possible environment. Thus, for a given set of individual orderings the result of the process is a particular social value system in the sense of Part I; that is, a rule for making selections out of all possible environments. The first condition may be termed that of

> *Collective Rationality:* For any given set of orderings, the social choice function is derivable from an ordering.

In other words, social choice system has the same structure as that which we have already assumed for individual value systems. The next condition is one that has been little disputed and is advanced by almost every writer in the economic literature:

> *Pareto Principle:* If alternative A is preferred to alternative B by every single individual according to his ordering, then the social ordering also ranks A above B.

Notice that we can use the term "social ordering" in view of the previous condition of Collective Rationality. The next condition is perhaps the most important, as well as the most controversial. For my own part, I am less tempted to regard it as ultimately satisfactory than I formerly did, but it has strong pragmatic justification:

> *Independence of Irrelevant Alternatives:* The social choice made from any environment depends only on the orderings of individuals with respect to the alternatives in that environment.

To take an extreme case, suppose that individuals are informed that there are a certain number of social actions available. They are not even aware that there are other conceivable social actions. They develop their own preference systems for the alternatives contained in this particular environment, and then the constitution generates a choice. Later they are told that in fact there were alternatives that were logically possible but were not in fact available. For example, a city is taking a poll of individual preferences on alternative methods of transportation (rapid transit, automobile, bus, etc.). Someone suggests that in evaluating these preferences they also ought to ask individual preferences for instantaneous transportation by dissolving the individual into molecules in a ray gun and reforming him elsewhere in the city as desired. There is no pretense that this method is in any way an available alternative. The assumption of Independence of Irrelevant Alternatives is that such preferences have no bearing on the choice to be made.

It is of course obvious that ordinary political decision-making methods satisfy this condition. When choosing among candidates for an elected office, all that is asked are the preferences among the actual candidates, not also preferences among other individuals who are not candidates and who are not available for office.

It will also be worth noting that the allocation of resources through the price system satisfies the condition of Independence of Irrelevant Alternatives. If we alter the utility functions of individuals with respect to allocations that are socially infeasible, we do not alter any competitive equilibrium. Indeed, decentralization of knowledge, which is such a virtue in the market mechanism, is incompatible with the use of utility comparisons among irrelevant alternatives in arriving at resource allocations.[7]

Finally, we enunciate probably the least controversial of all the conditions:

Non-Dictatorship: There is no individual whose preferences are automatically society's preferences independent of the preferences of all other individuals.

There is a difference between the first two conditions and the last two that is worth noting. The assumptions of Collective Rationality and the Pareto Principle are statements that apply to any fixed set of individual orderings. They do not involve comparisons between social orderings based on different sets of individual orderings. On the contrary, the condition of Independence of Irrelevant Alternatives and of Non-Dictatorship are assertions about the responsiveness of the social ordering to variations in individual orderings.

2. *Impossibility Theorem*

The conditions of Collective Rationality and of the Independence of Irrelevant Alternatives taken together imply that in a generalized sense all methods of social choice are of the type of voting. If we consider environments composed of two alternatives alone, then the condition of Independence of Irrelevant Alternatives tells us that the choice is determined solely by the preferences of the members of the community as between those two alternatives, and no other preferences are involved. Define a set of individuals to be *decisive* for alternative A over alternative B if the constitution prescribes that A is chosen over B whenever all individuals in the set prefer A to B and all others prefer B to A. Then the rule for choosing from any two-member environment has the form of specifying which sets of individuals are decisive for A over B and which for B over A. The majority-voting principle, for example, states simply that any set containing a majority of the voters is decisive for any alternative over any other.

Then, if the social value system is generated by a social ordering, all social preferences are determined by the choices made for two-member environments, and hence by pairwise votes (thus systems like plurality voting are excluded).

Now it has been known for a long time that the system of majority voting can give rise to paradoxical consequences. Consider the following example. There are three alternatives, A, B, and C, among which choice is to be made. One-third of the voters prefer A to B and B to C, one-third prefer B to C and C to A, and one-third prefer C to A and A to B. Then A will be preferred to B by a majority, B to C by a majority, and C to A by a majority.[8]

One might be tempted to suppose that the paradox of voting is an imperfection in the particular system of majority voting, and more ingenious methods could avoid it. But unfortunately this is not so. The following general theorem may be stated:

> *There can be no constitution simultaneously satisfying the condition of Collective Rationality, the Pareto Principle, the Independence of Irrelevant Alternatives, and Non-Dictatorship.*[9]

This conclusion is quite embarrassing, and it forces us to examine the conditions that have been stated as reasonable. It's hard to imagine anyone quarreling either with the Pareto Principle or the condition of Non-Dictatorship. The principle of Collective Rationality may indeed be questioned. One might be prepared to allow that the choice from a given environment be independent of the history of previous choices made in earlier environments, but I think many would find that situation unstatisfactory. There remains, therefore, only the Independence of Irrelevant Alternatives, which we will now examine in greater detail.

3. *The Independence of Irrelevant Alternatives and Interpersonal Comparisons of Intensity*

Modern economic theory has insisted on the ordinal concept of utility; that is, only orderings can be observed, and therefore no measurement of utility independent of these orderings has any significance. In the field of consumer's-demand theory the ordinalist position turned out to create no problem; cardinal utility had no explanatory power above and beyond ordinal. Leibniz's Principle of the Identity of Indiscernibles demanded then the excision of cardinal utility from our thought patterns. Bergson's formulation of the social welfare function carried out the same principle in the analysis of social welfare. Social choices were to depend only on individual orderings; hence, welfare judgments were based only on interpersonally observable behavior.

The condition of Independence of Irrelevant Alternatives extends the requirement of observability one step farther. Given the set of alternatives available for society to choose among, it could be expected that ideally one could observe all preferences among the available alternatives, but there would be no way to observe preferences among alternatives not feasible for society.

I now feel, however, that the austerity imposed by this condition is stricter than desirable; in many situations we do have information on preferences for nonfeasible alternatives. It can certainly be argued that when available this information should be used in social choice. Unfortunately, it is clear, as I have already suggested, that social decision processes that are independent of irrelevant alternatives have strong practical advantages, and it remains to be seen whether a satisfactory social decision procedure can really be based on other information.

The potential usefulness of irrelevant alternatives is that they may permit empirically meaningful interpersonal comparisons. The information that might enable us to assert that one individual prefers alternative A to alternative B more strongly than a second individual prefers B to A must be based on comparisons by the two individuals of the two alternatives, not only with respect to each other but also to other alternatives.

Let me conclude by suggesting one type of use of irrelevant alternatives, which may be termed "extended sympathy." We do seem prepared to make comparisons of the form: Action A is better (or worse) for me than Action B is for you. This is probably in fact the standard way in which people make judgments about appropriate income distributions; if I am richer than you, I may find it easy to make the judgment that it is better for you to have the marginal dollar than for me.

How is this consistent with our general point of view that

all value judgments are at least hypothetical choices among alternative actions? Interpersonal comparisons of the extended sympathy type can be put in operational form. The judgment takes the form: It is better (in my judgment) to be myself under Action A than to be you under Action B.

In this form, the characteristics that define an individual are included in the comparison. In effect, these characteristics are put on a par with the items usually regarded as constituting an individual's wealth. The possession of tools is ordinarily regarded as part of the social state that is being evaluated; why not the possession of the skills to use those tools, and the intelligence that lies behind those skills? Individuals, in appraising each other's states of well-being, consider not only material possessions but also find themselves "desiring this man's scope and that man's art." [10] The principle of extended sympathy as a basis for interpersonal comparisons seems basic to many of the welfare judgments made in ordinary practice. It remains to be seen whether an adequate theory of social choice can be derived from this and other acceptable principles.

NOTES

1. For technical mathematical reasons one must admit that sometimes more than one action should be regarded as chosen in a given environment, by which is meant the individual does not care which of the chosen actions is in fact adopted in a particular set of circumstances. We must also allow for the fact that there may be no chosen action; for example of the latter, consider an individual with a normal desire for money who can choose any amount of gold less than (but not equal to) one ounce.

2. "A Reformulation of Certain Aspects of Welfare Economics," *Quarterly Journal of Economics*, LII (1938), 310–34; reprinted in A. Bergson, *Essays in Normative Economics* (Cambridge, Mass.: Harvard University Press, 1966), pp. 1–49.

3. This point has been well stressed by I. M. D. Little, "Social Choice and Individual Values," *Journal of Political Economy*, LX (1952), 422–32.

4. A. Bergson, "On the Concept of Social Welfare," *Quarterly Journal of Economics*, LXIII (1954), 233–52; reprinted in *Essays in Normative Economics, loc. cit.*, pp. 27–49, especially pp. 35–36.

5. A. Bergson, "On the Concept of Social Welfare," *Quarterly Journal of Economics*, p. 242; *Essays*, pp. 37–38.

6. The analysis that follows is based on my book, *Social Choice and Individual Values*, New York, London, and Sydney: Wiley, 1st ed., 1951; 2nd ed., 1963.

7. Since the market mechanism does satisfy the condition of Independence of Irrelevant Alternatives it must, in accordance with the Impossibility Theorem to be discussed in Section 2, violate another condition, that of Collective Rationality. This violation is precisely the well-known intersection of community indifference curves. Samuelson's social indifference curves (see P. A. Samuelson, "Social Indifference Curves," *Quarterly Journal of Economics*, LXX [1956] 1–22) satisfy the condition of Collective Rationality but violate that of Independence of Irrelevant Alternatives; the income redistribution associated with each change in social production possibilities requires a high degree of centralization of knowledge about individual preferences.

8. This paradox seems to have been first observed by the Marquis de Condorcet, *Essai sur l'application de l'analyse à la probabilité des décisions rendues à la pluralité des voix*, Paris, 1785. That a rational voting scheme requires knowledge of all preferences among the candidates and not only the first choice was already argued even earlier by Jean-Charles de Borda, "Mémoire sur les élections au scrutin," *Mémoires de l'Académie Royale des Sciences*, 1781, pp. 657–65. For a modern analysis of Condorcet's work on voting, see G.-G. Granger, *La Mathématique social du Marquis de Condorcet* (Paris: Presses Universitaires de France, 1956), especially pp. 94–129. For an English translation of Borda's work, see A. de Grazia, "Mathematical Derivation of an Election System," *Isis*, XLIV (1953), 42–51. For a general history of the theory of social choice, see D. Black, *The Theory of Committees and Elections* (Cambridge, England: Cambridge University Press, 1958), Part II.

9. Arrow, *op. cit.*, pp. 97–100.

10. The moral implications of the position that many attributes of the individual are similar in nature to external possessions have been discussed by V. C. Walsh, *Scarcity and Evil*, Englewood Cliffs, N.J.: Prentice-Hall, 1961.

B

Personal Values and the Justification of Institutions

RICHARD B. BRANDT
University of Michigan

PROFESSOR ARROW'S PAPER raises a number of questions that are of central concern to the moral, social, and political philosopher. I am by no means sure, however, that all of these questions are major concerns of Professor Arrow, or even that he was intending his paper as a contribution to the discussion of them. Since I believe, however, that the chief interest of his paper for the philosopher lies in its bearing on these issues, I propose to concentrate my attention on them. Hopefully, what I say may help to provide a bridge between the traditional problems and Professor Arrow's theoretical work.

I shall discuss two questions raised by the latter half of Arrow's paper: (1) Is a social institution or policy right or rational if and only if it is some function of the "rational preference-orderings" of all individuals? (2) If, in determining which of two "social actions" is right or rational, we are allowed to take into account not only individual preferences between their consequences but also between other things, to an unlimited extent, are we able to surmount the traditional problem of interpersonal comparisons? In order to explain some difficulties I find in his answers to these questions, I shall consider still a third question: (3) Is a person's transitive and complete ordering of alternatives for choice necessarily an order of better-and-worse from the point of view of the individual's own welfare?

For simplicity, Arrow has chosen to ignore the fact that choices are usually or always made in the face of some uncertainty as to outcomes. I shall follow him in this.

THE WELFARE OF INDIVIDUAL PERSONS

The first thing we must do is get before us what economists tend to mean by a "transitive and complete preference-ordering" by individuals.

When a person acts, he believes that his bodily behavior will initiate a chain of consequences, and that the world as a whole will be different, in view of this chain of consequences, from what it would have been otherwise.

A person does not, of course, have prevision, to any considerable extent, of the more remote repercussions of the chain of consequences that his bodily behavior sets in motion. But, at the time of choice, he *conceives* of his action as bringing about a world different in certain respects from what the world would be if he did something else, say a world with features F_1 as distinct from a world with features F_2. To that extent we may think of an action as the "selection" of a world.

We must, of course, make a distinction between the anticipated outcomes of bodily behavior, and the actual ones. This is necessary even for differentiating between intentional and unintentional behavior. For instance, if in my anxiety to be helpful to my hostess at tea, I inadvertently upset a tray and break her best china, we hardly wish to say that I "chose" to break the china. I *did* this ("Look what you did!"), but I did not *choose* to do it. In order to explain *choice*, we need the concept of "acting *in the belief* that . . ." To this extent, we cannot be behaviorists, although to the committed, doubtless a long story would be required to make this clear.

The selection of a world F_1 over F_2 (in the sense of deliberate initiation of a chain of consequences with that anticipated differential outcome) may be said to demonstrate the agent's *preference* for F_1 over F_2 in the sense of "is deliberately chosen in the face of clear awareness of the other possible set of outcomes." (We should be quite clear, however, that there is another ordinary sense of "prefers" that is not necessarily revealed by a person's deliberate behavior; we often say that a person does what he would much prefer not to do, e.g., when his obligations or duties conflict with what he personally wants or likes. We shall come back to this.)

Once we have this conception of a "preference" before us, we can consider a person's preferences as between various "worlds" (say a world conceived as F_3 over one conceived as F_4) when he does not in fact "choose" between them in his behavior. We can consider how he *would* choose between different worlds if he had the choice, and had the concepts of these different worlds before him. With a stretch of our imaginations, we can think of his comparing alternatives of indefinitely great complexity—say, two total alternative future biographies of the universe. We can think of our individual as either preferring one, or being indifferent as between every possible state of affairs in this sense. If his set of "preferences" is complete in this sense, and transitive (if he would choose A over B and B over C, he would choose A over C, and so on, *mutatis mutandis*, for indifference), it will then be said that the individual has a "rational preference-ordering" of possible worlds. (Obviously we do not know much about individuals' preference-ordering in this sense; and it is certain that human intellectual capacities are too small to entertain the concepts of alternatives beyond a certain degree of complexity, so that it is not clear what can be meant by their having a "preference" between them. But let us ignore this.)

As I understand Arrow, he is suggesting that a person's *value system* is very close to a person's rational preference-ordering in this sense, for he says that a person's value system is "a rule giving his hypothetical choice for many or all possible environments."

With apologies to extreme behaviorists, it should be noticed that among the features of alternative worlds that are important for action are subjective states of other persons. I may choose to do one thing, because I think the world produced by that action will contain joy in my daughter; I may do something else with the thought it will make someone angry. If we are to give a complete account of the kinds of alternatives between which people make choices, we must include these things; indeed, they are probably the most important grounds for choice. Whether we can know or how we know that our bodily behavior will eventuate in such states of affairs is a question of great importance, but that we do have "preferences" in the above sense that can be described only by mentioning the states of mind of other persons is beyond question.

I believe, or hope, that the foregoing conception of a "rational preference-ordering" is familiar and acceptable to writers on the theory of decisions. I wish now to sketch some distinctions that some such writers sometimes appear not to make, although it seems obvious, on reflection, that they ought to do so.

It is consistent with the foregoing conception to distinguish between that part of the anticipated outcome of bodily behavior which is motivating, and that part which is not. We sometimes know that some feature of a world was not a ground or reason for our choosing that world, and that had this feature been the only difference between two worlds, we should have been indifferent as between them. In contrast, there are other features that are reasons for choice; these features are pro or con points with respect to choice. These are the *motivating* features of the anticipated outcomes. We can subdivide these. Some features are motivating only because of further beliefs about them (say, about consequences), whereas some other features are motivating in themselves. These latter we may call *ultimate* grounds for choice. My anticipation that the selection of a crabmeat dinner will eventuate in a stomachache is such an ultimate ground for choice. It is not always easy to decide whether a feature of an expected outcome is an ultimate ground for choice; possibly most grounds for choice that are ultimate are *also* motivating for further reasons. For instance, I believe the anticipated stomachache will reduce my effectiveness at work tomorrow, and this thought about that outcome adds to its motivating power. Philosophers sometimes call a person's ultimate reasons for choice his "intrinsic values." In ordinary speech, I suspect, such intrinsic values are more what we have in mind when we talk of a person's "values" than the preference-ordering made on account of them, which Arrow identifies with a person's "values."

There is a sense in which the features of a world that motivate a person, and those that are ultimately motivating for him (his intrinsic values) are prior to preference-orderings of complex sets of outcomes. For if we are deciding whether to choose one world over another, we make up our minds by considering the features each incorporates that motivate us or that we consider grounds for choice. Moreover, in such reflection it is necessary to distinguish between ultimate reasons for choice, and nonultimate reasons. A person making up a list of pro-points and con-points in connection with a given choice would be hopelessly lost if he did not know what he valued on its own account and what he valued for some other reason. For instance, if a student is deciding whether to attend a movie rather than study, he is hopelessly confused if, given that his only ultimate reason for working is a promised trip to Europe if he gets an A in a certain course, he counts as reasons for working, not only the trip to Europe but also the A in the course, the turning in of a paper on time, etc. For clear thinking, it is at least often necessary to make up one's mind what are basic objectives and what are not.

I want now to point out that the motivating grounds for a decision may be of two quite different kinds. Suppose you are preparing your income-tax report, and the question is whether to declare some sources of income that will never be known unless you declare them. Suppose you declare this income on the ground that otherwise you will be swearing to a false statement, or that it is unfair not to pay one's full share determined by one's actual income. It seems clear that doing this is not enhancing *your own welfare,* in any identifiable sense. You do not wish to pay the extra money (you'd much prefer to have an air-conditioner in your car); nor are you under the illusion that making the declaration is the cheapest way to avoid the discomforts of an uneasy conscience. You think, rather, that there are certain self-imposed restrictions on welfare-enhancing behavior, and that the imposition of these restrictions can be justified to a rational person and that they ought to be accepted by everyone. In contrast, there are decisions you make because you *want* or *like* some feature: the company of friends, physical activities like music, sex, tennis, and eating. These are things you want in the sense that you normally enjoy having or experiencing them, that you feel joy in the prospect of getting them, that you are disappointed when you miss them, etc. No one in his senses, however, thrills to paying extra income tax. Let us mark this distinction by saying that some choices are motivated by the prospect of enhanced *personal welfare* (this may include the happiness of children, etc.), whereas others are motivated by considerations of *moral principle.*

Utilitarian philosophers (I cannot speak about utilitarian economists) have normally made this distinction quite carefully. They take the fact that people *want* or *like* certain things for themselves as basic. The occurrence of these things is what is to be counted as "utility" for the person. As J. S. Mill put it, one thing is more desirable than another when it is preferred by people "irrespective of any feeling of moral obligation to prefer it." In contrast, utilitarians regard moral principles as rules that must be obeyed if, in a society, the intrinsically desirable is to be maximized. But a person's following a moral principle need not maximize *his* utility; for him it may be a serious sacrifice.

The concept of a "rational preference-ordering" is usually explained (and this seems true of Arrow's paper) in such a way as to omit this distinction. This is unfortunate, for it does seem that at least part of what justifies institutions and social policies is their promise of maximizing *personal welfare,* whereas it is not at all obvious that an institution is justified by its relation to persons' rational preference-orderings—the fact that they rank certain states of affairs above others, for any kind of reason.

Why is the distinction not drawn? This is an interesting question. (1) One possible answer is that economic theory does not *need* it; the points or predictions economists wish to make concern bargaining problems or equilibrium problems that arise only *after* an individual or firm has already, by whatever means, come to conclusions about its preference order, for whatever reason. This, of course, is no reason for rejecting the distinction, if there are other reasons for making it. (2) Another possible answer is that the distinction smacks of introspection. And so it does; but, as already remarked, we cannot be extreme behaviorists anyway, and there is no point in denying that we know what obviously we do know. (3) Another possible reason is that it must be conceded by all that both considerations of personal welfare, and of moral principle, are *motivating*. So, it may be said, why bother with the distinction? But the fact that two things have one property in common does not show that it is unimportant to distinguish them. It is surely not for nothing that Freud distinguished the *id* from the *superego*, or that Lewinian psychologists distinguish wants from values. More important, there are persuasive grounds for thinking that when a person wants or likes something for itself, there is some reason for getting it for him; there is no comparable ground for thinking that when a person supposes something *ought* to occur, that is some reason for producing it, for his benefit. Incidentally, it does not *follow* from the fact that some consideration is motivating, that the agent *wants* the event in question to occur; for to say that a consideration is motivating is to comment on its causal role in a decision process, whereas to say that a person wants a certain event is to say, among other things, that he will be disappointed if it does not occur.

Having drawn these distinctions, let us now revert to the third of the questions formulated in the initial paragraph of this paper: Is a person's transitive and complete preference-ordering (in Arrow's sense) of alternatives for choice necessarily an order of better-and-worse from the point of view of the person's welfare?

We should commence by conceding that if a person's

ordering of pairs of possible worlds that are alternatives for choice is not transitive, something is radically wrong. If an ordering is not transitive, further reflection, and revision, are called for. Transitivity is a necessary condition for an acceptable ordering.

But it is equally clear that a transitive ordering of alternatives can be far from a better-and-worse order from the point of view of an agent's welfare. One example is sufficient to show this. We must remember, of course, that the ordering, in Arrow's sense, is simply a description of what *would* be chosen, by the agent, *for whatever reason,* including reasons of moral obligation, as between various pairs of alternative worlds. The example is this: a man considers that it is his moral obligation to sacrifice his life for the sake of others (say, he falls on a grenade in order to save others standing nearby); it is obviously absurd to suppose that this choice is better from the point of view of his personal welfare.

A transitive preference-ordering could with more plausibility be claimed to be a better-and-worse order from the point of view of an agent's welfare if the order were established by *preference* not in the sense of "would choose for whatever reason" but in the sense of "*wants* more" or "would like more"— the relation suggested above as fundamental for utilitarian conceptions, especially for the concept of personal welfare, or of happiness. But it must be kept clearly in mind that this is *not* what Arrow, along with many or most writers on rational decision, have in mind, when they speak of "preference."

Even if we adopted this amendment, a person's transitive ordering of possible worlds may still diverge from an ordering of better-and-worse from the point of view of the person's welfare. This is, for one thing, because the assumption usually made by writers on decision theory, that a person's preference-ordering may be viewed as permanent or unchanging, happens to be an oversimplification. Persons' preference-orderings change: whenever children or friends are acquired, during periods of anxiety, and whenever a physical need is satiated, to take only a few cases. A choice that will contribute most to the agent's (long-term) welfare is one that will make provision not only for what the agent now prefers, in his present ordering, but also for what he *will* prefer—assuming he can know about this—at a later time, and on an equal basis. Obviously it would be arbitrary for a person who is choosing to give the preference-ordering of that particular time priority and to define his welfare in terms of it, when he knows that he is going to live through times at which he will have different preference-orderings. A systematic theory of welfare, incorporating the traditional conception of "preference" as "wanting more," that accepts this point (and others of similar force that could be made), is a complicated matter that can only be regarded, at present, as a program. Indeed, whether one thinks of a "preference"-order in this traditional sense of "wants more" or in the sense of "would choose, for whatever reason" of many contemporary decision theorists, the problem of changes of preference, and ignorance of future preferences, is one that demands attention. It is worth noting that some economists, e.g., T. C. Koopmans, have made some helpful suggestions along this line.[1]

However it may be with the identification of a transitive preference-order in Arrow's sense with an order of greater-and-less welfare of the agent, might one still say that a person's action that corresponds with his transitive and complete ordering of alternatives at the time is *rational*? Arrow notes that economists tend to identify it as such. On this point there are several comments to be made. First, economists use the word "rational" in a special technical sense, such that it is an analytic proposition that such an action is rational. In *that* sense of "rational" the answer to our question is obviously affirmative. But, second, in calling an action "rational" the economist is not merely classifying the action in accordance with his official definition; he is using a familiar word with complex associations, and therefore in calling an action rational he tends to suggest or imply that the behavior in question is to be *recommended*, that it is *desirable* (perhaps from the point of view of the agent's welfare), and so on, for whatever properties we ordinarily associate with "rational." It can hardly be an accident that the economist uses the word "rational" in these contexts, and does not confine himself to the more technical term "transitive." So it looks as if the thought the economist is expressing when he says a preference-ordering is rational may be a bit more complex than that the preference is transitive.

There are dangers in choosing a word with an established, if somewhat vague, connotation for some technical purpose: one may slide unwittingly from one use to the other. In the present case the danger is especially serious because a person can hardly be acting rationally in the ordinary sense, if his acts correspond to a preference-ordering that is not transitive. But we should be quite clear that it does not *follow*, from the fact that an act is rational in the economist's technical sense, that it is rational in the ordinary sense of this term, that it is desirable or to be recommended, and so on. So, although an action that corresponds with a person's transitive and complete ordering of alternatives is necessarily rational in the economist's official technical sense, it remains to be shown that it is rational in the ordinary sense.

THE JUSTIFICATION OF INSTITUTIONS

Thus far I have been discussing Professor Arrow's conceptual tools and presuppositions, which he shares with many writers in the field, and not the specific contentions of his paper, his thesis about social actions. Let us now turn to the issues of primary concern in his paper.

One question that one must answer prior to appraising the plausibility of Arrow's position is what precise positive affirmation he is making. There is room for misinterpretation on this point, but I believe he is making an assertion about the conditions in which a *social action is morally justified or rational* (I am not sure which of these terms he would pick, or precisely what he would mean by them). His view is roughly that a social action is justified or rational if and only if it is a certain function of individual rational preference-orderings of the kind discussed above; he does not say what function, and indeed leaves us only with some conclusions about what functions must be discarded, supplemented with some speculations about a possible useful line to take. I shall amplify this summary in a moment.

In stating Arrow's problem, I have used the phrase "social action." Arrow does not, in his paper, discuss the scope of social actions about which he wishes to frame a theory. But he can hardly be urging that the rulings of a judge in a court of criminal law, or of the Federal Reserve Board, should be justified, much less decided, in the way he describes. Nor do I think he means that the actions of individuals that affect others should be decided or justified in this way. My supposition is that his interest is in the *institutions* of a society, or in the *general policies* of its government. What he is asking about is the justification or rationality of things like the divorce law in New York State or the economic institutions of society or of a code of morality that might restrict individual decisions, or of the aims of U.S. foreign policy. I shall construe Arrow's remarks as a thesis about social actions in this sense.[2]

If I am correct in construing Arrow's thesis in this way, then his view is entered in the lists with some ancient and well-known competitors: natural-law theories, contract theories of the authority of governments, retributive theories of the rectitude of systems of criminal law, egalitarian and meritarian views about the justice of systems of economic distributions, utilitarian theories of all institutions, and so on. All of these are theories about when, or in what conditions, a social action is morally justified or rational.

Let me now state what I take to be Arrow's thesis a bit more completely. First, he holds that a particular social action (policy, institution) is rational or justified if and only if it corresponds to a rational or justified social ordering of all possible actions (policies, institutions), for the situation at hand. Second, Arrow thinks that a social ordering is rational or justified if and only if it is a certain mathematical function of the rational preference-orderings in his sense of individuals (and, as I understand him, of *all* individuals, past, present, and future)—in other words, if the social ordering could be determined by a computer that was given information about the individual orderings and was programmed in a certain way. Programmed in what way? It is to be programmed (this restriction is to be put on the mathematical function) so that it will give only transitive orderings, will satisfy the Pareto Principle, the Principle of Non-Dictatorship, and ideally the Independence of Irrelevant Alternatives. The possibility is left open for other restrictions, but Arrow does not mention any, and in fact, he holds that the above list is already too long: his celebrated "impossibility theorem" has shown that it is not generally true, for all logically possible individual orderings, that a machine could be programmed in any way at all so that it could meet all these conditions. In his present paper, Arrow suggests that the last of these requirements be dropped. (One might suppose, for reasons stated by Von Neumann and Morgenstern and others, that this suggestion would lead him to hold that cardinal numbers could be attached to the "votes" of an individual, but he does not seem to draw this inference although he thinks —a point to be discussed below—that his suggestion overcomes the traditional difficulty of interpersonal comparisons.) His view seems to be that a social ordering is rational or morally justified if it is this kind of function of the transitive orderings of individuals. This is his normative theory of social action.

The above proposal can, however, be interpreted in several ways, and it will be useful to contrast two such ways with what is apparently Arrow's interpretation, in order to bring his view into sharper focus. For this purpose, let us employ as an example the question whether the new New York State divorce law is justified as compared with the old one. (1) Arrow might mean that the law is justified if its adoption were indicated by some function (e.g., just by the majority) of the "votes" (hypothetical choices) of all persons (not just residents of New York State), where the hypothetical choice or vote of the individual is made on the basis of *his understanding* of the alternatives— not of his appraisal of them as he might appraise them if he knew what their consequences really are, but of his appraisal of them as he *thinks* they are. It is votes of this sort, of course, that determine such issues at the polls. Such a proposal might be called "extreme democracy." This proposal, however, seems *not* to be advocated by Arrow; and it should be noted that his view is not at all the thesis that a social action is justified if it is favored by the majority, given their actual understanding of the issue. (2) A second view is also not espoused by Arrow although it is closer to his proposal: the utilitarian view. Roughly, the utilitarian says that a social action is justified if it will maximize utility. According to this view, to determine the justification of an institution we first determine what the world will be like if we adopt it, and compare it with what the world will be like if we adopt the alternative; we compare what will be produced by one but not by the other, with what will be produced by the other and not by the one. We then assign utility-numbers to these effects. That is, we first develop a cardinal scale of utilities for each person, based upon assigning to the indifference point the number zero, and assigning arbitrarily some other number to some other point. These utilities are based on the nonmoral preferences (in the sense of "wants more") of individuals, *not* on preferences in the sense of "would choose for whatever reason." (This proposal makes the assumption, criticized above, that an individual has a fixed system of preferences.) It is assumed that interpersonal comparisons are possible, sufficient to standardize the zero (indifference) point and *some* point on the scales of each pair of persons (when the event defining this point is judged to be wanted equally by both parties). We can then determine which institution will produce the greater per person utility for sentient creatures generally. This institution is the justified one. The theory faces the familiar difficulty that it is not easy to justify interpersonal comparisons of the required sort—at least precise ones—and many persons think that the assumptions necessary for cardinal measurement for individuals are unrealistic. (3) We now come to the view that, as I understand him, Arrow is defending. Suppose we think of the intelligence of individuals being expanded, so that they could grasp entire world-biographies, and decide, for any given pair of these, which one they would choose, everything considered and for whatever reason. Now let us suppose that they consider the class of world-biographies containing the old divorce law, and the class containing the new law. Unfortunately, each class will contain an indefinitely large membership, since the world can be varied in an indefinitely large number of ways otherwise than in there being a certain divorce law in New York State. In order to get relevant "voting," we shall pair a world-biography containing the new law with a world-biography containing the old law, where the two biographies are exactly matched except for the divorce law and its consequences. We can, then, register the pro or con "votes" of each individual, past, present, or future. Obviously, in order to operate this system, someone first has to know what the effects of each system will be, and then we have to find whether the votes of each person (past, present, and future) would favor one relevant world-biography over the other (assuming they can visualize it as a whole). What are the differences between this proposal and utilitarianism? First, an individual preference-ordering is determined by what an individual "would choose, for whatever reason," and not by what he "wants more." This is the familiar difference between Arrow's concept and the concept of personal welfare. Second, although both views accept the Pareto Principle (each interpreting it in its own way), the utilitarian has a proposal about what to do in case an institution affects some people favorably, others adversely: he resorts to arithmetic, and figures out the per person gains. But this move requires cardinal utility, at least for some possible situations. Professor Arrow seems not to permit cardinal measures of utility. Professor Arrow is, as I shall explain below, willing to go along with the utilitarian view about the possibility of interpersonal comparisons; but short of also going to cardinal measures for the individual, it appears impossible to provide a computer with information about individual voting that will, in all cases, enable the machine to arrive at a transitive social ordering.

How persuasive is Arrow's proposal? (I postpone the details about interpersonal comparisons for the moment.) Let me first make the obvious point that his view that a rational or morally justified social ordering is some kind of function of individual orderings, in his sense, is not an analytic proposition, or one confirmable by observation—at least not until some crucial definitions have been provided and supported. Arrow offers no reason for accepting the view. The proposal is his alternative to traditional theories such as those mentioned above. It seems to be his own value judgment about which social orderings are justified. It is, of course, no worse for that. Persons sympathetic to utilitarianism may incline to agree with his view because of its apparent similarity to utilitarianism. But the similarity is more apparent than real. The utilitarian affirms that an institution is rational or morally justified if it will—or, on the evidence, probably will—maximize the average per person utility (in the sense of *personal welfare*, as explained above), as compared with the alternatives. Arrow, in contrast, makes the rationality or rightness of an institution depend on whether people would *choose* it in preference to any other, *for whatever reasons*, including confused and insupportable ethical reasons. This view strikes me, intuitively, as objectionable: social institutions should minister to personal welfare and be judged by their ability to do so, but they need not be the ones individuals would *choose* for whatever reasons. Indeed, the hypothetical choices of individuals in this sense are relevant to the justification of an institution, largely or wholly, because they tend to reflect the impact of institutions on the individual's personal welfare. Arrow's theory, as I understand it, has the implication that a sales tax as the only form of taxation is right and best if people favor it, perhaps because of some complex and confused line of reasoning about equal obligations and equal benefits; the utilitarian will rightly reject this form of tax as failing to maximize welfare, irrespective of what most people think of it. (Erroneous ethical reasoning is not eliminated by having a clear view of the alternative worlds between which one is choosing.) These views of Arrow's stem from his failure, pointed out earlier, to make some distinctions: primarily between personal welfare and moral principles.

Arrow's theory, insofar as it is close to utilitarianism, may be vulnerable to some attacks, on grounds of justice and equality, which have been leveled at utilitarianism. Some of these attacks, I think, are worthy of very serious consideration, but it is only possible to mention their existence here.

I shall conclude with some comments on Arrow's suggestions about interpersonal comparisons. I have already suggested doubts that Arrow's problem of basing a social ordering on individual orderings can be solved short of a system of cardinal measures for individuals. But let us consider his view about interpersonal comparisons. Arrow's proposal is that dropping the Principle of the Independence of Irrelevant Alternatives may be a clue to the solution of the problem of interpersonal comparisons. Let us see how good a clue it is.

What is the "problem" of interpersonal comparisons? The utilitarian needs to know, for his calculus, whether Mr. X's desire for A as compared with B is greater than Mr. Y's desire for B as compared with A. If we knew this, we should be over the hump of the *inter*personal problem, however far we might yet be from cardinal utility measures. Now *desire* is a theoretical construct, which is measured by such phenomena as intensity of disappointment, intensity of joy, etc.[3] If we could know whether Mr. X's disappointment at getting B rather than A would be more intense than Mr. Y's disappointment at getting A rather than B, we should be on our way toward comparing the relative intensity of their desires. But the trouble is that no one can observe the disappointment of both Mr. X and Mr. Y directly; even these gentlemen themselves can each observe only half of what is wanted.

Arrow's problem seems in one respect more difficult than that of the utilitarian. He needs to know whether Mr. X's *hypothetical choice* of A over B is stronger than Mr. Y's hypothetical choice of B over A. But whereas we understand "desire" well enough to be clear what experiences are a measure of strength of desire, it is not clear what experience or observation would in principle be a measure of strength of hypothetical choice. Perhaps some physical facts are a perfectly good measure of it, in which case there is no "problem" of intersubjective comparison at all. There is such a thing as choice, and hypothetical choice, but it is not clear that there is such a thing as *strength* of choice, *degree* of choice—anything beyond the fact that A, which is chosen over B, would also be chosen over many other things, perhaps, that would be chosen over B.

Let us assume, however, that in Arrow's case, as in the utilitarian's case, the difficulty is that we can make a comparative judgment of the intensity of the relevant variable only by knowing the comparative intensity of some subjective experience, such as disappointment, joy, etc. The "problem," then, is that such judgments are not based on direct observation. Need we worry about this? My own opinion is that many behavioristically oriented economists have gone far overboard on this matter, and that we have very often quite good reason for making such comparative judgments. Nobody doubts that we can make reliable judgments about unobservables in physics; and, as far as I can see, nobody has shown that this is in principle more difficult in psychology. The logic is essentially the same.

The question, however, is about Arrow's suggestion that we can surmount the difficulties if we permit individuals involved not only to express their hypothetical choices as between the alternatives being appraised, but also as between these and other things. It is not clear to me how these additional expressed preferences will help.

Arrow's suggestion seems to come to this: Suppose the question is whether I get an extra $5.00, or whether my newsboy does. Each of us is asked to consider how I will be affected by getting the $5.00, and also how the newsboy will be affected. The contemporary professor, doubtless both wealthy and jaded, knows he will get no thrill from what he can buy with $5.00, whereas he knows the newsboy will; and the newsboy knows the same. So it is put to both individuals whether their hypothetical choice will be for the nothing the professor will get from the $5.00, or for the thrill the newsboy will get from it. Hopefully, if the professor is sympathetic, he will choose the newsboy's experience; and presumably the newsboy will do the same. So the newsboy gets the $5.00.

I do not see, however, how this suggestion solves the problem of interpersonal comparisons; it rather presupposes that it has already been solved. For it is assumed that each party can know that the newsboy will get more of a thrill from the $5.00 than the professor will. It is on this assumption that each makes his hypothetical choice. But precisely this knowledge is what is needed for interpersonal comparisons; with it, we can at least solve, in the traditional way, the utilitarian's problem about whether the professor desires what he can get with the $5.00 as much as the newsboy desires what he can get.

It may be that Arrow thinks the problem is solved without any *knowledge:* he may think it enough if the professor sympathetically prefers a world-biography containing the newsboy thrilled and himself jaded to a biography containing himself jaded and the newsboy bored—and the same for the newsboy. But these hypothetical choices are not enough. Someone, in order to show the relevance of these world-biographies to the actual situation, has to know that they correspond to the real world. And to know this requires precisely the solution of the "problem" of interpersonal comparisons.

NOTES

1. T. C. Koopmans, "On Flexibility of Future Preference," in M. W. Shelly and G. L. Bryan, *Human Judgments and Optimality,* New York: Wiley and Sons, 1964.

2. It may be, however, that here my wish is father to my

thought! Perhaps I should say that I think Arrow's theory is much more plausible *if* it is interpreted in this way. For considerations supporting this view see John Rawls' "Two Concepts of Rules" (*Philosophical Review*, LXIV [1955], 3–32) and "Justice as Fairness" (*Philosophical Review*, LXVII [1958], 164–94); Richard Wasserstrom, *The Judicial Decision*, 1961; and R. B. Brandt, *Ethical Theory*, 1959, Ch. 15, and "Some Merits of One Form of Rule-Utilitarianism" (forthcoming, University of Colorado Publications in Philosophy). A criticism of the distinction is contained in David Lyons, *Forms and Limits of Utilitarianism*, 1965.

3. See R. Brandt and J. Kim, "Wants as Explanations of Actions," *Journal of Philosophy*, LX (1963), 425–35.

C

Arrow's Mathematical Politics

PAUL SAMUELSON

Massachusetts Institute of Technology

I. INTRODUCTION

PROFESSOR ARROW'S PAPER is essentially a summarizing description of the fundamental work he has done in connection with Welfare Economics. I am not able to judge how easy or difficult it is for a noneconomist—say, a philosopher—to apprehend the nuances of such a description. But I very much hope that philosophers, sociologists, and political scientists will become familiar with Arrow's analysis.

I say this because I believe that Kenneth Arrow has made a first-rate contribution to man's body of knowledge. In the middle of the twentieth century there are not to be found many new milestones in the history of ideas. *The Theory of Games* by Von Neumann does represent an imperishable advance upon a problem that intelligent men have brooded over since the beginning of intelligence. The analysis of personal, subjective probability, in its relationship to decision-making, is another intellectual breakthrough that should bring lasting fame to Ramsey, Savage, and Marschak. If the Muse of history has its wits about it and succeeds in doing justice— two hypotheses of a somewhat romantic nature—I believe that Kenneth Arrow's name will be long remembered for a new and important insight into the permanent problem of the nature of democracy.

My sense of justice requires me to bestow this high praise. In addition I must admit that my vanity as an economist is gratified that one of the soldiers in our regiment should have made a contribution of universal interest. Indeed, I shall argue again here the thesis that the Arrow result is much more a contribution to the infant discipline of mathematical politics than to the traditional mathematical theory of welfare economics. I export Arrow from economics to politics because I do not believe that he has proved the impossibility of the traditional Bergson welfare function of economics, even though many of his less expert readers seem inevitably drawn into thinking so.

II. A WELL-BEHAVED (INDIVIDUAL) ORDERING

Some re–exposition will, I think, be helpful. Consider three alternative states of the world: A or B or C. Suppose that you, Man i, have an ordering of them: you like A better than B or C, you like B better than C. Write this ordering as $(A, B, C)^1$. This is a shorthand description of several choices that you would make, namely: (A over B); (A over C); (B over C). Alternatively, suppose that some of the states of the world were "tied" for your affections: A indifferent to B; either better than C. Deliberately omitting commas in order to show indifference, write this as $(AB,C)^1$. The meaning of $(ABC)^1$ will now be clear, where of course the order of the letters *between* commas is immaterial.

How many different complete orderings could you have? Omitting your identifying superscript for brevity, we can list only thirteen alternative patterns that your tastes or values might take:

(A,B,C); (A,C,B); (B,A,C); (B,C,A); (C,A,B); (C,B,A);
(AB,C); (AC,B); (A,BC); (BC,A); (B,AC); (C,AB);
(ABC).

Although this may seem a great variety of possibilities, it is actually less than half the number of patterns that would be possible if we did not insist that all orderings be *transitive*. To see this, list a matrix of all possible pairs:

$$
\begin{array}{c}
\quad\quad\quad A \quad\quad B \quad\quad C \\
\begin{array}{c} A \\[20pt] B \\[28pt] C \end{array}
\left[
\begin{array}{ccc}
\cdot & \cdot & \cdot \\
\begin{matrix} +1 \\ 0 \\ -1 \end{matrix} & \cdot & \cdot \\
\begin{matrix} +1 \\ 0 \\ -1 \end{matrix} & \begin{matrix} +1 \\ 0 \\ -1 \end{matrix} & \cdot
\end{array}
\right]
= [a_{AB}, \ldots]
\end{array}
$$

Only the cells below the diagonal line need be considered. If B is preferred to A, select in the first cell $+1$; if they are indifferent, select 0; if A is preferred to B, select -1. In each of these 3 cells, there are 3 independent possibilities. Hence, in all there are $3^3 = 27$ different binary matrices possible. But only 13 of them are consistent with the transitivity requirement: if A is at least as good as B, and B is at least as good as C, then it must already be predictable that A is at least as good as C. Thus, of the following matrices, only the first is admissible in a "well-behaved" (transitive) ordering:

$$
\begin{bmatrix} \cdot & \cdot & \cdot \\ -1 & \cdot & \cdot \\ -1 & -1 & \cdot \end{bmatrix} ;
\begin{bmatrix} \cdot & \cdot & \cdot \\ -1 & \cdot & \cdot \\ 0 & -1 & \cdot \end{bmatrix} ;
\begin{bmatrix} \cdot & \cdot & \cdot \\ -1 & \cdot & \cdot \\ +1 & 0 & \cdot \end{bmatrix} ;
\begin{bmatrix} \cdot & \cdot & \cdot \\ 0 & \cdot & \cdot \\ +1 & 0 & \cdot \end{bmatrix}
$$

If we go from 3 to 4 states of the world, the admissible orderings will be evident. E.g., (A,B,C,D); . . . (D,C,B,A); (AB,C,D); . . . ; (ABCD). There will be much less than the $3^6 = 729$ matrix possibilities; and generally for N states of the world, only a small subset of the $3^{N(N-1)/2}$ possible matrices will correspond to a well-behaved transitive ordering.

One final observation. If the ordering is transitive, it *automatically* satisfies the condition called "independence of irrelevant alternatives." Thus, omitting C from any of the 13 patterns for A or B or C, leaves us with the *same* $+1$, 0, or -1 matrix element in the cell for B's row and A/s colu-n as we had when C was included. Likewise for leaving out any other one of the 3 states. Likewise for leaving out any $N-2$ of N states of the world.

Now consider the case of 3 different men. Each can have 13 possible orderings for A and B and C. There are thus $13 \times 13 \times 13 = 2,197$ possible situations that could confront us for ajudication. Given R persons, there are 13^R different contingencies that could arise. Clearly for many persons and many alternative states the total number of possibilities that could arise is vast in number (but computable as a finite integer).

Professor Brandt is within his rights in questioning whether what has here been called a well-behaved ordering should be dignified with the name "a rational preference-ordering." There is no need to do so. And if he wishes to discern "intrinsic values," let him. Furthermore, suppose I always choose to forego fish on Friday even though I love fish, in order to live up to some code of obligation; or suppose I would always enter a burning house to rescue my baby even at the cost of my own life; or would sacrifice future pleasures of living in order to fall on a bomb that threatens my companions-at-arms. So long as my acts fit in with a well-behaved ordering, there is no particular need to take note of the distinctions that Brandt may himself want to take note of. By all means, let him consider what we ignore.

III. A WELL-BEHAVED SOCIAL ORDERING

Now I shall consider a (Bergson) Social Welfare Function, contrasting it with a (Arrow) Constitutional Function. Conventionally, either of these somehow defines, in addition to the 3 persons' individual ordering, a new fourth ordering. [Or, if there are R persons, there is an $(R+1)$th "social" ordering to be considered.] Note that it, *if it is well-behaved*, can take on only 1 of our 13 possibilities.

Now it is a "natural" requirement in a culture obsessed by "individualism" to require that the social ordering be somehow defined in terms of the specified individual's orderings. E.g., if we are given $[(A,B,C)^1; (A,B,C)^2; (A,B,C)^3]$, representing unanimous agreement of all individuals, the social ordering might be required to be $(A,B,C)^0$, where the "o" superscript refers to the social ordering. Where unanimity is lacking—as in the case $(A,B,C)^1$, $(C,B,A)^2$, $(ABC)^3$—it is not so easy to find the "natural" corresponding social ordering. But from the artificial symmetry of the example, perhaps $(ABC)^0$ might be the tempting choice as the corresponding social ordering.

What needs stressing is that Arrow, and Bergson for that matter, specify that only the *order* relations of individuals determine the social ordering.

Suppose we learn that, although Man 1 "slightly" prefers A to B and B to C, and Man 3 is quite indifferent among all three, Man 2 "strongly" prefers C to B and B to A. Many ethical observers might in this case be willing to have $(ABC)^0$ be replaced by $(C,B,A)^0$.

But this appeal to cardinality—to quantitative intensity of preference that underlies the qualitative ordering—is not consistent with Arrow's first and basic Axiom. A number of people, confronted with Arrow's Impossibility Theorem and their natural feeling that cardinal intensity of preference ought to count (at least to break "ties"), have contemplated replacing mere ordinality by a cardinality formulation, thereby rejecting Arrow's very first Axiom.

Thus, Brandt refers to utilitarianism or hedonism and to "intensity of joy, etc." Even Arrow, in his final section, seems to be ready to explore use of cardinality, if some interpersonal comparisons can somehow be made. Professor A. K. Sen, of the Delhi School of Economics, at the 1966 Biarritz Meeting of the International Economic Association, has raised the question whether an escape from the Impossibility Theorem may be found through cardinalism. As I remarked at Biarritz, I think that cardinality will not so much provide an escape from the Impossibility Theorem as a plunge into a new Impossibility Theorem of cardinal type.

IV. ARROW'S CONSTITUTIONAL FUNCTION

What Arrow seeks is a way of going from *any* possible pattern of well-behaved individuals' orderings—all 2,197 of them when N=3 and 3 persons are involved—to a well-behaved social ordering. A Constitution Function is a way of mapping *any one* of the 2,179 points in individuals' space into 1 (and 1 only) of the 13 points of the social space.

What "reasonable" restrictions on the Constitution Function are we tempted to stipulate? Arrow lists them in 4 Axioms. I present the same content in 3 Axioms.

> Axiom 1. The well-behaved social ordering matrix $[a_{AB}, \ldots]^0$ is to be, element for element, a unique function of the *corresponding* elements of the individuals' $[a_{AB}, \ldots]^1$, $[a_{AB}, \ldots]^2, \ldots$ matrices *for each and all admissible patterns of those matrices.*

This merely restates the definition of an individualistic well-behaved cardinality-free social ordering. But note that my Axiom 1 *already* implies the full content of Arrow's Axiom on Independence of Irrelevant Alternatives. This is because each binary cell, such as a_{AB}^0, depends only on the corresponding cells a_{AB}^1, $a_{AB}^2, \ldots$ and not at all on other cells such as a_{BC}^1, plus the stipulation that the resulting social $[a_{AB}, \ldots]^0$ matrix belong to the class of 13 *"well-behaved"* "transitive" matrices.

Already Axiom 1 makes almost impossible the task of finding a well-behaved Constitution Function. If you try most rules of mapping the 2,179 points on to the 13, you will find the result is *not* a transitive ordering. However, there are some trivial exceptions. Try the rule: "Disregard all choices but Man 1's, and use his ordering." That will certainly meet the test of Axiom 1. But that is Dictatorship, and neither appealing nor logically nontrivial. Hence, the following is stipulated:

Axiom 2. (Non-Dictatorship) The Social Constitution is not to be dictatorial, merely reflecting one chosen man's ordering.

Does this rule out all remaining Constitution Functions? Not quite. Suppose we make the social ordering $[a_{AB}, \ldots]^0$ reflect no individuals' choices, being imposed by some outsider's ordering. That gives us 13 admissible Constitutions. But such an imposed matrix is hardly compatible with the individualistic notion that people's tastes and values are to be respected provided they don't interfere with other people's. Hence, the final requirement.

Axiom 3 (Non-imposition and Pareto-optimality or unanimity). Any $a_{AB}{}^0$ element is to be a non-decreasing function of each and every corresponding individual $a_{AB}{}^1$ element, so that if *all* men prefer A to B, so will the social ordering.

This says that if A moves from being worse than B to being as good or better for some people, while staying as before for the rest of the people, then the social ordering must *not* now demote A and make it worse in comparison with B than it was before.

All three Axioms seem reasonable. Arrow's great feat was to prove that no Constitution Function can satisfy them all.[1] The problems that have vaguely plagued us in connection with democracy—voting paradoxes, etc.—are apparently permanent ones. Which Axiom should we reject? It is like asking which triplet one should put up for adoption.

Many people think that the Independence of Irrelevant Alternatives is the one that must go. I cannot agree. My formulation builds it *from the beginning* into Axiom 1. Give up Axiom 1—a well-behaved ordering with transitivity—and the whole problem vanishes into thin air. It is not solved; it is evaded. In a moment I shall comment on the suggestion that cardinal intensities of preference be brought in, to make the impossible possible; little comfort will, I fear, be found from this approach. A third avenue of escape from the Impossibility Theorem is to retreat to the Possible, by narrowing down the domain of possible individuals' preferences from the full 2,197 possibilities to some more limited set.

V. THE BERGSON SOCIAL WELFARE FUNCTION

The Social Welfare Function of conventional economics, although named and analyzed by A. Bergson in the classic 1938 article cited by Arrow, was used in special form by writers since the time of Jeremy Bentham and before. I deem it a misfortune that Arrow chose to call what I have here dubbed a Constitution Function by the same name as Bergson's Social Welfare Function. In consequence, many readers can be forgiven for thinking that Arrow has proved the impossibility of a Bergson Social Welfare Function, thereby dealing a death blow to the magnificent edifice of modern welfare economics.

Orally and in writing, many authors (including me and I. M. D. Little) have criticized this usage of Arrow's as unfortunate and confusing. In his 1963 new chapter (pp. 104–105) Arrow stands his ground, asserting in effect that if Bergson did not have in mind the same concept, he should have. After rereading a dozen times the 1963 words, I fail to find in them arguments that I can accept.

Now it is fruitless to argue about word usage. (How do we know Uranus is "really" Uranus? Should America be called a Republic or a Democracy? Etc.) But it is important to be able to recognize when different things are indeed different. My previous exposition of the relation between a well-behaved social ordering $[a_{AB}, \ldots]^0$ and individuals' orderings $[a_{AB}, \ldots]^1$, $[a_{AB}, \ldots]^2, \ldots$ is well designed to bring out the difference between a Bergson Social Welfare Function and an Arrow Constitutional Function (or so-called "social welfare function").

For Bergson, one and only one of the 2,197 possible patterns of individuals' orderings is needed. It could be *any* one, but it is *only* one. From *it* (not from each of them all) comes a social ordering. Thus, a Bergson ethical observer need only know how to map 1 particular of the 2,197 points in individuals' space into 1 of the 13 points in social space. The only Axiom restricting a Bergson Social Welfare Function (of individualistic type) is a "tree" property of Pareto-optimality type.

Axiom A. The social ordering over the states of the world, $[a_{AB}, \ldots]^0$ must put A over B, i.e., $a_{AB}^0 = -1$, if every individual ordering does so, $a^i_{AB} = -1$ for all i; more generally, if no $a^i_{AB} = +1$, $a^0_{AB} \leqq 0$, the strong inequality being required if, with no $a^i_{AB} = +1$, $\Sigma_i a^i_{AB} < 0$.

This looks like the conjunction of Arrow's Axioms 1 and 3. But it is not. Thus, the point out of the 2,197 possibilities specified for the Bergson problem will—in all likelihood—not be subjected to any restriction by this Pareto Axiom A. Example: let the specified point be $[(A,B,C)^1; (B,C,A)^2; (C,A,B)^3]$. No state can be excluded by the Pareto-optimality principle of optimality. Any of the 13 outcomes are possible for $(\quad)^0$. Where Pareto-optimality acquires content in Bergsonian welfare economics is in cases, hardly mentioned in Arrow's paper for this conference, where each individual's tastes depend on variables of consumption that are all *his* alone, without altruism or envy being involved. In such cases, two different states—say C and D—are indifferent to all but Man 1, and his choice among them becomes decisive for the social ordering. Example: Consider $[A,B,C,D]^1$, $[B,CD,A]^2$, $[CD,A,B]^3$. Whatever else is decided, Axiom A tells us that $a_{CD}^0 = -1$ and socially C is preferred to D—because Man 1 ranks them that way and *all* other men are indifferent.

It is the "decomposability," or "tree," or (to use Arrow's happy phrase) "factorability" property of individualistic consumption that makes possible efficient use of a market-price system. The miracle is not that a pricing system works, but that the strong conditions for it to work are approximately present in nature. It was for this reason that I, in the discussion of Milton Friedman's discussion of Kenneth Boulding's paper, referred to Friedman's analogy between free pricing and free speech as poetry not prose. Not merely is such poetry not good poetry; not merely is it not persuasive; worst of all is the fact that such analogy denigrates, to the knowing ear, the genuine beauty and efficiency of market pricing in those situations where special "decomposability" properties are present.

VI. THE IMPOSSIBILITY OF CARDINALITY

Since space is short, let me jot down my conjecture that a full-fledged formulation of the Constitutional Function in terms of cardinal intensity will lead again to an Impossibility Theorem.

Replace the 13 patterns of A or B or C by all possible triplets of numbers (U_A, U_B, U_C) where

$$(A,B) \leftrightarrow U_A > U_B$$
$$(AB) \leftrightarrow U_A = U_B$$

The origin and scaling of the U numbers is unimportant, so long as the ratio $(U_A - U_B)/(U_B - U_C)$ is kept invariant. This will be the case only if we confine ourselves to linear transformations of the U's. For simplicity, assume that these $(U_A - U_B)/(U_B - U_C)$ intensity-differences are definable operationally by stochastic betting experiments: thus, $U_A - U_B = U_B - U_C$ if B with certainty is deemed indifferent to an even chance of A or C.

Now we can always add a fourth or Nth state to the sequence and find its new U number. Also, we can drop as many states as we like.

Let each man's cardinal ordering be identified by his triplet of numbers $(U_A, U_B, U_C)^1$. The problem now is to define a social cardinal ordering $(U_A, U_B, U_C)^0$, whose intensity-difference ratio $(U_A{}^0 - U_B{}^0)/(U_B{}^0 - U_C{}^0)$ is determinate as a function of the point in 3×3, or generally $N \times R$, dimensional space of the individuals' U's.

Let us place 3 or 4 reasonable Axioms on the functional relations

$$U_A{}^0 = f_A(U_A{}^1, \ldots)$$
$$U_B{}^0 = f_B(U_A{}^1, \ldots)$$

Thus $(f_A - f_B)/(f_B - f_C)$ must be a determinant function. It must not be dictatorial or imposed. It must have the Pareto-optimality property, etc.

Do there exist any $(f_A, f_B, \ldots)$ functions satisfying these restrictions? My conjecture is, No. An Impossibility Theorem can be proved for such cardinal cases just as in the ordinality case.

NOTES

1. See K. Arrow, *Social Choice and Individual Values* (New York: Wiley, 1951 and 1963), pp. 75–77, 80 for discussion of Duncan Black's case of "single-peaked" preferences. A trivial case would be where we consider only cases where "all (wise!) men think alike" and $[a_{AB}, \ldots]^i \equiv [a_{AB}, \ldots]^j$ for all i and j. Then an Arrow function is possible and Axiom 3 tells us it is $[a_{AB}, \ldots]^0 = [a_{AB}, \ldots]^1$.

PART II

The Basis of Value Judgments
in Economics

A

The Basis of Value Judgments
in Economics

KENNETH E. BOULDING
University of Michigan

THERE ARE a number of different concepts of value in economics. The most fundamental is that of the exchange ratio,
or terms of trade, which is the ratio of the quantities of two
things exchanged. The concept may be extended to ratios of
indices, for instance, of quantities of heterogeneous exports
and imports for an individual or a group. The terms of trade,
then, measure how much is received per unit of what is given
up. When one of the objects exchanged in the transaction is
money, the ratio of exchange is the price. The price set, or the
list of all prices in the society, is one of the major concerns of
economics, and a great deal of effort has gone into the question of what determines it. If we know the price set, we know
also the rates of exchange of all commodities for each other,
by simple arithmetic. Thus if a carpenter's wage is five dollars an hour, and butter is a dollar a pound, an hour of
carpentering can be exchanged for five pounds of butter, not
perhaps directly but through the medium of money. It is this
aspect of money that gives it the name medium of exchange.
All this is very elementary, yet it is surprising what confusion
these simple principles have occasionally caused. When
economists, for instance, have talked about the "theory of
value," contrasting it with the theory of price, all they have
usually meant is a theory of relative prices. Thus, suppose in
the previous instance that after an inflation the wage of
carpenters was ten dollars an hour and the price of butter
two dollars a pound. An hour of carpentering would still be

worth five pounds of butter, and the relative price structure would be unchanged, in spite of the fact that the two prices concerned had doubled. In fact, of course, inflation never leaves the relative price structure completely unchanged; otherwise it would have very little effect at all. Nevertheless, it is true that the relative price structure is much more invariant in the system than the absolute level of prices. A hyperinflation can take the absolute level of prices almost to infinity, yet the relative price structure will not be changed by more than would involve, say, the doubling or halving of some ratios, with the exception of contractual obligations in money terms, such as bonds, the relative price of which may fall almost to zero in a hyperinflation.

Exchange is only one method of transformation, so the concept of an exchange ratio is easily extended to that of a transformation coefficient or rate of substitution. Thus if giving up a beaver, in Adam Smith's little society of hunters,[1] enables them to get two more deer, the alternative cost or rate of substitution in the forest is two deer per beaver. The set of rates of substitution in production in the absence of monopoly or other restrictive conditions tends to be an *equilibrium* set of market prices. Suppose giving up a beaver nets us two deer in the woods; then if the market price in the village is three deer per beaver, it will pay to transfer resources from the deer industry into the beaver industry, for giving up a beaver nets us only two deer in the woods and three deer in the market place. Hence people will transfer into beaver and out of deer, the number of beaver coming to market will increase, the number of deer will diminish, and this will soon bring down the price of beaver to two deer per beaver. If the price of beaver were below this, the reverse would happen: beaver would get scarcer in the market and deer more plentiful, and the price of beaver would rise.

If the alternative costs or rates of transformation in production were independent of the amounts produced, the problem of the equilibrium price system is solved then and there; it simply corresponds to the rates of substitution in production.

In fact, however, we have nonconstant transformation ratios, and even in the deer and beaver case, if either industry expands beyond a certain point, its costs are likely to increase. Hence the set of relative prices in the market depends not only on the transformation ratios in production but also on demand; and this depends on transformation ratios in evaluation, or what is called the rate of indifferent substitution. This is the amount of one thing that we can substitute for another and leave our welfare or utility unchanged. The rate of indifferent substitution, therefore, is a measure of subjective evaluation. Here again, if the rate of exchange in the market does not equal the rate of indifferent substitution of any of the marketers who come into the market to buy and to sell, this will change both the market prices and their rates of indifferent substitution as they get more of what they prefer and give up what they do not prefer, until the market price and the rates of indifferent substitution are equal. Thus, suppose at a moment when the market price was two deer per beaver one of the marketers felt that with his existing stocks of beaver and deer he would be just as well off if he were to give up one beaver and receive three deer. If now he sells three deer in the market he gets one and a half beaver, so that he is, as it were, half a beaver to the good, and he will sell deer and buy beaver. As he goes on with this, however, following the great universal principle of diminishing marginal utility, he has fewer deer and they become more valuable to him, more beaver and they become less valuable to him, and his personal rate of indifferent substitution will shift until it is equal to two deer per beaver, at which point he will cease exchanging. Each individual, that is, adjusts his quantities exchanged up to the point at which his personal rate of indifferent substitution is equal to the market price.

Figure 1 will perhaps clarify these principles. Here we measure the output of beaver along OB and of deer along OD. If the society devoted all its resources to beaver, it could produce OB; if it devoted all to deer, it could produce OD. The line BB′D′D is what economists call a production possi-

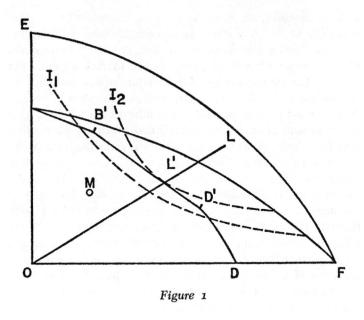

Figure 1

bility curve. Any combination of beaver and deer inside this line is possible; any combination outside it is not. This line represents, therefore, the fundamental scarcities under which the society operates. Between B' and D' we suppose constant costs, that is, a shift in the proportion of beaver and deer produced does not alter the marginal rate of substitution in production. From B' to B we suppose that beaver production is getting difficult, as the society has to go farther out into the woods, whereas deer production is getting easier as the deer are coming right into the village. Hence the rate of substitution in production changes to the advantage of deer, that is, we would get more deer per beaver given up. Similarly, between D' and D beaver are getting easier to get, deer are getting harder to get, and we get fewer deer per beaver. The actual proportions of beaver to deer produced, that is, the allocation of resources in the society, depends on the demand. If the demand for beaver increases, the equilibrium point will move toward B; if the demand for deer increases, it will move toward D. As long as it lies between B′ and D′, a change in demand will not change the alternative cost or the equilibrium market price structure. If, however, the demand for beaver is so great that the equilibrium point moves between B′ and B, the great demand for beaver will cause a rise in its relative price. Similarly, if the demand for deer is great enough so that the equilibrium point moves between D′ and D, the relative price of deer will rise. We can represent the aggregate demand structure roughly by a demand proportion line such as OL. The point of equilibrium is then at L′, where this intersects the production possibility curve. If there is an increase in demand for deer, OL swings toward OD; an increase in demand for beaver swings it toward OB, and the equilibrium changes accordingly. It is easy to extend this principle to *n* dimensions for *n* commodities, and the whole theory of equilibrium price is thereby developed.

For a single individual, we may suppose that BD represents his exchange opportunity line, and his preference structure is represented by a family of indifference curves such as I_1, I_2, each of which represents those combinations of beaver and deer to which he is indifferent, and the whole set of which represents the contours of a utility surface. The slope of an indifference curve at any point is the rate of indifferent substitution, or subjective valuation. He will always try to move toward a "higher" indifference curve, and hence the highest indifference curve that he can get onto while remaining on his exchange opportunity line is the one that touches it as at L′. At this point his rate of indifferent substitution is equal to the rate of exchange in the market. If this point of equilibrium is in the range B′D′, the market for the individual is "perfect" in the sense that transactions which he makes will not affect the rate of exchange itself. Beyond B′ or D′ the market becomes imperfect, and the transactions affect the rate of exchange.

One or two minor points that emerge out of this analysis may be clarified. One is the relation of this type of analysis to the famous labor theory of value. Here Adam Smith is perhaps responsible for a good deal of eventual intellectual confusion, when he said, in the chapter referred to above, "If among a nation of hunters, for example, it usually costs twice the labor to kill a beaver which it does to kill a deer, one beaver should naturally exchange for or be worth two deer." This natural rate of exchange is, of course, the alternative production cost as we have defined it, and it by no means follows that this is invariantly related to the relative quantities of labor embodied in the two commodities, though labor embodied is not a bad first approximation. If we want to explain to a ten-year-old why a Volkswagen is worth about a ton of butter, it will usually satisfy him to say that they cost about the same amount of labor to produce; and this explanation is certainly good enough to explain why a Volkswagen is worth one ton of butter and not ten. On the other hand, at more refined levels of analysis, the labor theory breaks down, simply because labor is not the only scarce resource. The fundamental problem is what creates a production opportunity boundary with a negative slope. The general answer is *scarcity* of some kind, and certainly one of the major sources of scarcity is the fact that any society only has so many hours a day to spend, and what we spend on one thing we cannot spend on another. On the other hand, other sources of scarcity have also come to be recognized. Ricardo, for instance, introduced the "time taken to bring the commodity to market" as a modifier of the labor theory, and in effect Marx accepted this. This is what Marshall afterwards called "waiting." If one had to go a long way into the woods to get the beaver, so that it took a year to bring it to market, we would have to add a time preference or interest factor to get the equilibrium market price, for if the commodities exchanged only in proportion to the quantities of labor embodied, those that involve a lot of waiting in addition would simply not be produced, and their price would therefore rise until it was sufficient to compensate for the waiting. Similarly, we may wish to identify other elements in society, the scarcity of which limits the production possibility curve.

Certain natural abilities, for instance, may be scarce and incapable of reproduction. Limitations of available land, of organizational skills, means of communication, willingness to take risks, and so on, may all be factors limiting the production possibility curve as well as labor as such, or simple human time. In reality therefore the production possibility curve in its *n* space is going to have a lot of kinks, discontinuities, and holes in it, which mess up the beautiful simplicities of price theory.

The whole theory of value in economics assumes scarcity in the sense that the preferred position of all individuals and the society in general is beyond the production possibility curve, and hence the equilibrium position will always be on the curve itself. We conceive the society as always wanting more than it can get, and hence being limited by its production possibilities. It is this limitation that produces the price system and value in the economic sense of the word. Suppose, however, that either the society is so affluent or its desires are so undeveloped that its optimum position lies within the production possibility set, that is, within the area BOD in Figure 1. Suppose, for instance, that the point M represented the satiation point, both for beaver and for deer, in the society. The indifference curves would be roughly circular around M; there would be nothing to prevent the society moving to its point of maximum preference at M; and it would never expand to the production possibility curve at all. Under these circumstances the whole theory of value collapses, simply because there is no scarcity, because we can have all our cakes and eat them too, because we do not have to give up anything in order to get something. All prices would be zero, and exchange would simply disappear. Beaver and deer would roam the village and expire blissfully like schmoo on the front door of every household. Continued economic development makes this eventuality not so absurd as it might at one time have seemed, for economic development means pushing the production possibility curve "out," for instance from BD to EF. Assuming there are any points of satiety at all, that is, assuming that the general preference function has a maximum in the field of commodities, if this process is continued long enough the production possibility curve would eventually pass over the maximum of the preference function and the value system will disappear. This indeed is not unlike Marx's vision of the ultimate communist society, in which affluence simply destroys the price system and everyone has as much as he wants of everything. This indeed is the Big Rock Candy Mountain, and whether it is a utopian dream or a nightmare, depends very much on who is looking at it.

Whether this dream or nightmare will ever become reality is another question altogether. I must confess myself to be highly skeptical about the possibility of even the eventual disappearance of the value problem, that is, of scarcity in the economic sense. In the first place, the developmental process is ultimately self-limiting, and even though we are at the moment in the midst of a great transition in human productivity, this does not mean that the process is endless. Furthermore, it is clear that in the course of economic development, even though labor or human time and energy as a source of limitation may become less important, other sources of limitation become more important. Land as a limiting factor, for instance, is becoming increasingly important with the expansion of the human population, and we may easily end up with a land theory of value rather than a labor theory of value, in which the sheer difficulty of finding space for anything is the thing that forces us into a production possibility function. If we do A, we cannot find the space to do B. We will have to face also in the next few hundred years the development of what I have elsewhere called a "space-ship economy," that is, an economy that no longer depends on inputs of material from mines and geological accumulations or on output of material to pollutable reservoirs, but that has to maintain a place for man in a closed ecological cycle. In the space-ship economy, scarcity may be a very acute factor indeed, and I have suggested that what we may have to look forward to is a peculiar combination of affluence and parsimony, affluence in regard to the general environment or state, parsimony in respect to the through-put of materials through it. It by no means follows, therefore, that economic development inevitably leads to the disappearance of scarcity. Nevertheless, it may lead to the development of different kinds of scarcity, and in particular to a very different system of relative prices than what we are now accustomed to. Even the course of economic development so far has profoundly changed the structure of relative prices, simply because the productivity in some lines changes much faster than in others. Thus, because the most technologically progressive industry has been agriculture, the relative prices of agricultural commodities have tended to fall very sharply by contrast with the prices of the unprogressive industries, such as education. Jean Fourastié has pointed this out in a masterly, though rather neglected work.[2] These marked changes in the relative price structure create real difficulties in cross-cultural communication between, say, more developed and less developed societies.

The problem of the shift in the relative price structure with development can also be illustrated by Figure 1. If development is relatively uniform for both beaver and deer, the production possibility curve will move from BD, say, to EF, and there will not be much change in the relative price structure. If, however, the beaver industry, shall we say, is stagnant and the deer industry is progressive, the production possibility curve will be anchored at B and will move, say, from BD to BF, thereby increasing the relative price of beaver, diminishing that of deer. This incidentally illustrates why parity in agricultural policy is such a foolish concept, from the point of view at least of economic justice; for it assumes that the relative price structure of one period is sacred for all time, whereas in fact if agriculture, as indeed it is, is more progressive than the rest of the economy in improving its technology, the relative price of agricultural commodities ought to fall, and the maintenance of parity would be a gross injustice.

Arising out of, and largely based on, the set of relative prices, is another important set of valuation coefficients, that is, the ratios by which we can multiply the items of a hetero-geneous aggregate to transform each quantity into a common measure, such as money. Thus two elephants plus three wrist-watches are not five of anything very much, but if we can multiply each by its valuation coefficient, if elephants, say, are a thousand dollars each and wristwatches a hundred dollars each, then the total of two elephants and three wristwatches is $2,300. Money is not the only possible measure of value; value can be expressed, of course, in any single commodity, or "numeraire." We could even use a thing like density as a valuation coefficient, or weight per unit, to get a sum total of weight, which might be highly relevant if we were shipping the items by air freight. In this sense, however, valuation always implies reducing a heterogeneous aggregate to a com-mon uniform measure.

The usefulness of these concepts extends far beyond the usual limits of economics. They apply, indeed, wherever choices have to be made and wherever, therefore, we must compare one aggregate with another and say which we prefer. Decision theory is a large mathematical apparatus resting like an inverted cone on the delicate point that everybody does what he thinks is best at the time; and it is astonishing that a principle apparently so empty could produce such an enormous mass of mathematical content. The trick, of course, lies in the assumption of regular sequences in the variables and of well-behaved preference functions that permit marginal adjust-ments or maximum extreme points. This is what Wordsworth describes as "the lore of nicely calculated less or more," which today is known as Operations Research. In linear, and even more in nonlinear programming, we have developed out of what are essentially the basic principles of economic value theory, an elaborate set of mathematical tools devised to re-duce complex problems to quantitative form in which they can be solved. The principle is a relatively simple one. We identify a field of choice; we associate each position in the field with some quantity or number such that the bigger the num-ber, the better the case; and then by a wide range of mathematical devices we identify that element in the field of choice which bears the biggest number of the value function. This, we say, is the solution of the problem. Techniques of this kind have been applied to problems as diverse as the routing of ships, the mix of products of a gasoline refining plant, the organization of traffic through a tunnel, or the planning of a whole public transportation system. It is not surprising that in the light of the extraordinary eloquence and beauty of these principles, the economist tends to regard the price system with an almost superstitious awe and to regard maximizing behavior as virtually the moral law within, for the subtle order that is revealed in the making and interaction of human decisions is as great as that of the starry universe without.

In the face of the wonder and beauty of economics, it is somewhat of a shock to the economist to be brought up against the proposition, to enlarge the quotation from Wordsworth, that high heaven rejects the lore of nicely calculated less or more.[3] Here we have economics confronted with what I suppose might be called theonomics. In this rejection of the whole kit and kaboodle of the economic ethic, economic behavior, rational choice, maximizing utility, and this whole apparatus of nice calculation of gain and loss, the poet is joined by the preachers, prophets, lovers, and military men, who unite with high heaven against the economist, insisting on fine frenzy, unconfined joy, giving without cost, and not reasoning why. When this united blast has swept all the papers off his desk, the economist may pick them up again and argue that he can still reduce these objections to rational mathematics. The protests of high heaven, as reflected for instance in the exhortation to give without counting the cost and to labor without asking any reward, or in the advice to take no thought for the morrow or to let the dead bury their dead, unquestionably arises out of a sense of the infinity of spiritual resources and the enormous spiritual riches available for those who take the plunge in the baptism of divine love. One finds this sense of the infinity of the spiritual resources especially in the New Testament and in St. Francis and other recapitulators of the

Gospel, and where this sense is strong and spiritual coin is plentiful, the faithful can have their spiritual cakes and eat them too, and choice is unnecessary, and the niggling problems of economic scarcity do not arise. We could interpret this, of course, and it is particularly tempting to interpret St. Francis in this way, as a deliberate moving of the position of maximum utility within the production possibility line so that ordinary economic considerations become meaningless. However, economics has usually taken its toll of spiritual and utopian communities that have rejected it, and both the early church of Jerusalem and the Franciscan Order had to come to terms very soon with the dismal theorems of material scarcity, and even perhaps ultimately with spiritual scarcities.

In political and military life the protest against economics as we find it, say, in the "Charge of the Light Brigade," or even in the late President Kennedy's exhortation that we "ask not what our country can do for us but what we can do for our country" arises from a sense of certain discontinuities in the production functions or the preference functions. In the market place or the bargaining table one may have nicely calculated less or more. In the political arena, however, there develops a certain ideology of "winner take all." What we are running into here is absolute values, that is, infinite rates of substitution, in which no amount of monetary or other economic ointment in the way of returns could compensate for the loss of national integrity or personal pride. In all three religious, political, and military, life the heroic ethic has always stressed the possibility, indeed the necessity, of certain absolute values. If we once admit that it is possible to die for anything, nicely calculated less or more seems to go out the window. The economist can retort, of course, that even if utility functions have discontinuities and infinite rates of substitution, they are still utility functions, and the formal theory applies. However, this makes the theory so formal as to be virtually without any content. The economist might go even further, of course, and denounce these heroic utility functions as in some sense abnormal or malign, and he may add that even in the Charge of the Light Brigade somebody will ask the reason why, and somebody might even ask if it makes any sense to regard one's country in a different light from the way one regards General Motors, which is exceeded by only eleven countries in its GNP, and is a good deal more useful than most of them. The economist has a certain sneaking suspicion that economic man has perfect mental health, having no delusions of grandeur, no Freudian complexes, no heroic attitudinizing, and at least an Olympian neutrality toward his exchange mates. Superman is only a costume, and Batman a mask; and after all their heroic exploits they will have to go back to economic Mama and count their costs, ask their rewards, pay the bills, and face the inexorable consequences of real scarcities, which their heroic antics have actually increased. There is unquestionably a demand for the heroic, a lot of which perhaps rises out of a subconscious protest against the disgreeable fact of scarcity itself. There is more to it than this, however. The demand for the heroic cannot merely be dismissed as irrational, for without it human life would be deprived of a great deal that makes it worth living. What we have to achieve, however, is a creative tension between heroic man and, dare we say it, economic woman. Economics, if we remember, in Greek is the science of householdry, and the demands of domesticity are perhaps the best check on the excesses of the heroic.

Is there any sense, then, in which human values can really be contrasted with economic values, in the sense, for instance, in which Oscar Wilde, I think it was, accused the cynic of knowing the price of everything and the value of nothing? Economists have always recognized, of course, that market prices could diverge from some ideal evaluation or exchange ratio. The distorting effects of monopoly have been long recognized, and so has the problem of "neighborhood effects," in which there are real costs and benefits that do not get into the accounting system—the smoke nuisance, river pollution on the one side, private gardens in public view and just being a nice guy on the other side. There is also an uneasiness among economists about speculative instabilities in the market, especially in highly organized competitive markets such as the stock exchange or the wheat market. From Dutch bulbs to Florida land booms, certain diseases of the market have been apparent, mostly those that result technically from positive feedback, where rising prices induce the belief that prices will go on rising, and vice versa. Many of these diseases of the market can be corrected, perhaps by regulation, perhaps by countervailing power, perhaps by counterspeculation, perhaps through the tax system. On the other hand, both the diagnosis and the cure of these ills requires an information system of a delicacy that we do not always possess, and economics has always been curiously indifferent to the nature of its information system. We have long advocated, for instance, the taxation of economic rent, without investigating very much how we know where to find it.

Suppose, however, that we cure all these ills of the market, what then? No matter how well we take care of all neighborhood effects and external economies and diseconomies, no matter how exactly the seven marginal conditions of welfare economics are fulfilled, there remains a residue of elements in social relations that are not accounted for by exchange. It is these residues (the concept is not unlike that of Pareto) that constitute what I call the integrative system, involving such things as status, respect, love, honor, community, identity, legitimacy, and so on. I would argue indeed that without an integrative framework, exchange itself cannot develop, because exchange, even in its most primitive forms, involves trust and credibility; and this demands at least elementary forms of the integrative system. If therefore there is a contrast between economic values and human values, it is precisely at this point. Economic values are those that involve exchange, that is, a situation in which a quid is given for a quo. In economic terms, the integrative system is best measured, perhaps, by what I have called the "grants economy" in which quids are given without any quos, simply because of status, identity, community, love, and so on. The sense that pervades a great deal of human literature, especially of the more romantic and heroic kind, that human values are in some sense superior to economic values, arises, I think, out of the sense that exchange without an integrative system is strongly self-limiting, even self-defeating. There is not much point in being rich, for instance, if we do not have legitimacy. Threat systems likewise cannot establish themselves in the absence of an integrative framework. How the integrative system is established, maintained, and developed, is of course another story altogether. It is not unrelated to the exchange system; wealth, for instance, often creates legitimacy, even if it does not insure love. If the terms of trade between the partners to a marriage, a citizen and his government, an employee and his employer, are too unfavorable, the integrative system will be undermined. On the other hand, if the integrative system is strong, this permits unfavorable terms of trade. It is clear that these relationships are both complex and reciprocal. Their clarification, however, can clear up a good deal of confusion about values.

Even though the principles that govern the integrative system are somewhat different from those that govern exchange, for a good many of its aspects the general principles of economic analysis can be applied. The general theory of preference can take care of benevolence and even malevolence just as well as it can deal with selfishness. If we identify the welfare of another as our own, we can take care of this in formal theory by simply supposing that the preference function that governs our behavior has goods possessed by others in its domain as well as goods that we possess ourselves. If we make a gift, it is presumably because we prefer the distribution in which we have less and another more to the one from which we started. There is nothing irrational in this; indeed, because community is one of the supreme achievements of man, it is highly rational. Economics is thus seen to go far beyond the limits of Jevons, who defined it as the mechanics of utility and self-interest. It might be better defined as the mechanics of reflective choice, which by no means assumes self-interest, at least in any narrow sense of the self.

These principles can be illustrated in Figure 2, in which

we plot A's welfare vertically and B's welfare horizontally. The point P represents a given position in the field, and we may suppose that one of the parties, say A, has a range of choice open to him that can be mapped in the field as something like the shaded area; that is, he can move from P to any point within the shaded area. If now he is completely selfish, his indifference curves will be horizontal, that is, he will be indifferent to B's welfare and will always prefer an increase of his own. In that case his decision will be to move from P to P_1, where the boundary of the area of choice is touched by a horizontal indifference curve. If he is benevolent, his indifference curves will be negatively sloped, indicating that he would prepare to sacrifice some of his welfare for a gain in B's welfare, the extent of his benevolence being measured by the slope of the indifference curve. In such a case he might move to a point such as P_2, in which his own welfare increases a little less than it would do to P_1, but in which B's welfare increases also. If he is malevolent, his indifference curve will be positively sloped, indicating that he will give up his own welfare in order to reduce B's welfare. In such a case he might move to a position such as P_3.

An important conclusion follows from this analysis, that under some circumstances, namely, where the slope of the opportunity line or the boundary of the area of possibility is roughly the same as the slope of the indifference curve, a very small change in preference may result in a large change in the decision.[4] Thus in Figure 2, a relatively slight increase in benevolence might move him from P_2 to P_4. Even quite extreme cases can be handled by this analysis. If we suppose a total altruism, so that A values only B's welfare and not his own, his indifference curves will be vertical, and he would move, say, to P_5. If we suppose total malevolence, the indifference curves will again be vertical, only this time the utility will increase as B's welfare declines, and he will move to P_6. We could even suppose A to be governed by self-hatred and indifference to B, in which case he would go to P_7. Virtually any combination, therefore, of attitudes toward himself and

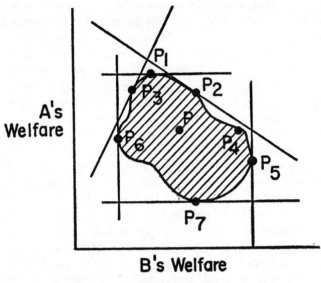

A's Welfare

B's Welfare

Figure 2

others can be taken care of by the nature of the preference function, provided, of course, that we have some kind of objective measure of both A's and B's welfare; otherwise the analysis breaks down. In economic terms, these objective measures are not too difficult to get, for instance in terms of something like per capita real income. In the case of political and the more complex integrative relations, the measures are much harder and this type of analysis less applicable.

A strong case can be made, therefore, for the extension at least of the method of economics into the integrative system, in which case all human values become at least subject to economic analysis, even if we may wish to distinguish between what we might call "ordinary" economics and the more exotic cases of the integrative system. The very capacity of economics for analysis, furthermore, produces a substantial impact on the nature of our preferences themselves. This is something that economists have rather neglected, with the notable exception of Veblen, who perceived very clearly that preferences were not "given" but were themselves products of the social system, and that in any dynamic social science we had to take account of the fact that the price system, for instance, determines preferences just as preferences determine the price system. We sometimes decide not to want what we can't get (the sour-grapes principle), or sometimes our inability to get something spurs desire still further, as in romantic love. One of the things that affects our preferences is precisely, however, the ability to analyze them, which comes out of economics itself. In this sense economics may turn out to be the real enemy of the heroic. In Marx, oddly enough, economics became the excuse for a heroic ideology. As operations research takes over, the heroic aspects fade, and even heroic Marxism becomes, in the words of Gerard Manley Hopkins, "bleared, smeared by trade." In spite of Manley Hopkins, however, who was, after all, a poet and a romantic, trade makes us reasonable, if not sweet. On this profoundly ambiguous note I had better conclude, before I am totally incapacitated by my internal fight between the poet and the economist.

NOTES

1. Adam Smith, *The Wealth of Nations,* Book I, Chapter 6.
2. *The Causes of Wealth,* by Jean Fourastié, translated by Theodore Caplow, Glencoe, Illinois: The Free Press, 1960.
3. William Wordsworth, sonnet on King's College Chapel, *Collected Poems,* Oxford Edition, 1917, p. 451.
4. K. E. Boulding, "Some Contributions of Economics to the General Theory of Value," *Philosophy of Science,* XXIII, 1 (January 1956), 1–14.

B

Preference, Evaluation, and Reflective Choice

ERNEST NAGEL
Columbia University

IN THE FINAL SENTENCE of his paper Professor Boulding suggests, what is evident in any case, that it is the work of a thinker who is both an economist and a poet. Since I am neither one nor the other, I am clearly unqualified to comment on his contribution, even though I feel generally able to distinguish the things in it that are properly economics from those that are poetry. But I must also confess to some disappointment with his essay. For despite its title, there seems to me little in it that deals centrally with problems in the evaluation (or validation) of what Professor Boulding, like most professional economists, calls "value judgments" in economics; on the contrary, he devotes himself mainly to expounding the uses made in economic analysis of a formal calculus of postulated preferences. The rationale of evaluating preferences undoubtedly is a theme on which philosophers might be expected to have something to say; but a discussion of this problem would be only remotely relevant to the substance of the present essay. Moreover, many of the views expressed in the paper are summary statements of positions Professor Boulding has developed at considerable length elsewhere; and while some of his present formulations of points call for fuller explanations and justifications than he here gives them, under the circumstances it would be a gratuitous exercise to raise questions about them. My comments will therefore be few and brief, and my primary intent in making them is to persuade

Professor Boulding to expand on some views he holds that, to my knowledge, he has nowhere stated except in outline.

I

My first set of remarks is concerned with matters I am confident belong to problems of economic analysis or of its methodology. The task suggested by the title of Boulding's paper can be construed in two ways. First, as an analysis of the nature and role of various sorts of so-called "value judgments" that are presumably found as components in the *subject-matter* of *positive* economics, as materials that the economist can objectively identify, so that the task is somewhat analogous to those attempted by social anthropologists who seek to disclose the place and function of various systems of values held by members of a community in the operations of the society. Secondly, the task can be taken to be that of analyzing the ways in which, and the grounds on which, economists as *students* of economic behavior (as distinct from agents of such activity) make explicit or tacit commitments to various "values," whether in their theoretical constructions or in their policy recommendations. On the face of it, these are different tasks, even if they should prove to be related ones; and I understand Boulding's paper to be concerned in the main with the first of them.

However, it is frequently alleged (though of course not by Boulding) that the value commitments of social scientists in general and of economists in particular enter constitutively into their analyses of human transactions. It is therefore claimed not only that a "value-free" positive economics is impossible, but also that a distinction cannot be drawn between the values allegedly held by the agents who form part of the economist's subject matter and his own value judgments. The issues raised by this claim are complex—they are partly factual, partly logical—and this is not the place to go into them, and I must content myself with asserting without argument that none of the reasons that have been advanced for the claim seem to me cogent. On the other hand, rejection of view that a value-free economic analysis is *in principle* impossible does *not* exclude the possibility that the value preconceptions of economists may *in fact* influence their theoretical analyses. However, whether such influence is operative in a given theory cannot be settled a priori one way or another, and can be ascertained only by a detailed examination of the theory under discussion. But it is pertinent to add that since recommendations of economic policy are sometimes alleged to be based exclusively on considerations of positive economics, it is important to make sure whether tacitly accepted policy goals are not antecedently built into the assumptions of an ostensible positive theory.

But however this may be, I will take for granted that the value judgments whose nature and basis Boulding is examining are conceived by him to be in some manner identifiable in the *subject matter* of economic analysis, whether or not he himself subscribes to those values. He notes, however, that the word "value" is ambiguous even when it occurs in economic discussions, and a good fraction of his paper is taken up with distinguishing four important senses in which the term is employed by theoretical economists. Let me briefly summarize these senses. The first is the notion of value as the ratio in which quantities of commodities are exchanged in the market—according to Boulding, this is the fundamental sense of "value," for it is a major objective of economic theory to explain the structure of exchange ratios. The second sense of the word is based on the first, and is associated with a "valuational coefficient" or ratio with the help of which the items of a heterogeneous aggregate of commodities are assigned a common quantitative measure, such as money. The third is the notion of value as the ratio of substitution of commodities (or alternative costs) in production. The fourth is the notion of value as the ratio of indifferent substitution of commodities in consumption that leaves "the welfare or utility" of individual consumers unchanged; and on the assumption that these ratios can be linearly ordered for each individual, value in this sense is taken to be the "measure of subjective evaluation" (or preference) that individuals (or other economic units) supposedly associate with commodities. The substance of Boulding's paper then expounds in broad outline the way in which current economic theory explains the structure of exchange ratios (or prices), the explanation offered involving in part reference to the relative utilities or preferences that economic units allegedly associate with different commodities.

The adequacy of explanations of the type to which Boulding subscribes is the subject of continuing controversy among economists, but the question is not discussed by him, and I will therefore ignore it as not germane to his paper. However, since in any case the various senses of "value" he distinguishes, and especially the notion of value as relative preference, play a fundamental role in his account, some comment on them is appropriate.

a) "Value judgments" as commonly understood in moral philosophy are statements expressing a reasoned approval (or disapproval) of something by someone, in the light of deliberation concerning what is desirable. However, when "value" is used in any of the first three meanings Boulding notes, statements he calls "value judgments" (in conformity with established usage in economics) have no such connotation; for although they *may* be the outcome of such deliberation, this is not essential to them by virtue of their explicit definition, so that they must apparently be construed simply as morally neutral descriptions of certain facts of economic behavior. Thus, the sense in which it is a value judgment to say, for example, that two commodities are exchanged in the market in some given ratio of their quantities, is basically similar to the sense in which it is a value judgment to assert that the complete turns each of a pair of meshed cog wheels makes are in a specified ratio to one another. Accordingly, value judgments as predications of comparative measure are not distinctive of economic analysis, and are as pervasive in the natural as in the social sciences.

b) The assumption central to the type of explanation Boulding expounds in his paper—namely, that each consumer entering into the economic market comes provided with a definite schedule of indifference curves that are ordered according to preference—has been frequently criticized by institutionalists in economics as "unrealistic" or false to fact. Indeed, Boulding himself notes that the preferences of individuals are not just "given but [are] themselves products of the social system," and that the price system "determines preferences just as preferences determine the price system." However, although the unrealistic character of this assumption is generally admitted, in my opinion as in Boulding's this by itself is not a sufficient reason for rejecting (as many critics believe) the explanations in which the assumption is incorporated—any more than the unrealistic character of numerous assumptions in physical theories (e.g., hypotheses formulated in terms of frictionless surfaces or perfectly elastic bodies) is adequate ground for rejecting those theories.

On the other hand, the use of such assumptions does call for methodological clarification, with the intent of showing just how, despite their lack of "realism," the assumptions are relevant for understanding the actual operations of the economic market. The need for such clarification seems to me especially pressing in view of Boulding's own claims. For according to the account he has given in another work, ". . . marginal analysis, in its generalized form, is *not* an analysis of *behavior* but analysis of *advantage*. It is not a psychology or an analysis of actual behavior. It is more akin to an *ethic* or an analysis of normative positions. It only becomes an analysis of behavior if we make the further assumption that people always act according to their best advantage." [1] However, this further assumption is itself hardly a true descriptive statement about people in general. Professor Boulding therefore owes his readers a fuller explanation than he has thus far given in any of his publications (at any rate, in those with which I am familiar) of how, from a normative theory of maximum advantage conjoined with a patently false factual assumption, he thinks it is possible to account for actual economic behavior.

c) The ratios of indifferent substitutions that enter into Boulding's fourth sense of "value" are said by him to be measures of "subjective evaluations" of commodities that leave "our welfare or utility" unchanged. Provided a terminology is clear, it would be silly to quarrel with it, and I do not propose to do so. However, it is important to note that in their technical economic use the words "evaluation," "welfare," and "utility" do not have their ordinary meanings, but are employed in a Pickwickian sense. For in their formal expositions of the analytic technique of constructing and ordering indifference surfaces most contemporary economists (including, so I believe, Professor Boulding) stress the point that whether two bundles of commodities are to be placed on the same indifference curve for a given individual or on different curves is not a question whose determination requires a reflectively grounded decision as to whether the commodities *satisfy* the individual's *needs* or are even sources of *pleasure* to him—the question is settled by whether or not the individual *prefers* one bundle to another, irrespective of the reasons or lack of reasons for his preference. Accordingly, while there may be some consumers who form their preferences in the light of careful estimates of the satisfactions different combinations of commodities may yield, economic theory does not differentiate between such consumers and those whose preferences are uninformed by any knowledge of the likely consequences of alternative choices but are the expressions of unreflective impulse. To be sure, some economists maintain (though apparently not Boulding) that the preferences postulated by marginal theory are assumed to be made in the light of full knowledge of the innumerable consequences resulting from the choices open to consumers. But on this assumption the theory outflanks the reservations just noted, only to raise others. A theory of rational consumer choice that stipulates ideally complete knowledge and absence of any uncertainty may be a useful guide to omniscient beings; it is not obviously relevant to the problems of mortal men.

Nevertheless, though it is not clear in what sense uninformed preferences or desires may be said to be *evaluations*, or in what way questions of *welfare* are allegedly settled by such evaluations, it is certainly legitimate to develop a theory of the type Boulding has outlined, *if* the intent is to use the theory to describe and explain economic phenomena. On the other hand, when such a theory comes to be employed as a basis for policy recommendations, it becomes obviously pertinent to ask what credentials an ostensibly positive theory has for making any recommendations and whether they ought to be accepted. For it may not be to the best advantage of anyone to adopt such recommendations—unless, indeed, advantage (or welfare) is equated by definition with the fulfillment of the preferences prescribed by the theory, however arbitrary those preferences may otherwise be.

The question is difficult to answer, for it involves complex moral and social issues; but in any case, it cannot be settled by purely economic considerations that deliberately abstract, for legitimate limited purposes, from other aspects of human life. It is certainly not a question that economists (including Boulding) have generally ignored. It has been recently raised in a forthright way by Professor Abram Bergson when he asks, in the context of discussing the applicability of the maximizing principle to problems dealing with the allocation of resources, "To what extent should one be guided here by overt preferences such as the individual himself expresses in the market?"; and he makes clear that the principle of consumer sovereignty is by no means ethically neutral.[2]

Boulding himself carefully notes in some of his publications that when economists advocate specific economic policies, they do so not simply on the basis of some positive theory but only by postulating further certain objectives (e.g., the goal of increasing the rate of real income per capita, or equalizing income), since those objectives cannot be read out of the economic theory. However, he is far less explicit on this point in the present paper, even if for quite understandable reasons. Thus, in his brief discussion of the policy of maintaining parity of prices in agriculture (i.e., a constancy in the ratio of the prices at which farmers sell their produce to the prices at which farmers buy their commodities), he declares that it is foolish to assume that "the relative price structure of one period is sacred for all time"; and he notes that because of technological development in farming, the productivity in agriculture has increased much more rapidly than in other industries, so that the relative price of agricultural goods has declined just as economic theory requires it should. Boulding therefore concludes that since "the relative price of agricultural commodities *ought* to fall," the maintenance of parity would be "a gross injustice." (Italics added.) I am aware that elsewhere Boulding has supplied the missing steps in this argument, and that in particular he has indicated the social objectives relative to which he believes the policy of maintaining parity creates injustices. However, as the argument is presented in the present paper, the conclusion is a non sequitur—except on the generally indefensible assumption that a structure of prices that positive economic theory asserts *should* obtain as a matter of fact is necessarily the structure of prices that *ought* to obtain as the *just* one when measured in the light of some accepted moral or social ideal.

In short, economists whose policy recommendations rest in part on considerations drawn from positive theory must guard themselves against confusing the formal "values" that are imputed to economic agents for purposes of theoretical analysis and the "values" that are being served in the advocacy of some policy. But just how these prima facie different sorts of value judgments are related is not fully clear from Boulding's paper; and it is my hope that in his extended comments he will make it so.

II

Boulding maintains that the distinctions and mode of analysis presented in the first half of his paper can be usefully extended into areas far beyond the usual limits of economics. Indeed, he declares that the analytic tools described in it can be applied "wherever choices have to be made and wherever, therefore, we must compare one aggregate with another and say which we prefer." This claim is perhaps advanced by him only as a bit of deliberate poetry, but I am taking it seriously. Men have long been searching for a general logic of reflective choice, and it would be glad tidings if they were true that the principles of marginal analysis and consumer choice are at least a good first approximation to the objective of this quest. However, while I do not challenge Boulding's statement that the basic ideas underlying these principles (especially in the forms they have assumed in recent developments of decision theory) have been successfully employed outside the traditional domain of economics, there seems to me ground for doubt that their scope is quite as universal as he declares it to be.

The type of analysis Boulding's paper outlines reduces the problem of making a rational decision between alternative possibilities of choice to the problem of ascertaining by means of a straightforward mathematical calculation which of these possibilities is associated with the maximum value of some index of value. Accordingly, as the paper makes entirely clear, an indispensable condition for the effective application of the decision procedure to a given problem is the institution of a common measure of value for the heterogeneous aggregates of items between which a choice is to be made. And this is the point at which Boulding's account begins to waver in its clarity, and to leave his readers with puzzles on which he throws little light. There is certainly no doubt that such a common measure of value for different items can often be devised, especially in contexts in which the items belong to some system of exchange, or in which they can be substituted for one another for certain purposes. But it is not at all evident that such a measure can always be constructed in a nonarbitrary manner, or if it can, how it might be specified even if only in principle—especially when the items under consideration embody "multidimensional" values that are not separable from one another, or when they satisfy needs or interests that may not be substitutable for each other.

For all I know, Boulding may have discussed this critical point in satisfactory detail elsewhere. But he deals with it only sketchily in his paper, and what he says about it does not seem to me very helpful. He asserts that "the general theory of preference can take care of benevolence and even malevolence just as well as it can deal with selfishness"; and he suggests that the theory can do this if we identify the welfare of another person with our own "by simply supposing that the preference function that governs our behavior has goods possessed by others in its domain as well as goods that we possess ourselves." And he illustrates these dicta by introducing a diagram in which the "welfares" of two individuals A and B are represented by points within a certain area, while different "degrees" of A's selfishness are represented by the positions and slopes of A's indifference curves. However, none of this seems to me to speak to the issue. I confess to no difficulty in following Boulding's exposition of his diagram, once the diagram is taken for granted. My difficulty lies in understanding how the diagram has been *constructed*—for example, how the welfares of the individuals have been estimated so that points on the diagram can serve to represent them, how "degrees" are assigned to selfishness so that they can be mapped into slopes, and how an individual's concerns for himself and others are compared so that his indifference curves can be plotted. Provided that the relevant utility functions of the individuals have been specified, everything else is clear sailing. But the construction of those functions for the admittedly heterogenous collection of items that enter into the consideration of an individual's welfare presupposes an ordering of his preferences—an ordering whose existence seems to me in general problematic, though without which the theory of preference is inapplicable.

A less abstract example may help to make plainer the grounds for skepticism of Boulding's large claim for the theory of preference. Suppose that individual liberty and security from want are two factors contributing to a person's welfare, that each of these items has a number of components or "dimensions" (e.g., individual liberty includes, among other things, the possibility of making choices in political, economic, and religious matters), and that they are causally interrelated (e.g., restrictions on effective choice in organizing the economy may affect men's chances of suffering from want). Suppose further that in order to assess the import of some proposed social legislation a person undertakes to construct his schedule of indifference curves for these items. How is he to proceed? Since each item has several dimensions, it is at least an open question whether, say, alternative "forms" of individual liberty can be specified, where each form consists of some selection of its various dimensions; and in view of their causal interdependence, which precludes their effective separation and recombination, it is even less clear whether different bundles of forms of freedom and security can be enumerated. But it is impossible for a person to arrange in linear order his preferences for these items (whether taken singly or jointly), unless such listing of different bundles of them is first presented. The difficulty stems from the fact that there appear to be no "units" of freedom or of security (as there are in the case of commodities in the economic market) by the addition or subtraction of which a person's freedom or security can be significantly said to be either augmented or diminished; and it is therefore not evident what meaning, if any, is to be attached to the supposition (integrally involved in preference theory) that the substitution of so much freedom for so much security leaves invariant a person's utility (or welfare, or state of indifference as to preference). These difficulties may all have satisfactory answers, though if so I do not happen to be familiar with them. But unless or until they are resolved, the claim that the theory of preference constitutes a general logic of reflective choice has not been established.

NOTES

1. *The Skills of the Economist*, p. 60.

2. *Essays in Normative Economics* (Cambridge, Mass.: Harvard University Press, 1966), p. 53.

C

Value Judgments in Economics

MILTON FRIEDMAN
University of Chicago

I FIND myself in the pleasant position of agreeing fully with Kenneth Boulding's comments, except for a couple of technical quibbles that I shall relegate to a footnote.[1] Hence, I shall use this comment in part to supplement his remarks and in part to carry them in directions where he may not be willing to follow me.

I have been impressed by the tendency at this symposium for the philosophers and the economists to speak at cross purposes. The philosophers, I am sure, have somewhat the impression that the economists are avoiding what they regard as the basic issue, namely, the value judgments that affect and enter into private and public policy. And by value judgments, the philosophers do not mean relative exchange value. They mean "moral" or "ethical" values. The philosophers in my opinion are correct. To help explain why we have been avoiding "their" issue and to contribute a little to bridge the gap, I shall discuss three points: (1) The basic reason for the avoidance is that there are no value judgments in economics; (2) The appearance to the contrary arises partly from the tendency to use alleged differences in value judgments as an evasion in explaining differences in policy conclusions; (3) The market itself, broadly conceived, is a mechanism for the development and not merely the reflection of value judgments.

1) *The absence of value judgments in economics.* This point has been made by Professor Nagel in his comment and

85

I am fully in agreement with him. *In principle,* economics as a special discipline is concerned with the consequences of changes in circumstances on the course of events, with prediction and analysis, not with evaluation. It has something to say about whether specified objectives can be achieved and if so, how, but not, strictly speaking, with whether they are good or bad objectives.

Yet economics has something to say about value judgments. In the first place, no objectives are really fully defined. They are partly revealed in their consequences. In the second place, we never "really" know all our values. As my revered teacher Frank H. Knight is wont to say, though we all repeat "de gustibus non est disputandum," in practice we spend our time arguing about little else. And such discussion is relevant and fruitful. Its aim is to see what the implications of our value judgments are, whether they are internally consistent. This is the contribution of Arrow's important and fundamental work and of much of what is called welfare economics.

Further, economists are not solely that but also human beings, and their own values undoubtedly affect their economics. A "wert-frei" economics is an ideal and like most ideals often honored in the breach. The economist's value judgments doubtless influence the subjects he works on and perhaps also at times the conclusions he reaches. And, as already suggested, his conclusions react on his value judgments. Yet this does not alter the fundamental point that, in principle, there are no value judgments in economics, despite the title of this session.

2) *The resort to alleged value judgments as evasions.* I have been much impressed, in the course of much controversy about issues of economic policy, that most differences in economic policy in the United States do not reflect differences in value judgments, but differences in positive economic analysis. I have found time and again that in mixed company—i.e., a company of economists and noneconomists such as is here today—the economists present, although initially one would tend to regard them as covering a wide range

of political views, tend to form a coalition vis-à-vis the non-economists, and, often much to their surprise, to find themselves on the same side. They may argue among themselves on the fine points, but these differences disappear when they confront the lay world.

But even within the profession, the same point applies. Paul Samuelson and I have often disagreed in recent years about the relative weight to be put on monetary and fiscal policy. This difference does not reflect—as I trust Paul Samuelson will agree—any difference in our basic or even reasonably proximate objectives. It reflects a difference in the tentative hypotheses we accept about the relation between monetary and fiscal changes on the one hand and economic changes on the other.

An example I have often used that brings out the same point is the minimum wage rate. If we leave aside those who have special interests in the issue, the difference between those who favor and those who oppose minimum wage rates is not about the objective but about the effect. Both groups would like to see poverty reduced. Those who, like myself, are opposed to minimum-wage laws predict that the effect of the laws will be to render people unemployed and hence to increase poverty; those who favor them predict that the effect will be to reduce poverty. If they agreed on effects they would agree on policy. The difference is not a moral one but a scientific one, in principle capable of being resolved by empirical evidence.

The reason why, in my opinion, apparent differences in policy judgments between people in the same culture are largely of this kind is the point raised in the discussion of Arrow's paper and in Boulding's paper: the need for agreement on basic values to avoid the "impossibility" theorem. Differences in opinion among people from different cultures would probably more frequently reflect "real" differences in value judgments.

The fact—or what I allege to be a fact—that differences about policy reflect mostly differences in predictions is concealed by the widespread tendency to attribute policy differences to differences in value judgments. This tendency arises because it is often so much easier to question a man's motives than to meet his arguments or counter his evidence. We can shortcut the hard process of analysis and collection of evidence, and at the same time bring the support of indignation and moral fervor to our views, by regarding the man who differs with us as a "bad" man who wants to achieve "bad" objectives. I was particularly impressed by the seductiveness of this approach during the 1964 presidential election, when most of the intellectuals, of all people, largely cut off the possibility of rational discussion by refusing to recognize the possibility that Senator Goldwater might have much the same objectives as they and simply differ in his judgment about how to achieve them.

To avoid misunderstanding, let me emphasize that I am not asserting that all policy differences are attributable to differences in positive analysis. Some clearly do reflect differences in value judgments. But I submit, the cause of reaching rational agreement will be furthered if we leave that explanation as a last resort rather than using it as the first.

Let me also note that there undoubtedly is a relation between men's value judgments and their presumptions about matters of fact. There is a subtle and complex relation that needs further study but on which I have nothing but platitudes to offer.

3) *Role of market in developing value judgments.* My third point is more closely related to Boulding's paper. Boulding takes as the essence of economic exchange, the "nicely calculated less or more." His position on the limitations of economic exchange is very similar to that which J. M. Clark so felicitously summarized in his famous remark that "an irrational passion for dispassionate rationality takes the joy out of life." Boulding ends by discussing the "integrative" system that is necessary to complement market exchange narrowly conceived.

Valid and important as Boulding's comments are, they are

confined to only one dimension of the relation between economic analysis and value judgments. Another, and a very different dimension, is the role of the market as a device for the voluntary cooperation of many individuals in the establishment of common values, whether these be ratios of exchange in the market or the components of the integrative system to which Boulding refers. In this dimension, "exchange" and the "market" cover a far broader range than the narrowly economic. The aim of my comments is to direct attention to the broader relevance of what seem at first like narrowly economic constructs.

Boulding emphasizes the "quid-pro-quo" character of market exchange. This characteristic is precisely the requirement for an exchange to be voluntary. Unless each participant receives something he values more than what he gives up, he will not enter into a transaction—if the transaction is to take place, he will have to be coerced. In a "free" market, he must be "persuaded," which is the same as "bribed."

For exchange to take place, the values of the participants must differ. If Mr. A has X and Mr. B has Y and both agree that X is to be preferred to Y, no exchange of X for Y can take place. Exchange of X for Y only takes place if Mr. A values Y more than X and Mr. B values X more than Y. In that case, both A and B benefit from the exchange of X for Y and the exchange will take place, unless prevented by some third party. As this trivial example illustrates, the essence of exchange is the reconciliation of divergent values; of achievement of unanimity without conformity. If instead of the one act of exchanging all of X for all of Y, we conceive of X and Y as divisible magnitudes and of exchange proceeding piecemeal, then exchange between Mr. A and Mr. B will continue until, *at the margin,* both attach the same relative value to a little more of X or of Y. In this sense they have been brought to agreement about value through exchange. Yet this agreement is only at the remaining point of contact between them. Both can be well satisfied with the prior exchanges even though that leaves Mr. A, say, having most of the Y and

Mr. B having most of the X. Introduce other participants, and the process of achieving unanimity without conformity is broadened: throughout the whole market, all participants will come to have common values at the margin. It takes a difference of opinion to make a horse race, as the saying goes, and the opportunity to wager on the outcome enables the difference of opinion to be a source of mutual satisfaction rather than an occasion for conflict.

The same analysis applies immediately to free speech and free discussion. Here again, the freedom to speak does not imply having an audience, just as the freedom to sell does not mean having a buyer, only the opportunity to seek one. Only if speaker and listener can mutually benefit will transactions take place in the market for ideas. And again, it will generally require a difference of opinions for the transaction to be consummated. Few experiences are duller than communicating with someone with whom you are in complete agreement on everything—though that concept is clearly a nonexistent ideal type. None of us even agrees completely with himself.

The essence of free speech as of free exchange is the mutual benefit to the participants. The hope is that it will enable us to reconcile our differences while each of us gains in the process. Indeed, I should not say "of free speech as of free exchange," for free speech is a special case of free exchange.

Similarly, consider "academic freedom" or freedom to pursue the bent of one's intellectual interests in research and writing. If intellectuals applied to this area the kind of analysis they bring to the market in goods and services, many or perhaps most would have to oppose such freedom. They would be led to deplore the "chaos" involved in letting each man decide for himself what is important, the "duplication" and "wastes of competition" involved in different scholars studying the same problems, the lack of "social priorities" in determining which are the "important" problems to be studied. They would be led to call for "central planning," with a governmental body to decide what topics most need investigation, to assign scholars to the areas in which they could, as judged by that body, contribute most, to see to it that there is no wasteful duplication of effort, and so on.

Because this comes close to home, intellectuals know better. They know that if there were complete agreement on values and on knowledge in this area, such central planning would be harmless—and also unnecessary. But with the present extent of disagreement and of ignorance, they prefer the "wastes" of a free competitive market to the coercion of central planning, and they reinforce their preference by the rationalization, which conforms to my prejudices too, that this is a surer way to add to our knowledge than reliance on a few chosen agents. Unfortunately, they do not recognize their inconsistency in applying wholly different standards to the market for goods.

Boulding emphasizes that "the economist tends to regard the price system with an almost superstitious awe" and to marvel at "the subtle order that is revealed in the making and interaction of human decisions." These same sentiments are evoked by the more generalized application of free exchange. The whole wondrous body of modern scientific knowledge has been built up by free exchange in the market place for ideas. Or consider another example, the development of language. Here is a complex interrelated structure capable of gradual evolution. Yet no one "planned" it that way. It just grew through the voluntary cooperation of millions of individuals coordinated by free verbal exchange. The structure of common law is yet another splendid example.

Which brings me full circle to the point made by Boulding that set me off: the need for an "integrative" system, which I interpret to mean, the need for a common set of values that must be unthinkingly accepted by the bulk of the people the bulk of the time in order for any stable society to exist. How have these values developed and changed and come to be accepted? What is a desirable mechanism for the preservation of such a set of values, which yet retains the possibility for change?

Here is where I suggest that economic analysis can contribute most to the political scientist and the philosopher. For it brings out how such a structure can emerge and develop from the spontaneous and voluntary cooperation of individual human beings and need not be imposed or constructed or legislated by philosopher-kings, or aristocrats, or presidents, or legislators, though all of these have much to contribute to its development. In many ways, this is the basic role of the free market in both goods and ideas—to enable mankind to cooperate in this process of searching for and developing values.

Needless to say, the process of social evolution of values does not guarantee that the integrative system that develops will be consistent with the kind of society that you or I with our values would prefer—indeed, the evidence of experience suggests that it is most unlikely to. Most of mankind at all times has lived in misery and under tyranny. One of the urgent questions requiring investigation is, indeed, what integrative system will be consistent with the kind of society we value, what circumstances contribute to the development of such a system, and to what extent the key element is the process itself—such as free discussion—or the substantive content of the integrative system.

Each of us, as he attempts to influence the values of his fellows, is part of this process of development of integrative systems. Each of us, also, is proceeding, as he must, on the basis of tentative answers to the questions just suggested. So in such sessions as these we are simultaneously actor and audience, observer and observed, teacher and student.

NOTES

1. 1) Boulding implies that the existence of more than one limitational factor means that there will be "kinks, discontinuities, and holes" in the "production possibility curve in its n space." This is wrong. The production possibility curve *can* be perfectly well behaved, without kinks, discontinuities, or holes, regardless of the

number of limitational factors; and, on the other hand, it may *have* kinks and discontinuities even if there is only one limitational factor. Mathematically, the production possibility curve is a function

$$1) \quad f(X_1, \ldots, X_n) = 0$$

where $X_1, \ldots, X_n$ consists of the n services in the economy, of which some will end up as products and some as factors of production. The existence of some limitational factors simply means that the values of some of the variables are fixed, so that the production possibility curve is an $n - m$ dimensional cross section of function (1), where m is the number of factors fixed. That cross-section can be well-behaved or not whether m is equal to or greater than unity.

2) Boulding says that without scarcity "all prices would be zero," without specifying the "numeraire" in terms of which prices are to be measured. However, no matter how the "numeraire" is chosen, the statement seems to me wrong. What is true is that, if there be a point of complete satiety, at that point the marginal utilities of all goods are zero. *Relative* prices, being equal to the ratios of marginal utilities, are all indeterminate, not zero, as is readily seen from the fact that if the price of A in terms of B is zero, the price of B in terms of A would be infinite, so that all relative prices cannot be zero. What is true is that no one would care what the relative prices were. The reason Boulding's statement seems plausible at first glance is that if some goods are available in quantities greater than the satiety amount, while others are not, the price of the former will be zero in terms of the latter. But this clearly cannot be generalized to the case in which all goods, including the "numeraire," are available in quantities greater than the satiety amount.

1

Economic Values and the Value of Human Life

PETER S. ALBIN
New York University

GENERAL INTRODUCTION

I WISH to provide an extended statement on a line of argument that I feel is implicit in Professor Boulding's exposition of value theory, but which was not adequately developed in the discussion. After describing the basic operations of a market system and the analysis of these operations through the theory of price (or relative value), Professor Boulding focused on areas in which the failure to apply economic reasoning was apparent. Certain actions could be explained as choices of rational men only if it was assumed that infinite or near-infinite values were attached to certain principles or attributes, ideological, romantic, or heroic as the case might be. The analysis is straightforward. One can count the resources devoted to the pursuit of the principle. If we assume rationality, the expected benefits (the value of the principle upheld) exceed the costs. In the cases cited by Boulding there seems to be no limit to the willingness to bear costs in pursuit of principle; therefore, the principle must implicitly have assigned to it an infinite value (or the rationality assumption must be discarded). Boulding stresses that too often implied valuations are such as to suggest a tragic departure from rationality. The point that I feel was neglected is that there is a considerable number of cases in which values attached to abstract principles or attributes can be calculated. That is, one can reason backwards from actions to presumed underlying values and find that the implicit values have an apparent upper bound and are so scaled that the rationality assumption is plausible. The values so derived may be compared to explicit prices generated in the market place and can (with some qualification) be included in the formal structure of relative values.

One can apply this line of analysis in a surprising variety of contexts. Consider, for example, government health or safety programs. Appropriations and expenditures are generated by a political process, transactions take place and resources are used up. Can we not analyze the economic events *as if* they were the results of a conventional market process with the usual relative value implications? The implicit values would be comparable to explicit values (prices) in the market place at a given point of time. The stability of such implicit values over time and the consistency of valuations among related attributes would be useful information in a description or evaluation of the functioning of the political process or other means of command outside of the market place.[1] Presumably any attribute that enters into a decision with economic effects can be valued by the appropriate counting of costs. It is useful, however, to focus on a single attribute that enters into a wide range of decisions through a variety of decision mechanisms. For this reason the value of preserving a human life seems particularly appropriate as a subject. This seeming abstraction is a datum in a wide range of decisions both public and private and yet may be susceptible to fairly precise measurement.

IMPLICIT VALUE CALCULATIONS

A highway commission decides to pave the shoulders on highway 101 but not on highway 102. The decision was based on findings by safety engineers that the improvement of highway 101 will probably prevent four fatalities over a planning period, while improvement of highway 102 will be likely to save three lives. Both improvements have dollar costs of one million and no side benefits or drawbacks. Can we infer from the decision of the authority that a human life has an implicit worth of at least $250,000 but is not worth as much as $333,-333.33? Do we find that the same approximate valuation is implicit in other areas of expenditure or do we find perhaps that motorists' lives are implicitly worth more than pedestrians', or perhaps that government authorities in general hold life more dear than parties in the private sector?

Study of this general type of problem takes us into a shadow area of analysis, but one in which results significant to the economist, political analyst, social critic, and philosopher are likely to be generated. The theory of relative values can only be applied with caution, more by way of metaphor than as a predictive device. We are not quite into an area of activity in which ideology or the heroic impulse dominates to the extent that "nicely calculated less or more . . . [is] . . . out the window." The highway planner is sufficiently bound by budget so that a crusade against death on wheels can be no more than a limited war. Within the limits and because of them he is forced to economize, ration, allocate, and reckon.[2]

ANALYTICAL VIEWPOINTS

Where the heroic, ideological, or romantic impulses prevail over rationality, we can say little more than that resources or life are assigned negligible costs or that the impulse commands an infinite valuation—no finer calculations are possible. In the area of analysis discussed here, value ranges corresponding to those ordinarily generated in the goods and services economy are at issue and the domain and scope of significant analysis and judgment are correspondingly wide. The actual analysis can take one of several forms, according to a normative or positive viewpoint.

It is possible to develop an extensive normative calculus similar to the cost-benefit methodology currently being perfected. Attention would focus on the efficiency requirement that the number of lives saved per dollar of expenditure should be equal at the margin for all social and private expenditure. Difficult and interesting questions would concern the analysis of activities involving multiple benefits or costs and the design of institutions and command mechanisms that would be most effective in promoting the efficiency goal.

The descriptive-positive approach followed here involves study of the functioning of existing mechanisms that set values on human life. The interest is primarily in the value implications (in the broader sense) of lapses from efficiency—why for example is the value of life perhaps different in medical research than it is in traffic safety? What other values enter the implicit calculations? I have little to provide in the way of empirical substance; the remainder of this paper is basically taxonomic, identifying the agencies involved in costing lives and some of the more interesting problem areas.

DECISIONS INVOLVING THE VALUATION OF LIFE

A surprisingly large number of decisions within the private sector of the economy involve implicit valuation of life. Increases in income generally lead to purchases of superior qualities and increased quantities of medical care. Such purchases involve the exchange of cash for reduction in uncertainties and improved life expectancy; a calculation of implicit life value is feasible. Similar reasoning applies to transactions in transportation safety-equipment and home repairs. The demand for compensating wage differentials for dangerous work is another manifestation of life valuation within the private market sector.

The list of public activities involving the valuation of life includes safety expenditures, such as the highway example previously cited, expenditures on public health or medical research, military action, and the setting of safety standards that in turn require private expenditure.

In all of the instances cited, the value of preserving a life at the margin of decision can be calculated as the ratio of expenditure change over change in life expectancy for a standardized base period. Deviations from the efficiency standard, which asserts that values should tend toward equality, can then be analyzed. The empirical research has yet to be carried out, but we can speculate on some value comparisons that are likely to prove illuminating.

COMPARISONS WITHIN THE PUBLIC SECTOR— INTERAGENCY COMPARISONS AND COMPARISONS AT DIFFERENT LEVELS OF GOVERNMENT

On one hand we might find gross inconsistencies among valuations—an indication of basic inefficiency in the political and budgetary allocation of resources. On the other hand we may find patterns of consistent valuation—an indication that the bargaining, logrolling, and balancing of powers within politics and administration may be responsive to social preferences (or establish consistent values that are independent of social preferences). Assuming consistent response, we might expect to see significantly different values established in agencies responsible for different program areas: public health, medical research, highway safety, and defense.[3] On the state and local level we might hypothesize that the wealthier areas would tend to place higher values on life and that patterns of bias and discrimination would have their image in values underlying expenditure patterns.

COMPARISONS WITHIN THE PRIVATE SECTOR

Interesting questions arise as to how individuals implicitly value their own lives in one class of expenditures and the lives of either close associates or strangers in other classes of expenditures. One might expect that social and moral pressures could be identified by analysis of the observed value structure and that cross-cultural comparisons would be meaningful. Other fruitful areas for hypotheses concern implicit life values in various population cross sections (wealth, income, location, social classes), differences between private and public valuations and differences between implicit values and approximations of such valuations that might be set by the courts in damage judgments. Finally, one would expect to see significant value differences where expenditures are made by an individual in his own behalf or where expenditures are made for the benefit of others by an individual acting in a trust or administrative capacity or under coercion of legal standards.

SUMMARY AND CONCLUSIONS

The above examples should indicate that it is not unreasonable to hypothesize a structure of implicit economic values, indirectly observed, that corresponds, in effect, to the structure of observed prices and is subject (presumably) to economic analysis. The examples somewhat exaggerate the possibilities for empirical analysis, however; it is unlikely that there are more than a few areas in which life values are consistent and systematically determined. Even so, the arguments have some meaningful content: a finding of inconsistency in public-sector valuations would be important in itself and suggestive of a need to develop the mechanics of administration, budget, and expenditure along lines of greater efficiency in the economic sense and greater responsiveness to underlying social valuations. In short, this note serves as a reminder that there may be patterns of rationality of "nicely calculated less or more" in significant areas of public and private activity that are at some distance from the conventional market places and that border on areas in which the heroic, romantic, and ideological impulses are unchecked.

NOTES

1. Following Arrow's analysis of the political process, one does not expect to be able to reason from individual preferences to explicit behavior, as one can using the value theory applicable to economic markets. For example, shifts of power from one coalition to another may lead to dramatic jumps in calculated implicit values without any change in the structure of people's preferences.

2. He may never directly calculate a life-value or even know that such a value is implicit in his budget. However, if the need for safety is communicated to him as one of a number of planning requirements, each manifest as political or internal-administrative pressure, the resolution of these forces in his decision can be likened to a bargaining outcome.

3. Life valuations in cases such as the highway expenditure enter into decisions made under conditions of *risk* where outcomes are subject to fairly well-defined probability distributions and expected benefits can be calculated with relative confidence. Benefits deriving from expenditures in medical research, however, are subject to greater *uncertainty* (as are many classes of individual expenditures). The errors in measuring valuations in the uncertainty cases are likely to be relatively high, particularly in such examples as medical research, where values are imputed to the activity for its own sake.

2

Human Values and Economists' Values

SIDNEY S. ALEXANDER
Massachusetts Institute of Technology

I'M AFRAID I must rise to bring a serious charge—a charge of misleading advertising. We are invited here to discuss *Human Values and Economic Policy*. We have talked instead of *Human Choice and Economic Value*. Human values concern the Good Life, economic policy concerns what we should do in an economic context. Yet there was little mention in today's discussion either of the Good Life or of "should." Instead, we heard how economists describe the optimal satisfaction of wants constrained by limited resources, and we were told that a social welfare judgment must lack at least one of the properties we would like it to have, if we base it on purely ordinal aspects of individuals' preferences.

Perhaps I too may be accused of fraud, in that, invited to this conference as an economist, I am impersonating a philosopher in criticizing economists for excluding almost all human values from economics. My defense, however, is that the rule against an economist's making value judgments professionally lacks legitimacy, that the exclusion from economics of normative judgments embodying human values is based only on an arbitrary definition of economics. In this forum, at least, I claim the right, even the duty, to follow where the argument leads.

I charge misleading advertising, not Bad Faith. Our chairman and convenor has certainly acted in the best of good faith. He would, I am sure, be delighted to have his distinguished economists tell us how economic institutions can be made better to serve the Good Life. At the worst, Professor Hook can be accused of ignorance of the ways of economists, a defect from which, after today's lesson, he can no longer be presumed to suffer. He did not know, before today, that if you ask an economist about human values and policy you will be told about the theory of choice, or about the problems of making welfare judgments on the basis of ordinal information, a constraint imposed by the exclusion of almost all human values.

As for our economist speakers, they have faithfully delivered, with a considerable show of brilliance, what they thought the topic called for. And while the relation of human values to economic policy has not been discussed, it certainly has been revealed, if only between the lines. Between the lines is indeed the sole abode of human values in economics these days. For economics is now almost as "value free" as its practitioners can make it.

Philosophers should understand this tendency with sympathy, especially if old enough, or historically minded enough, for their memory to go back thirty years or so, since the economist's calendar of philosophy lies open to the year 1936. If you wonder whatever has happened to that old verification principle, you will find it ruling the roost in the social studies, or, to use the preferred term, the social sciences. Economists, and those who seek to honor economists, are fond of quoting Keynes' dictum that practical men are only the slaves of some defunct economist. It may afford philosophers in turn some mischievous amusement to see the power of defunct philosophies in economics and the other social studies.

The guilt of our economists in evading the requirements of the topic set for discussion may be ascribed to society rather than to the individual, to that social force which has driven normative judgments out of the social studies. Our convenor's mistake was in asking economists to talk about the Good Life, and "should." That is the sort of talk the economist expects to get from the philosopher, not to give to him. But some philosophers, indeed the dominant school of Anglo-Saxon philosophy today, would turn the economist away, declaring that questions of policy are for the moralist, not for the moral philosopher.

He will tell you how to talk, not how to live. The philosophers of ordinary language have settled for the job of janitors in the Mansions of Truth, leaving the premises otherwise untenanted. Meanwhile from Europe comes another line of thought, or at least of feeling, that would indeed answer questions of policy, but from such murky Existentialist depths as hardly to offer an acceptable solution of the problems of economic policy. We want hardheaded answers.

There are other possibilities, at least one of them closer to home. The philosophic work of our distinguished convenor, it seems to me, has been dedicated to the proposition that you *can* talk about values in a sensible, hardheaded way. His example offers an approach to policy problems that might indeed find an honorable place in economics and the social studies. My complaint is that economists, and more generally social scientists, have failed to take this offer seriously. I am by no means proposing that Professor Hook be given a blank check to dictate to the social sciences the normative principles they require to become sciences of policy. I *am* suggesting that along the lines that he has worked, we social scientists should work too, by evaluating the actual and potential operations of our social institutions according to the best normative standards we can find.

These standards need not appeal to any transcendental authority. It is not inconsistent with the doctrine that all knowledge comes from experience to hold that we have knowledge of good and evil. We may even admit, or rather insist, that such normative knowledge differs in its validation or vindication, or, in general, in its rational support, from our knowledge of what is and what is not. But we should recognize that sensible men can reasonably discuss normative questions, and can cooperate in the study of how our social institutions can best be brought to serve the Good Life. Belief to the contrary comes from the recognition that a normative judgment is interpersonally valid only among those who share some common point of view. This is not mistaken. What is mistaken is the assumption that a positive judgment is interpersonally valid among those who share no common point of view. A positive judgment is believed to be founded on a rock, the normative adrift on the sea. Deeper consideration will find both positive and normative "in the same leaky boat." [1]

The misrepresentation in the title of these discussions thus proceeds from a deep defect in social scientists, treason to their normative responsibilities. There was good reason, as Max Weber argued, for driving the normative away from interfering with the study of the descriptive. He was undoubtedly right, when he insisted, presumably with Treitschke in mind, that "the investigator and teacher should keep unconditionally separate the establishment of empirical facts . . . and *his* own practical evaluations, i.e., his evaluation of these facts as satisfactory or unsatisfactory." [2] But when he, followed by two generations of social scientists and at least half a generation of philosophers, inferred that there was no place in rational discourse for cooperative formation of normative judgments, a mistake was made. That normative judgments have no place in rational inquiry into *how* social institutions work does not imply that they have no place in the social studies. There remains the question of how *well* they work.

The economist does not really think that the philosopher can supply him with the basic normative principles that, together with the economist's findings on how economic institutions work, can answer this question of better or worse. When the social scientist sends you to the philosopher, he doesn't really expect you to come back with a normative basis for social policy. He doesn't expect you to come back at all; he's sending you to Siberia, or is it Coventry? If you do come back with a normative basis for social policy, he will regard it as just one man's opinion. This is the social scientist's homemade philosophy, and he wants no exotic imports.

The emphasis on *his* in the quotation from Weber lies at the heart of the problem. Social scientists just about unanimously follow Hume in recognizing two little men in each of us, Reason and Will. Reason is interpersonally valid, Will is personally arbitrary. When a man judges that which is, whether it is or is not, he does so by employing Reason, and so is the agent of all men. But when he judges that which should be, he sends *his* Will to do the job, and Will works for him alone. So Weber finds that a man's judgments of empirical facts are not his but mankind's, while his evaluations are *his* evaluations. The possibility that a man might have some normative beliefs that are no more exclusively *his* beliefs than are his beliefs about the atomic weights of the elements has not been given a fair hearing in the social studies. It has been assumed away with the Humian separation of Reason from Will, a separation that may be questioned.

As Professor Friedman's remarks have illustrated, economists generally regard value judgments as essentially personal and irreconcilable. I think it is scandalous that, in a roomful of philosophers, it should fall to me, an economist, to point out that when men differ over values there may be an alternative to the barricades. But among social scientists there is widespread acceptance of the belief that values are indiscutable. *Non disputandum* has, in the social studies, been raised to the position of a first principle. The pernicious effects of this belief, or in my opinion, this error, are seriously compounded by a widespread mistake that may be called the Fallacy of Misplaced Values.

The differences of values that might underlie differences over social policy must lie very deep. But we find, in practical discussions of social policy, that values seem to be vested shallowly, in instruments rather than in ends. One man is "for" a progressive tax, and another "against." It is hardly credible that the protagonists really regard either of these taxes as having intrinsic value, surely they regard them as instruments to other ends. By progressively examining those other ends, also presumed to be vesting points of values, we will usually find, I think, that they constitute a chain extending back to a concept of the Good Life.

So what is prematurely labeled as a difference in values, even as between such broadly defined social systems as capitalism and communism, may be found, upon examination of what the disputants are *claiming*, to be differences not over values, but over descriptive, operational, predictions of the consequences of the alternatives in view. This is not to claim that the disputants' points of view can be strictly inferred from the conjunction of empirical beliefs with a particular characterization of the Good Life. We are not now talking about their psychological motivation, but about what they *claim* in their arguments. The apologist for capitalism does, I am asserting, *claim* that his position can be derived from a concern for what would promote a Good Life for man, and the apologist for communism makes the same claim for his position. If this is so, it is a fallacy of misplaced values to say that in their *argument* they have come to an irreconcilable difference of values. Their attitudes may in fact be irreconcilable from the point of view of depth psychology or the sociology of knowledge, but not from the logic of what they are *arguing*. Their difference is logically reconcilable in terms of a common conception of the Good Life. If they come to argue about *that*, they are no longer arguing capitalism versus communism, and it is necessary to inquire again if they are not differing over some empirical characterization of the nature of man or of the way a social system would work, rather than over some basic normative judgment of what is good for a man. And even such a basic normative judgment may not be ultimate. Indeed, from the point of view from which I am arguing no principle need be regarded as ultimate, even though every argument must start somewhere. As Quine has observed, presumably from a priori considerations, there are no points in Ohio that are by their nature starting points, even though every journey must start somewhere.

Professor Friedman has advanced, elsewhere, the opinion that most disagreements over economic policy are based on differences in positive rather than in normative judgments.[3] But the general practice of economists runs to the contrary, so that the verification principle is used to exclude from the main corpus of economic research questions of policy that depend essentially on positive rather than on normative issues, because the issues are mistakenly identified as normative. That the alleged mistake is indeed an error follows, of course, from the acceptance of some deeper normative principle that makes the particular issue, say excise versus income tax, a matter of positive identification of consequences. What is positive depends on a prior determination of the normative.

The trouble is, as I see it, a double one, like a mistaken court decision under a bad law. First, normative judgments are excluded from the social studies, and secondly, certain problems that turn on empirical issues are excluded in turn, because they are misidentified as normative rather than positive. This same point, I believe, underlies the Dewey-Hook argument that within a problematic situation the issues are empirical. They imply that any purely normative question lies at the next higher level. Indeed, if we are ready to accept an infinite regress, as I think we should be, we need never to go to barricades. For either we agree on the normative principle governing the problem before us and need only establish the empirical descriptive facts, or we differ on the normative principle. If we differ on the normative principle, we can construct a new problematic situation in which that normative principle is at issue, depending on still other empirical facts or on a still higher normative principle. We can repeat the process indefinitely, so long as we do not come to a normative principle that we refuse to discuss. If, as is increasingly being recognized, no particular principle is inherently a *first* principle, there is no necessary stopping place.

THE NORM IN ECONOMICS

The one first-level norm, as distinguished from such higher level, methodological, norms as the exclusion of value judgments, that still survives in economics is regarded as so obvious as hardly to be normative at all, and so it is exempt from the test of operational verification. That norm is sometimes referred to as the pig principle, that if you like something, more is better. Its corollary is the ethical value of efficiency—the only first-level ethical value normally admitted into economic discourse. Whatever you want, it is argued, you can have more of it if you respect the dictates of efficiency. As Professor Boulding says, even the heroic must come to terms with economic scarcity, so to the Kwakiutl the economist can say, in the spirit of Edwin Cannan's précis of Lionel Robbins, "Burn down your house if you want to, but mind you, don't use too many matches." [4]

Together with the belief in the personal autonomy of normative judgments the efficiency principle leads to Pareto-optimality. According to Pareto-optimality, state of the world A is better than state of world B if at least one person is better off in A and nobody worse off. A person is to be taken as better off in A than in B if he prefers to be in A rather than in B. As a normative principle Pareto-optimality corresponds roughly to a cooperative egoistic hedonism plus the assumption that the individual is the best judge of what will make him happy, an alliance among monads. Whether Pareto-optimality is right or wrong, it is normative to the core. And my charge against most economists is that they are ready to exclude other normative viewpoints as unscientific, while permitting this one to crawl under the fence because it is so obviously acceptable. In most other matters economists are in favor of free competition, but in this normative question they grant a monopoly to Pareto-optimality. If it had to compete in the marketplace for ethical ideas it could not, I believe, long survive. The strongest form of Protectionism is, of course, outright exclusion. And all other normative standards are excluded from economics because to be normative is to be personal.

As a consequence, economic analysis has concentrated on the quest for more. Its success was largely esthetic, almost anesthetic in paralysis of the will to social criticism. As both Boulding and Arrow have pointed out, the economists contemplate the operation of the ideal market system with the same sort of entrancement as the post-Newtonians viewing celestial mechanics, or Kant the moral law within. It *is* a beautiful system. And the actual market system has worked spectacularly well for all its imperfections relative to the ideal market system. Until recently, however, it was dubious whether the operation of the market system or its prodigies of production owed much to economic analysis, or whether the economist wasn't just lucky to have studied and understood a process that was so spectacularly successful.

More recently, however, the New Economics has apparently been able to overcome an imperfection in the market system that some observers, Dewey and Marx among them, thought would ruin the system. So positive economics, or at least not-too-normative economics, has paid off in its quest for more.

The consequence of the exclusion of normative questions other than Pareto-optimality from economics is that, by and large, those questions have nowhere else to go. Philosophers once studied them, and occasionally they do try to evaluate the moral worth of some of our economic institutions, but then the economists ridicule the naive ideas of the philosophers as to how the system works. One specialist presumably knows how the economy works, and the other knows what is good and what is bad, but they never get together.

What permitted Pareto-optimality to get by when all other normative standards were outlawed was the impersonality of its appeal. No one of those persons, each of whose normative standard is taken as final to himself, can reasonably object to Pareto-optimality. So it is universal, everyone can reasonably subscribe to it whatever his desires. This familiar Kantian idea, that if a norm is such as to be acceptable to any rational being independent of the particular things he wants it is interpersonally valid, can carry more and better normative baggage than Pareto-optimality. But it is not allowed to in the main body of the social studies. Arrow's Indian Summer affair with extended sympathy is a move in this direction, however. And in general, the notion that some normative judgments are impersonally, and hence interpersonally, valid, would open up for discussion many topics now closed out of the social sciences.

Both Professor Arrow and Professor Boulding have, in their

contributions, moved a fair distance away from the narrow bounds of Pareto-optimality. But still they have not satisfied the demands that a proper concern for human values makes upon the analysis of human welfare.

Thus, Boulding states that the problem of neighborhood effects has long been recognized in economics. But it has been recognized only from the point of view of Pareto-optimality: there are people who would pay to be rid of the smoke nuisance an amount more than it would cost the factory owners to abate it. He and other economists fail to notice that our whole culture is a smoke nuisance. Neighborhood effects concern the ways in which economic transactions affect those who are not parties to the transactions. If, as is generally agreed, our economic institutions play a leading role in shaping our culture, in determining what sort of men we turn out to be, that is all part of the neighborhood effect, and economists have *not* taken it into account in their approach to economic policy. The neighborhood effect of economic institutions in shaping what we in our culture-bound fashion call human nature is opaque to Pareto-optimality because a man is not likely to be prepared to pay for being made other than he is the amount that it would be worth to him to be a different man, a worth that he could recognize only if he *were* a different man. The pig will not want to pay anything to be made into a Socrates. He doesn't want to be Socrates.

That wants are generated by the social process, not in the trivial sense that they are affected by advertising, but in the profound sense of their dependence on the whole cultural matrix, certainly threatens the entire ethical basis of economics, striking in particular at Pareto-optimality. It challenges the principle that more is better, and opens up the question of what sort of wants we should generate, what sort of men we should make.

These are obvious questions that are asked, if not answered, in the first course of philosophy. In the study of our social system, and in economics in particular, they are systematically excluded, except for a few lonely voices such as

those of Frank Knight and J. M. Clark. That those voices remain lonely does reflect some strong process operating to keep
the normative evaluation of economic institutions out of economics, an interesting question for the sociology of knowledge.
That normative standards other than Pareto-optimality are excluded grants our social institutions immunity from criticism
other than on the grounds of efficiency. Economists have long
recognized that one of the principal gains of monopoly is a
quiet life, and the normative monopoly of Pareto-optimality is
no exception.

THE NORMATIVE BASIS OF ARROW'S SOCIAL JUDGMENT FUNCTION

Professor Arrow has studied a procedure for counseling a
public official, showing how to form a normative social welfare
judgment such as "A should be done rather than B." The
device he has proposed for consideration is, I believe, unac-
ceptable on normative grounds. It implies that A should be
done if a certain decisive group, possibly but not necessarily a
majority, prefers the consequences of A to B. I would argue
that a social scientist, or if that term be objectionable, a social-
policy specialist, asked by a public official whether it is better
to do A or B, should use a criterion different from a count, or
some similar function, of individual preference orderings,
whether ordinal or cardinal. The question of whether A or B
should be done is a question of whether it is better or worse
to do A or B, and not whether more people within some group
prefer A to B.

There is an implicit personalism, decisionism, or voluntar-
ism in Arrow's approach, that is, I maintain, objectionable. It
is clearly based on a positivist distinction between a descriptive
judgment and a welfare judgment. A similar function of people's orderings of the alternatives is not usually constructed to
find, say, the atomic weight of copper, although our delegation
of this social decision to certain scientists might possibly be so
regarded. But such delegation as is made to them is not to

them as persons, as a decisive set whose vote is to count, but as the community's agents for finding out this particular thing. The implicit assumption of Arrow's approach, when translated into a political proposal, would be that public officials should follow public-opinion polls rather than their own best judgment, that Burke's famous speech to the electors of Bristol was on the wrong track. There is no space here to argue this position, so I shall confine myself to stating that it is arguable, and that, in my judgment, it is ill-founded. The question of what should be done is one to be investigated in terms of what is good for man rather than what most people think. The question of what is to be done may be decided, and I think it should be, even in a democracy, by the people's representatives rather than by a public-opinion poll. And there is at least an argument to be made that the public official is responsible to use the best available judgment of what it is best to do.

Our distinguished chairman has stated, in attempting to reconcile the views of Dewey and the naturalists with those of their principal emotivist opponent: "If the good is defined in relation to human need or interest (or preference, desire, satisfaction)—if, in other words, the nature of morals is conceived as having any relation to human nature—then every statement about the good or better in any situation has a descriptive meaning, and in principle is decidable in reference to the needs and interests involved." [5]

We may boggle at the term "defined" in this statement, in view of the hullabaloo that has been made about the definist, or as it is rather misleadingly called, the "naturalistic fallacy." [6] But if we substitute "can be operationally specified" for "is defined" in Hook's statement we may leave open the question of just how we came to the normative judgment that what is good, and in this case, what should be done, can rightly be specified operationally in terms relating to the nature of man. As a particular example in the spirit of Hook's proposal, consider the following criterion: alternative A should be done rather than alternative B if and only if a reasonable, well-informed man, free of personal and cultural bias, would prefer to be anyone at random in the state consequent on A rather than in the state consequent on B. This device, which we may call the Humanist Criterion, appears to be rather similar to Arrow's social-judgment function but is fundamentally different. For the test would be made by operational psychological investigation rather than as a count of individuals' preferences.

Arrow's device, for example a simple majority vote, could be used to find it some decisive set of men, as they are, would prefer A to B. But it fails to require that the electorate be well informed, and it fails to eliminate personal and cultural bias, as well as failing to register any differences of intensity of preference. It is just this sort of nose counting that Broad tried, rather notoriously, to pin on Hume, the easier to demolish him with the judgment that "to me this kind of answer [statistics of how people in fact do feel] seems utterly irrelevant to this kind of question," of right and wrong.[7] While one might hope for more than this intuitive insight as a test of the validity of nose counting as a guide to what public officials should do, the fact that the matter could be left that way suggests that, upon investigation, strong considerations could be found against nose counting as a device for making normative judgments.

Under the Humanist Criterion, the question is also an operational one, in which state would a man of a certain temper prefer to live, rather than which one a decisive set of men would rank higher. Public-opinion polling is an inappropriate technique for answering such a question simply because each person is not in a similar position to know. Even among specialists a majority vote is not the appropriate test of validity.

Social scientists generally allow that it *is* permissible to advance a normative judgment professionally if you make your normative preconceptions explicit. It seems a little superfluous, however, in reporting the judgment that tax A is better than tax B, to add the qualification, "provided you subscribe to the Humanist Criterion." Why not require that a statement that water is composed of hydrogen and oxygen be qualified by "if you subscribe to certain specified methods of chemistry"? Suppose that all concerned agree that were the Humanist Criterion to be applied, using accepted scientific techniques, it would yield the judgment that A should be done, but a majority of the people in some group in our community rank B higher than A in their individual orderings. Why should I, as a social scientist, advise a public official that B should be done? If I advise A, is that "only a personal judgment"? Suppose I personally prefer B?

If we accept the Humanist Criterion, Arrow's device is inappropriate for any question of social policy that can be determined by that criterion. Is it an appropriate device for determining whether we should accept the Humanist Criterion itself? There may indeed be deontological arguments against exclusive use of the teleological Humanist Criterion. But is the venerable argument between deontology and teleology to be settled by an Arrow-type nose-counting device? Is *that* question (the one in the preceding sentence) to be so settled? And *that* question, and *that,* in the familiar infinite regress? It hardly seems so. The best way we have of settling such questions, and dealing with that regress, still seems to be the Socratic dialectic, the bringing to bear on the issue whatever we believe that appears to be relevant, and considering the joint implication for this question of those things we believe. This procedure can claim to be rational, even though not operational, and beliefs that emerge from this process are worthy of being designated as knowledge achieved by rational inquiry. No argument to the contrary can reasonably be based on other than normative principles, and it is hard to see how that higher-level argument could reasonably be conducted except within the framework of the dialectic.

The Socratic notion that men can sensibly discuss normative issues, that they can devise impersonal means, if not of verification, at least of evaluation of normative judgments, that they can cooperate in progressive rational inquiry directed toward making those judgments soundly, is still worthy of consideration even by hardheaded social scientists. From a practical point of view, recognition of the fallacy of misplaced values can reduce most apparently normative issues to empirical ones. If any purely normative issues remain, there is room for argument that they can most appropriately be impersonally evaluated by this dialectical process rather than being personally adopted by an arbitrary act of will. But this argument must be continued elsewhere. It, too, is normative.[8]

In sum, most issues of policy could be settled by operational means if only we could successfully perform the required operations. The widespread notion that differences over policy are based on differences in values is a consequence of the premature vesting of allegedly irreconcilable values in issues that can in fact be determined operationally against the background of more fundamental value judgments. Whether these more fundamental judgments are themselves irreconcilable or not becomes another question, or in Dewey-Hook terms, another problematic situation. It is at least a possibility that we may have an infinite regress here, benign in this case, since at the end of the regress we must, we are told, go to the barricades. But if at every point there is still room for discussion, so much the better, and we need go to the barricades only at infinity, which is never. Alternatively, we might even stop at, or near, the Humanist Criterion, just as, for practical purposes, we stop at inductive verification in the natural sciences. Do we, in practical discussions of social policy, *really* want to push the argument farther?

NOTES

1. Morton G. White, *Toward Reunion in Philosophy,* Cambridge, Mass.: Harvard University Press, 1956.

2. Max Weber, *The Methodology of the Social Sciences,* trans. Edward A. Shils and Henry A. Finch (Glencoe, Ill.: Free Press, 1949), p. 11. (Weber's italics.)

3. Milton Friedman, *Essays in Positive Economics* (Chicago, Ill.: University of Chicago Press, 1953), p. 5.

4. *Economic Journal,* XLII (September 1932), 425. The quotation has been tampered with.

5. Sidney Hook, *The Quest for Being* (New York: St. Martin's Press, 1961), p. 66.

6. W. K. Frankena, "The Naturalistic Fallacy," *Mind*, XLVIII, 1939; reprinted in Sellars and Hospers, *Readings in Ethical Theory*, New York, 1952.

7. C. D. Broad, *Five Types of Ethical Theory*, London and New York, 1930, 1956, pp. 114–115, and 85. See also Rachel M. Kydd, *Reason and Conduct in Hume's Treatise*, New York, 1964, p. 176, and Arthur M. Prior, *Logic and the Basis of Ethics*, Oxford, 1949 and 1961, pp. 86–87.

8. See, however, David Pole, *Conditions of Rational Inquiry*, London, 1961, for arguments that I believe to be in support of the position taken in these comments. See also Arthur E. Murphy, *The Uses of Reason*, New York, 1943, and *The Theory of Practical Reason*, LaSalle, Ill., 1965.

3

The Place of Moral Obligation in Preference Systems

KENNETH J. ARROW
Stanford University

PROFESSOR BRANDT'S PAPER raises a number of very interesting issues but I wish to concentrate here on only one, the place of moral obligation in the preference systems of individuals.

I should make it thoroughly clear that the preference systems of individuals that I regard as basic raw material for the formulation of social choice refer to what Professor Brandt calls "personal welfare," *not* moral principle. In the typical economic situation, it is true, issues of moral principle in the ordinary sense are not faced in any very explicit form (though they probably play a much larger role, even in narrowly economic circumstances, than is usually considered). We rather think of a set of individuals, each with his own personal preference scales, who have to make a collective decision of some kind. Suppose that they surmount all the difficulties of collective decision making and come to an agreement. In general, this agreement will not be the best possible decision for any single individual, according to his own personal preference scale. Each one carries out his part of the agreement, not because he wants to undertake this obligation for its own sake but because it is part of an agreement, the net result of which is beneficial to him as compared with the alternative of no agreement, though not as compared with the best state he could achieve if he were a perfect dictator.

To illustrate, consider two individuals living in a valley to which there is presently no road. I assume that the road brings each of them great benefits but neither enjoys the labor of building it. Obviously, from the point of view of either one the optimal situation is to have the other man build the road. Nevertheless, they may agree to share the labor of building a road because the alternative of failing to agree is worse for both of them; each one would rather have the road and do half the labor than not have the road at all. If one observes their behavior he might be tempted to say that they have not followed out their personal preferences in that they would have preferred not to work on the road. But in fact, considering the whole agreement, they are behaving in a preferred way, i.e., preferred to the actually possible alternatives, not to unattainable alternatives.

Thus, behavior in accordance with an agreement is compatible with judgment based on personal preference scales but might not appear to be so if the analysis is not complete enough. I now come to the key point: I interpret moral obligation as the carrying out of agreements which may, however, be implicit. Thus, a society in which everyone immediately executed his aggressive impulses would be untenable. Therefore, there is an agreement that I will refrain from aggressive actions, which in themselves give me satisfaction, in return for your not taking aggressive action against me. However, conscious agreements to achieve these ends are much too costly in terms of information and bargaining. Therefore, as societies have evolved they have found it economical to make these agreements at an unconscious, implicit level. Internalized feelings of guilt and right are essentially unconscious equivalents of agreements that represent social decisions.

In the light of changes in circumstances and the development of knowledge, it may indeed be important to rethink these past agreements. Many aspects of conventional morality are indeed being altered, partly consciously, partly unconsciously. What may be thought of as moral obligations to obey the law or to help the poor have come under increasing reexamination; in other words, a new decision based on the synthesis of individual preferences under an altered environment is being formed.

In regard to Professor Brandt's question, then, my answer would be the following: strictly speaking, the preference scales that I deal with are those relating to personal welfare only. The range of moral obligations is part of the social decision to be arrived at by the collective decision-making machinery. In practice, of course, we do not continually make decisions about everything, so that in any concrete instance some parts of a collective agreement and in particular some moral principles are left unexamined and taken as data while other matters are under discussion. But this is a matter of economy of thought and action, not of long-run immutable principles.

4

Welfare and Preference

KURT BAIER
University of Pittsburgh

ARROW'S IMPOSSIBILITY THEOREM is generally considered surprising and embarrassing.[1] For it appears to prove the impossibility of something widely held possible and desirable: a formula for translating the will of the people into social policy; or more technically, a formula for aggregating individual preferences concerning alternative states of society into corresponding collective, or social, preferences, such that the application of this formula always yields determinate (transitive) social preferences that satisfy at least the minimal, and surely very reasonable, requirements of democracy.

The problem raised by Arrow's Impossibility Theorem is much the same as that posed by the well-known voting paradoxes. Arrow himself formulates it as follows: "There are three alternatives, A, B, and C, among which choice is to be made. One-third of the voters prefer A to B and B to C, one-third prefer B to C and C to A, and one-third prefer C to A and A to B. Then A will be preferred to B by a majority, B to C by a majority, and C to A by a majority."[2] Each individual may have a perfectly consistent (transitive) set of preferences yet the group preference, as determined by a majority vote, is inconsistent (intransitive). Hence in some cases this method of arriving at social policy will not yield determinate results.

Recently, it has been shown [3] that the intransitivity of such results is due to a certain contingent matter of fact about the tastes of the individuals whose preferences are being aggregated: the results are intransitive if and only if "the profiles of preference orderings," that is, the patterns formed by the individual orderings of possible social states, lack certain specific features, such as "singlepeakedness." [4] However, since the reasonable democratic conditions imposed on the aggregating formula (Pareto Principle, Citizens' Sovereignty, and Non-Dictatorship) are all designed to insure dependence of the resulting social choice on that profile, it is not surprising that this profile is always reflected in the social choice. Is it really surprising then that the shape of some such profiles is reflected in the intransitivity of social preferences? On the face of it, this would seem to be no more surprising or paradoxical than the fact that an equal division of voters on some issue should show itself in a "contradictory social decision." In such cases there is then no genuine (transitive) social will or preference, however genuine (transitive) the individual wills or preferences may be.

All the same, it may be said, it surely is surprising when an individual has intransitive preferences. Why then is it *not* surprising when a *group* consisting entirely of individuals with transitive preferences has social preferences that, though quite adequately reflecting the individual transitive preferences, are themselves intransitive? It will help to make it completely clear why it is so surprising when individual preferences are intransitive. Note in the first place that, strictly speaking, what is intransitive is not *preferences* but *expressions of preference*. For, as economists define "preference," a person's real or genuine preferences (logically) cannot be intransitive, even though his expressions of preference are so. From the fact alone that his expressions of preference are intransitive, it does not of course follow that his preferences are intransitive; and in the economists' sense of "preference" such a consequence would be impossible. Thus, he may at t_1 *express* a preference for A over B, at t_2 for B over C, and at t_3 for C over A, and yet he may *have* genuine (transitive) preferences in relation to A, B, and C. For there may be an explanation of why his expressions of preference are intransitive. Perhaps the explanation is that he wishes to deceive someone about his real preferences, or that he has changed his mind or that he is unaware of the inconsistency. In any case, *his expressions of preference,* being intransitive, do not *express preferences.* Hence if he has genuine preferences, they must be different from what he says they are. In such a case, three questions arise: (1) whether or not he has any genuine preferences; (2) if so, what they are; and (3) what exactly is the explanation of the intransitivity.

The test of whether there is an adequate explanation of the intransitivity comes when he is confronted with it. If he gives an adequate explanation and withdraws one of the expressions of preference in favor of another that would make the set consistent, then we may assume that he has real or genuine preferences and that they are what he says they are. If he persists, then we are inclined to assume that he has no real preferences and that he is irrational. The irrationality must be ascribed to him, not to his preferences for, since preferences are by definition transitive, he has none. This point is not unimportant for it shows that having (transitive) preferences is one of the (minimal) achievements of a rational ordering of behavior. A greater achievement of such rational ordering would lie in having not just preferences, but rational preferences; not just dispositions to make consistent (transitive) choices, but dispositions (transitively) to choose what is really preferable for one, and not what is merely erroneously thought to be so.

Now, sometimes an individual's expressions of preference are intransitive because he is unaware of that intransitivity. This is *surprising* because we so confidently expect people to achieve transitivity in their expressions of preference. The surprise lies in the rarity of this deviation from the norm. Such a deviation is also *embarrassing* to the individual because he has been caught out in a performance that falls *below* the norm. Our surprise turns to alarm when the person so caught out, instead of being embarrassed, persists in his intransitive expressions of preference. For then he convicts himself not merely of lack of competence but of a high degree of irrationality, or perhaps worse. However, a person lays himself open to the charge of failing to achieve transitivity in the expression of preference only if, at the time of expressing a preference, he knows or should know what these expressions are, and so knows or should know whether they are transitive or intransitive. But a society, unlike an individual, cannot know what its (collective) preferences are until they have been "constructed" by the aggregation, in accordance with some chosen formula, of individual preference orderings. For there is not, of course, a "moi commun," a conscious common self analogous to an individual, and capable of knowing his (collective) preferences prior to and independently of the results of the aggregation procedure. And so at the time of constructing the collective preference there is no one whose failure to achieve transitivity of the expression of (collective) preferences could be censured or could cause a surprise. But what about afterwards, when the intransitivity of the results has transpired and the citizens nevertheless persist in their original choices? Is there not then cause for surprise, embarrassment, or even alarm? The problem is to see whose failure could give rise to it.

Let us retrace our steps. When someone proclaims that a certain person, whether himself or another, prefers oranges to pears, pears to bananas, and bananas to oranges, he lays himself open to the charge that his expressions of preference are intransitive. Such a charge amounts to one or other of the following three things. (1) That he has failed accurately to state what he actually does; that is to say, that, contrary to what he implies, he either does not really choose bananas in preference to oranges but actually chooses oranges in preference to bananas. (2) That he has failed to note and state the limiting conditions under which he makes the choices he implies he makes; that is to say, that, contrary to what he implies, he does not *always* prefer oranges to pears and so forth, but rather prefers oranges (and pears) to bananas only under some conditions, e.g., when he is thirsty, and prefers bananas to oranges when he is hungry. (3) Or, lastly, that he has failed to note that he does not have any settled preferences at all.

Now, such a failure amounts to inadequate self-knowledge or inadequate expression of it. It can be corrected by withdrawing one or the other of the inconsistent expressions of preference, or by the appropriate modification of (imposition of limiting conditions on) both of them, or by the abandonment of the word "preference," which amounts to an admission that the individual does not *have* (settled) preferences in this matter.

The parallel failure in the case of social preference would clearly be the expression, by an official or a social scientist, of the society's preference ordering of the alternative social states open to it. Such an expression would be in the nature of an imputation to the society of a certain preference ordering and, by implication, of its adoption of a certain social policy. Such an imputation is faulty if it fails to correspond to the policy actually adopted. However, the mere fact that the expression is intransitive or that it fails to correspond to one of the reasonable conditions imposed does not render it faulty since it may be the case that the employment of the aggregate procedure does in fact yield such results. For the reason already given, the parallel with the case of individual preferences here breaks down. For on the view so far presented, the social scientist and the official have merely the task of recording the collective will of the people. If that will, when aggregated, turns out to have the characteristics mentioned, then neither the scientist nor the official is at fault. If their function is merely to ascertain and record, the unsatisfactoriness, from some points of view, of what they find cannot be blamed on them. An individual differs from a scientist and an official, as so far conceived, in being not merely an observer and recorder, but a molder of his own preferences and behavior.

By now it should be perfectly clear that the cause of the surprise and embarrassment engendered by Arrow's theorem does not lie in the discovery of the inability of given scientists or officials to get the popular will right. The embarrassment rather lies in the content the popular will occasionally has and in the underlying implication of certain strands in democratic thought that the popular will is always *sacrosanct* and that, even if it is not, there are no clear principles available for dividing popular preferences into the more legitimate ones that must be reflected in social policy and the less legitimate that need or must not.

To repeat, the surprise and embarrassment are due not to the discovery of someone's ignorance or incompetence, but to the discovery of the very real possibility of an irreconcilable conflict between two basic democratic desiderata of social policy, conformity with the popular will and the requirements of fairness, as formulated in Arrow's axioms (Pareto Principle, Citizens' Sovereignty, Non-Dictatorship, and Independence of Irrelevant Alternatives). Given these (very reasonable) formulations of these desiderata, some possible, even likely, profiles of individual expressions of preference will not result in a determinate (transitive) collective preference ordering, satisfying all of Arrow's conditions. Thus whether we get satisfactory social decisions does not depend solely on democratic procedures, the good will of bureaucrats, and adequate scientific homework, but also on suitable tastes and attitudes of would-be-democratic citizens. Put in its simplest form, the lesson of Arrow's proof is that if we want consistent social policies, then officials may be required to choose without possible objective guidance between policies that are fair but unrepresentative of the popular will, and policies that are representative of the popular will, but unfair. In the remainder of this paper I want to suggest another alternative. It involves conceiving of Arrow's conditions, not as axioms, but as criteria or desiderata, that is, as prima facie principles. If we conceive of them in this way, we are prepared for occasional incompatibilities between them. We then do not ask which of these conditions should be altogether abandoned. We ask merely which of them should be set aside on those occasions and only those when they come into conflict with one another.

If I am right in what I have said so far, then we need only to find principles for settling the conflict between such desiderata for those occasions on which such conflicts arise. Indeed, the very technique for determining social policies, which employs the four (or five) desiderata spelled out by Arrow, itself rests on further value assumptions that must not be treated as wholly inflexible. But the more flexible they are the less embarrassing is the necessity to accept social policies that occasionally fail to satisfy all of the desiderata in question, provided only that there are principles determining when to set aside or in what manner to modify these assumptions. I have space for the discussion of only one of them. I mean the assumption that social action should be designed to maximize or at any rate increase the satisfactions of the members of the society, irrespective of the states of affairs, events, or activities from which they derive these satisfactions. If this were not accepted, then the axiom of citizen sovereignty would not be so plausible, for then we might grant that not all of the individual preferences need be reflected in the social preference orderings.

Here we may with profit examine one of the natural extensions of this assumption that is supposedly in conflict with one of the axioms necessary to Arrow's proof. I mean the assumption that since an individual must (presumably by the definition of "intensity of preference") derive greater satisfaction from developments based on a preference of greater intensity, social action should reflect not only individual preferences but also their relative intensities. It is widely held that this assumption, and the extension just mentioned, are sound, that a consideration of such "irrelevant" alternatives (those not actually open to the society) would enable us to determine not merely the preferences of individuals but also their intensities and that, since these should be taken into account in determining social policy, Arrow's axiom of the Independence of Irrelevant Alternatives should be waived. This would of course have the further consequence of removing Arrow's impossibility.[5] It is, however, a highly questionable value assumption that the collective preference ordering should *always* reflect not merely individual preference orderings but also their intensities. No doubt there are plausible cases, as when a minority prefers its principle much more passionately than the majority prefers a contrary alternative.[6] But suppose Jones, a wealthy man, is passionately opposed to any increase in the living standards of the poor and therefore passionately prefers policies that leave the poor in their miserable and apathetic state or make it worse. Is a social policy that does not adequately reflect the intensity of these preferences really worse, less fair, less democratic than one that does? Thus even if it is correct that by taking into account "irrelevant" alternatives, one can determine the intensities of individual preferences, still the main argument for relaxing Arrow's axiom of the Independence of Irrelevant Alternatives falls to the ground, because it is not morally defensible to argue that intensities of individual preferences *should* in all cases be reflected in social policies. On the other hand, it does seem true that in some cases, such as that of the minority just cited, the intensity of their preference should be taken into account. Hence neither the retention of the axiom of the Independence of Irrelevant Alternatives nor its replacement by some axiom of the Dependence on Irrelevant Alternatives would seem satisfactory.

Let us then return to the discussion of the basic value assumption: that social action should be designed to maximize the satisfactions of the members of the society, irrespective of the states of affairs, events, or activities from which these satisfactions are derived.

The point at issue is an old one. Many liberals reject the evaluative assumption just mentioned and insist that although social action should indeed aim at maximizing individual satisfactions, it should also take into account wherein individuals find their satisfaction. Liberals attempt to draw a distinction between those states, developments, and actions that affect an individual and that therefore are *his business* or *legitimate concern* and those that do not and therefore are not. Arrow denies that this distinction *can* be drawn. One need have no illusion about the ease of drawing it to find fault with the grounds for this contention put forward by Arrow.[7] It is of course true, as he says, that mankind is interdependent, but from this it does not follow that we cannot draw a line between what is and what is not a person's business. It does not seem true that "if my satisfaction is reduced by somebody else's poverty (or, for that matter, by somebody else's wealth), then I am injured in precisely the same sense as if my purchasing power were reduced." [8] Surely the wealthy man is not injured by the poor man's increase in income in the same sense in which he is injured by a reduction in his own purchasing power. In one case there is an economic (causal) connection between the poor man's getting more money and the rich man's having less purchasing power, attended by various psychological and other satisfactions and frustrations following upon these complex changes. In the other case there are only the psychological satisfactions and frustrations caused by the knowledge of the unwanted improvement in the poor man's condition. [9] The difference between the two lies in the fact that the former change affects the purchasing power of the rich man, whether or not he knows of that change and its causal impact, the latter affects him only by way of knowing of it. There is thus a meaningful way of distinguishing between the consequences of social actions that do and those that do not actually affect third persons. Hence if we are liberals and democrats and so subscribe to the view "that every individual should have the opportunity to find his own way to personal development and satisfaction," [10] then we can draw a further evaluative inference. We can infer that social actions should not reflect Jones's preferences as between the ways in which other individuals should seek or not seek their satisfaction, unless such seeking causally affects Jones's own opportunities. Arrow's examples are a mixed bag ignoring these important distinctions in liberal ethical and political thought. Thus, the example of the rich man's objection to social action improving the poor man's lot cannot (unlike the poor man's objection to the converse case) be based on considerations of injustice or even self-interest but simply on ill will. Such preferences, liberals might argue, need not, indeed should not, be reflected in social policy. Much the same is true for those differences in sexual taste that (assuming that they have no other socially undesirable causal consequences) when dwelt upon in the imagination may arouse disgust, anxiety, or anger. However, the same does not hold for Arrow's third case, a person's being disturbed about discriminations against Negroes, for discrimination is itself social policy differentially affecting classes of individuals, permitting or encouraging some individuals to seek their own satisfactions in ways that diminish the ability and opportunity of others to find theirs. Democratic and liberal theory need not treat in the same way these two kinds of frustration at, or dissatisfaction with, the way others find their satisfaction.

If social policy is to promote social welfare and social welfare is to be determined by aggregating, in accordance with a "constitution," the preference orderings of all members of the society, each member will naturally be vitally concerned not only about the formula of the constitution but also about the "raw material" to which this constitution is applied. For the constitution transforms all individual preference orderings into the social one. Such a transformation implies that the social preference will normally be different from each individual one. As far as each individual is concerned, the constitution sets aside his own preferences to accommodate those of others with whom he lives in the same society. Since social policy is, and often must be, enforced, each citizen will want to insure the "legitimacy" of the other persons' expressions of preference that are taken into account. He will hope not only that others refrain from forming illegitimate coalitions or from illegitimately modifying the expressions of their preferences lest such modifications of their *real* preference orderings jeopardize the representation of his *real* preference orderings in the social preference ordering, but he will also hope that the preferences of others in matters that are none of their business be regarded as illegitimate and therefore not taken into acount.

Our misgivings about the judgment that all preferences indiscriminately *ought* to be taken into account increase when we ask ourselves why this assumption should have been thought acceptable in the first place. Of the considerations apparently at work, two stand out, both unsound.

One of them is that by indiscriminately allowing all preferences to be aggregated, the difficulty of determining their legitimacy has been bypassed. But this is clearly not so. The decision to include all is tantamount to the judgment that all are equally legitimate and should therefore weigh equally, or in proportion to their intensity. However, as we have seen, this may sanction a policy that obligates a person to act against, for instance, his preferences in food, housing, sex, and so forth, because a majority (though directly unaffected by his doing so) intensely *dislikes* the thought that he should indulge them.

The second consideration seems to be this. It seems self-evident and generally accepted that governments *ought* to promote the social welfare. Moreover it is contended that social welfare is determined by the social preference ordering (sometimes called social-welfare function) as determined by the aggregation of individual preference orderings in accordance with a constitution. Hence the necessity of this enterprise. Hence the embarrassment when it is found impossible.

It is, however, doubtful whether governments *ought* in all situations and circumstances to promote social welfare. It is in any case a value judgment that is widely rejected, and that cannot therefore be defended on the ground of consensus. For many would maintain that when social welfare conflicts with certain higher aims or claims, such as Christian spiritual values, the free-enterprise system, basic human rights, international treaty obligations, and the like, then government policy ought to promote these higher ends and adhere to these higher principles even if such adherence fails to promote social welfare. The doctrine of basic human minority rights, of international treaty obligations, and international law is surely as much a part of the democratic tradition and quite as respectable in itself as the doctrine of citizen's sovereignty. If Arrow's proof tends to show that rigid adherence to the doctrine of consumer sovereignty could be self-stultifying, this need not be an embarrassment to rational democrats. They need only be prepared to substitute for *unconditional* adherence to the principle of consumer sovereignty adherence to it, *other things being equal,* and to include among the several exempting condtions the case in which expressed individual preferences turn out to aggregate into an intransitive social preference. We (as detached thinkers) may then agree that in such a case public officials should be allowed and required to select, by some other criterion, the policy that is best and we may advocate the inclusion of such a provision in our "constitution."

A second doubt is more radical. It arises not merely in exceptional cases when individual preference patterns aggregate into an intransitive social preference, but also in the standard case in which no such difficulties occur. It questions the very idea of determining social welfare through the aggregation of individual preference orderings of alternative possible social states. The main objection is that, as the economists use the term "welfare," the sentence "Governments ought, other things being equal, to promote the welfare of the society they govern" does not express the plausible value judgment ordinarily expressed by these words. Economists define "welfare" in terms of "preference," except that by "preference" they do not mean preference but "the order of priority in which a person chooses from a given set of alternatives." Thus if for example someones chooses to court financial ruin rather than let his daughter marry a wealthy member of a certain racial minority, then quite irrespective of why he chooses he *prefers* (in the economists' sense) the former to the latter. Ordinarily, we should contrast a choice made from preference with one made for religious or moral reasons. In the latter case our high-principled father chooses financial ruin, not indeed because he *prefers* it to the mixed marriage but because he feels he ought to choose it and *despite the fact that he prefers the other.* Even if we waive the question of preference, it would not be at all convincing to claim that the person who, for religious or moral reasons, chooses (prefers) financial ruin, thereby promotes his welfare. Yet that is what economists would have to say, in their technical senses of "preference" and "welfare." Now, there is of course no objection in principle to using a technical sense of "welfare" and "preference." But we must remember (which in practice is very difficult) that the reasons we normally have for favoring the promotion of welfare will not then always apply to cases of "welfare" (in the technical sense).

What is true for the welfare of individuals is true, by and large, also for the welfare of a society. Just as the actual choice pattern of an individual, however well informed he may be, is not identical with the promotion of his welfare, so *a fortiori* the "aggregation" of individual choice patterns into a so-called social-welfare function can hardly always be identical with social welfare. Now, in the case of an individual we often know what would promote his welfare (his interest, his good, his advantage) without knowing whether he would choose to do it. The explanation is of course that individuals, even when they have full information, often choose for reasons other than that they wish to promote their welfare. Thus, an individual's welfare is not constituted by his choice pattern even when he has full information. It would be really surprising if his actual choices, determined by his loves and hates for others, by moral, legal, and other considerations, by his inclinations, desires, impulses, and passions, were always to coincide with his choices based solely on his interest, good, or welfare, i.e., his nonerroneous judgments of what is in his interest, is for his good, or promotes his welfare, etc. But we could use even his actual choice patterns (or his nonerroneous declarations of intention to make certain choices) as perfectly reliable guides to what constitutes his interest, good, or welfare only if we could rely on the regular occurrence of this miracle. By parity of reasoning we could use a choice pattern based on aggregation of individual choice patterns as a guide to social welfare only if the two coincided or if social welfare was nothing but (nothing but another word for) the aggregation of individual choice patterns.

Coincidence here would be even more miraculous than in

the case examined above; particularly if one bears in mind the different possible bases of individual choice patterns just mentioned, e.g., those based on an individual's judgment (non-erroneous or otherwise) of what promotes his own welfare (Rousseau's Will of All) or based on an individual's judgment of what promotes the welfare of the society (Rousseau's General Will) or based on anything whatever (the economists' "preferential choice").[11]

Could it be that social welfare is *nothing but* the aggregation of individual choice patterns in accordance with a certain constitution? This is a tricky question that it would take a lengthy examination to settle. Here it must suffice to say that on the face of it, it does not seem so. We can point to a few rather obvious cases of promotion of social welfare, e.g., the raising of living standards, general health, life expectation, personal and economic security, education and amenities, lowering of the rate of violent crimes, elimination of dangerous and illness-causing types of work, and so on. And it is clear that we know that these are cases of the promotion of social welfare even though we do not know whether these are developments favored by the individuals of a given community, or whether there is a "constitution" that would aggregate individual preference orderings into a social choice pattern favoring these things. The epistemological basis for saying that some development promotes social welfare would thus seem to be other than the individual choice patterns and the "constitution." "Social welfare" can thus hardly mean the same as "social choice pattern derived from individual choice patterns in accordance with a reasonable constitution." But if it is granted that social welfare neither normally coincides with nor means the same as "social choice pattern derived by a certain method," then we should no longer feel quite so dependent on this particular method nor quite so embarrassed by the proven impossibility of always insuring its successful use.

Of course, the impossibility of aggregating individual preference orderings into social ones remains unaffected. But if social welfare cannot and therefore need not be determined by such an aggregation, then the impossibility is not troublesome and embarrassing. If what we determine by such an aggregation is not social welfare but merely social preference, we need not be embarrassed if aggregation of individual preferences in accordance with a formula satisfying Arrow's reasonable conditions does not produce *any* social preference orderings, i.e., produces an *intransitive* expression of social preference. For whereas we might well be surprised and embarrassed by the discovery that frequently no social policy was capable of promoting social welfare, we need not be surprised or embarrassed by the discovery that sometimes no acceptable aggregation of individual preferences will yield such a social policy, or indeed any social policy. For where no such settled social preference exists, officials can reasonably be authorized to decide, on the merits of the case, whether to implement any social policies or instead to allow social developments to take their own course; and if they decide the former, also to decide, on the merits of the case, which of Arrow's conditions should be set aside to make it possible to arrive at a social policy. Such a solution would be objectionable in serious matters but not in matters of *mere* preference.[12]

NOTES

1. For a full discussion, cf. Kenneth J. Arrow, *Social Change and Individual Values*, 2nd ed. (New York, London, and Sydney: Wiley, 1963); *id.*, "Public and Private Values," above (henceforward to be abbreviated as PV); R. Duncan Luce and Howard Raiffa, *Games and Decisions* (New York, London, and Sydney: Wiley, 1957), Ch. 14; Jerome Rothenberg, *The Measurement of Social Welfare* (Englewood Cliffs, N.J.: Prentice-Hall, 1961), or James M. Buchanan and Gordon Tullock, *The Calculus of Consent* (Ann Arbor Paperbacks: University of Michigan Press, 1965), especially Part III and Appendix 2; Robert A. Dahl and Charles E. Lindblom, *Politics, Economics, and Welfare* (New York: Harper Torchbooks, 1953); David Braybrooke and Charles E. Lindblom, *A Strategy of Decision* (Glencoe, Ill.: Free Press, 1963).

2. PV.

3. E.g., D. Black, *The Theory of Committees and Elections,* Cambridge, England; see also PV.

4. For details, cf., e.g., Luce and Raiffa, *op. cit.,* p. 332, and all of section 14.7.

5. Cf. Luce and Raiffa, *op. cit.,* pp. 335–38; also Robert A. Dahl, *A Preference to Democratic Theory* (University of Chicago Press, 1963), especially Ch. 4.

6. Robert A. Dahl, *op. cit.,* p. 90.

7. PV.

8. PV.

9. For a similar distinction, see H. L. A. Hart, *Law, Liberty, and Morality* (Stanford University Press, 1963), pp. 38–48.

10. PV.

11. We can now put the difference between the economists' and the ordinary use in this way: "preferential choice" ordinarily is a certain subclass of the class of choices, namely, those based on preference as opposed to other reasons, but as the economists use it, it is any freely made choice whatever it is based on.

12. Work on this paper was made possible by a research grant from the Carnegie Corporation of New York and the International Business Machines Corporation to the Department of Philosophy of the University of Pittsburgh to undertake a philosophical study of American values. I have greatly profited from helpful criticisms by David Braybrooke, Martin Bronfenbrenner, and Nicholas Rescher.

5

Some Questions on Human Values and Economic Policy

SHIRLEY B. JOHNSON
New York University

IN THE COURSE of the discussion on Human Values and Economic Policy a number of questions have been asked of the economists. The questions seem to resolve themselves into four main ones. Two of the questions, the ones which economists tend to ask themselves, have been answered elaborately by the papers and the formal commentators. The other two questions, which were asked in many ways, and thus appeared to be of great interest to many of the philosophers and some of the economists, were not and cannot be answered by the economists qua economist. And yet it is those questions that seem to be the most intriguing, yet most frequently misunderstood by the economists.

I should like to indicate the main forms of the questions raised as I understood them, differentiate between the ones that can and the ones that cannot be answered by the discipline of economics, and finally, comment briefly on why the unanswered questions cannot be answered in ways satisfying to the noneconomist.

The first question raised by economists, if not philosophers, was:

1) What do economists mean by the statement that "some individual, A, prefers X to Y and Y to Z, etc."?

The second question, perhaps of more interest to the topic under discussion was:

2) What do economists mean by the statement that "some group (a state or society), B, prefers X to Y"?

Both of these questions are in part questions about the use of language. Mr. Arrow's paper, his *Social Choice and Individual Values,* and the discussion of Mr. Samuelson gave some indication of what we as economists mean by these statements when we are trying to talk sense and some conditions under which we can say that "preferences have been revealed." Attempts to be precise, which led to the use of geometric and algebraic statements, may have convinced some members of the group that economists make the least sense when they are trying the hardest to make sense. However, I think it would be agreed that, given a long enough time period and enough translators, everyone in the room could see a certain logic in the axiomatic system presented. Whether everyone would also find the questions important is less clear.

The third type of question that was raised is a rather different one. It is a more personal question, perhaps even an embarrassing question, but one raised by almost all articulate noneconomists who have not been exposed to economists a great deal. I think the question can be simply stated as follows:

3) What do economists, acting in their capacity as professional experts, mean when they say not that A prefers X to Y but that *they* prefer X to Y, where, for instance, X is one policy recommendation and Y another?

Economists clearly do not mean that they prefer X to Y on any ethical or emotional grounds or grounds of esthetic merit. Rather, they are always talking about implicit if not explicit statements. For instance, an economist might say, "If one wants to accomplish a given end, one wants to do X instead of Y because X will lead to the desired goal more quickly, with fewer unhappy side effects upon the economy, with a higher probability of success in an uncertain world, or because X will involve a lower monetary cost than Y.

For economists all of the reasons given above for preferring X to Y can be reduced to what we call "lower costs." It seems to me that this is precisely what Mr. Friedman was talking about when he insisted that there is more apparent than real disagreement among economists. We are all concerned with models of maximizing returns at lowest cost. There can still be plenty of hearty disagreement among economists, given the state of imperfect knowledge. There is particularly likely to be disagreement about the aforementioned "side effects."

The most difficult of the questions raised, and one that some of the participants in the discussion would probably like to regard as a nonquestion, is the fourth:

4) What do economists as a group or guild think are right or good goals for society?

Or, put a little more irreverently:

Is there a professional point of view or bias among economists about social or political goals?

Surely this question is one that we as a profession must be willing to discuss now that we have achieved a place of prominence as advisors to governments, corporation presidents, and the like. Whether it is asked by those who seek some kind of "truth" that we are supposed to have or by those who are implicitly asking about the source of power of our modest discipline, it is a legitimate question.

There has been some reference to this question in the talk about maximizing, Pareto optima, and highest points on Social Welfare Functions yesterday and today. However, the reference has been somewhat oblique and, I think, largely obscured from those unused to the economist's way of using language. Because economists are talking about a calculus and are concerned with teaching its applications, we are forbidden from specifying priorities for goods for either an individual or a group. This is as true when the goods concerned are freedom versus paternalistic restraint as it is when the goods are apples versus oranges, for we are talking about an axiomatic system in which others or economists as "ordinary men" supply the goals or values to be assigned to goods. Thus, any poll of economists asking their views on Vietnam or preferences in cigarette brands will reveal their personal not their professional biases. If they claim otherwise, they are being bad economists and confused thinkers.

We can hardly speak of a credo of economists, unless it is the passion for maximizing of which Kenneth Boulding spoke. (However, in fairness, I think economists must often admit to a fascination with the market mechanism.) The philosophic tradition out of which the discipline of economics developed was the Empiricism of J. S. Mill and Bentham, not the Rationalism of Kant. As a result, we are blessed or cursed with having all imperatives except one forbidden to us. The one imperative is that our conclusions must not be biased by our passions.

6

Social Choice and Policy Formation

GAIL KENNEDY
Amherst College

PROFESSOR ARROW'S INTENT, as I understand it, is to construct
a model that will be useful in the determination of welfare
judgments. His model is derived from the type of analysis
employed by economists in determining under varying conditions the allocation of resources in a free market through the
operation of a price system. He intends it to be generally
applicable to any system of social organization exhibiting
similar characteristics and he thinks it could be widely applied
to the determination of social and political policies in a democratic society because there is a close analogy between
economic exchange and the preferences indicated by public-
opinion polls or by elections. To purchase beaver rather than
deer is sufficiently similar to voting for Smith instead of Jones.
Some modifications of the economic model are, of course,
necessary—for instance, he is envisaging here a pure democracy where each individual has an equal vote as against the
inequalities of income—but these, it seems to me, are mostly
technical and relatively unimportant.

The practical use of this mode of inquiry would be to
supply citizens or the officials of such a democracy with advice that would enable them to formulate formal social policies
that are "right," i.e., morally justifiable. This advice would be
in the form of what he calls welfare judgments, i.e., statements that assert any one possible alternative "social action"
or set of "social actions" to be preferable to another.

Nearly everyone, I assume, will grant the utility of the

construction of models for the purpose of analyzing complex situations; and many persons would assert that economics is more advanced than other social sciences, largely because of the comparative success economists have had in the construction of models descriptive of economic behavior. It is also recognized that, in general, models operate most successfully within a restricted context, one where the area of their concrete application is isolable. Finally, there is wide agreement that such modes of formalization have inherent limitations and that when their application is overextended they can lead to ambiguous and misleading interpretations of the situation to which they are applied. I have no doubt that the kind of model Professor Arrow here presents works well in determining the exchange ratios that express a relative preference for beaver vs. deer, but I wonder how well it can function when one attempts to apply it to the welter of circumstances involved in the case of many if not most formulations of social policy. At any rate, the easiest way to estimate the utility of Professor Arrow's model, or others like it, would be to ask how closely it corresponds to reasonably typical instances of policy formation, to what extent it *is* relevant to the exigencies of common sense as they press upon citizens who are trying to arrive at an opinion, or officials who are attempting to formulate and implement a policy concerning an issue that is a matter of public interest.

I

Professor Arrow begins his exposition with the Robinson Crusoe approach traditional among economists. What, he asks, "can be said about any imaginary, completely isolated individual?" His answer is, "To an economist, and I suppose to most philosophers, a value system would, in these terms, be simply the rule an individual uses to choose which of the mutually exclusive actions he will undertake."

Most of the inadequacies I find in his paper are, I think, the logical consequence of this starting point. Although he goes on to say that in fact "all significant actions involve joint participation of many individuals" and that "all nontrivial actions are essentially the property of society as a whole, not of individuals," the process of decision is for him essentially the same in both cases. He thinks this is true for two reasons: all actual decisions are made by individuals; and these decisions, although they involve the joint participation of many individuals, can be aggregated since "economic analysis has supplied us with a model of factorization of social actions, that achieved through the price system."

To me the most striking thing about these assumptions is what they omit:

1) All value judgments are treated as *de facto* preferences ranked in a certain order. No question is raised about their origin: they may be the expression of an instinct, momentary impulse, routine conditioning, a habit that is the consequence of prior deliberation, or a choice made now after an estimation of the consequences of alternative decisions. Any attempt to discriminate between that which is in fact valued and that which upon reflection might be found either valuable or the contrary is ignored. Professor Arrow does mention two possibilities: "An observer looking from the outside on our isolated individual may say that his decision was wrong either in the sense that there is some other standard of values to which it does not conform or in the sense that it was made on the grounds of insufficient information or improper calculation." The first he rejects, because: "For the single, isolated individual there can be no other standard than his own values"; the second he seems to consider irrelevant since what he is concerned with is an individual's preferences, not some hypothetical reason why he might be led to modify them. What is omitted, then, is any reference to either the cause or the rationale of individual choice, above all, even the intimation that rational choices are the result of prior inquiry.

2) A second striking omission is any mention of types or forms of association, such as interest groups, factions, regional blocs, or formal organizations, such as labor unions, corpora-

tions, and political parties—the associations that are the usual referents of the political scientist when he is discussing public opinion and policy formation. Professor Arrow seems to assume that we can arrive at welfare judgments without specific references to associations. Although the unit he chooses for the purpose of his analysis is what he calls "a social action, i.e., an action involving a large proportion or the entire domain of society," it is the individual, he says, "who plays a central role in social choices as the judge of alternative social actions according to his own standards. We presume that each individual has some way of ranking social actions according to his preferences for their consequences. These preferences constitute his value system." Again, the cause or rationale of the individual's preference is irrelevant. It does not matter whether his choice is the consequence of membership in an association, nor need we notice that the demands of groups, classes, and organizations are frequently antagonistic—and irreconcilable if dealt with merely as *de facto* claims.

Only two things, then, are needed, adequate information about individual choices of social actions, and a method for the aggregation of these "choices": the "problem of social choice is the aggregation of the multiplicity of individual preference scales about alternative social actions." Granted these two conditions it is possible to derive what he calls a "constitution," i.e., "a rule that associates to each possible set of individual offerings a social choice function, i.e., a rule for selecting a preferred action out of every possible environment." And a welfare judgment is then what he calls "a second-order evaluation," "it is an evaluation of the consequences to all individuals based on their evaluations."

For Professor Arrow, what does this really mean? By way of answering the question, he quotes a passage from a paper by A. Bergson in which two alternatives are presented. The first is that these judgments are intended to give advice to individual citizens, advice in which "reference is made to some ethical values which are appropriate for the counseling of the individual in question." Then he goes on to say: "But some may be inclined nevertheless to a different conception, which allows still another interpretation of Arrow's theorem. *According to this second view, the problem is to counsel not citizens generally but public officials.* [Emphasis added.] Furthermore, the values to be taken as data are not those which would guide the official if he were a private citizen. The official is envisaged instead as more or less neutral ethically. His one aim in life is to implement the values of other citizens as given by some rule of collective decision making." And to this Professor Arrow adds, "My interpretation of the social choice problem agrees fully with that given by Bergson beginning with the italicized statement . . ." I do not know what Bergson means by "some ethical values which are appropriate." Certainly the interpretation that seems to me consistent with Arrow's position is the one that he himself adopts.

II

I come now to the original question: to what degree is Professor Arrow's model applicable to the concrete process of arriving at equitable decisions in the formulating and implementing of social policies? I have no doubt the model could be applied within restricted areas for the purpose of describing and predicting some kinds of social behavior. It would work if the question before the government were whether fiscal policies should be adopted that would sharply increase the interest rate even though there were side effects such as concomitant decline in mortgage loans for the construction of private dwellings. But the welfare judgments that might be offered in instances of this sort seem to fall into the category of information rather than advice and express only an incidental obligation of the sort Kant calls a technical imperative—perhaps sometimes also, at least in a negative way, what he terms counsels of prudence.

I do not see, though, how use of the model could disclose any genuinely moral obligation. What we here need to know is how and to what degree decisions affecting the interest rate become a matter of public interest. As Dewey defines it, a public interest is involved when transactions "have extensive and enduring consequences which involve others beyond those directly engaged in them."[1] It is at this point that the need for certain kinds and types of governmental institutions arises, and for the elective or appointed officials whose primary responsibility is to ascertain what the public interest really is and to formulate policies for its enforcement. Here we can recognize a type of obligation that goes beyond technical advice and prudential monitions.

How can the public interest be derived simply by the application of "a rule that associates to each possible set of individual orderings a social choice function"? How is the "second order evaluation," the welfare judgment, derived? When Professor Arrow tells us that "it is an evaluation of the consequences to all individuals based on their evaluations" he seems to be adopting in the most literal and simplistic way possible the two notorious assertions of John Stuart Mill: "the sole evidence it is possible to produce that anything is desirable is that people do actually desire it"; and, "that each person's happiness is a good to that person and the general happiness, therefore, a good to the aggregate of all persons."[2]

Professor Arrow seems to think that information derived from election returns, a referendum, or an opinion poll can be fed into a computer and that the computer can "decide" what is the most justifiable choice function. If this is his opinion, it completely ignores the obvious fact that for a society most real choices cannot be factored in this way. If A wants X while B wants Y and C wants Z, what actually most often results from the complex interaction of their respective efforts to realize their aims is a set of consequences that no one initially intended or desired; and if this complex unintentional result could be predicted by some process using a "model of factorization of social actions" derived from economic analysis, does it follow that the result would be a judgment expressing what is actually in the public interest?

As a way of getting at the answer, consider the following

excerpt from a recent "Letter from Washington" by Richard H. Rovere. I choose this example because the President, we know, is so markedly sensitive to opinion polls that he inevitably reminds us of his predecessor, Andrew Johnson, for whom it was an article of faith that the voice of the people is the voice of God.

> The Lyndon Johnson of today, some hold, is a man seized with martial fever and a new dream—a messianic one, of himself as the scourge of Communism everywhere. He has sometimes sounded as if such a transformation had taken place, but those who have most often been right in predicting his behavior and his moods do not believe a word of it. They insist that he still regards himself as a victim of events, and that the frustration he feels is as intense as that of any of the doves and hawks who press in on him from opposite directions, compelling him to fight a rearguard political action on two fronts while in Vietnam itself he fights a bloody war that has no front at all. But no matter what his dreams may be, he remains the country's closest student of public opinion, and he is getting the message of the polls, which is that the war in Vietnam has shattered the very core of his consensus beyond any hope of early repair.[3]

Obviously, a situation of this kind is a fair, even though extreme, example. Confronted with such a fluid and inchoate state of affairs, one in which it is vitally important to make continual reassessments of policy, what should President Johnson do were he to think it his duty to act as an official whose "one aim in life is to implement the values of other citizens as given by some rule of collective decision making"? An accurate knowledge of the present state of public opinion does partially define the limits within which executive action is feasible. But does Professor Arrow seriously propose that the American people, sitting as a committee of the whole, should make the decision by employing an official to evaluate the consequences to all individuals based on their evaluation?

In general there are two types of evaluation. The first is in terms of predetermined standards. In very simple cases, where no serious or important uncertainty about objectives is involved, this method works. If for learning to type the agreed objectives are speed and accuracy, the requisite means are readily available by which one may evaluate the "hunt and pick" vs. the touch system. Consider, though, the following examples: (1) If one of the problems in the Simon-Binet test is the ability to repeat a number backward, then what is tested is the ability to repeat numbers backwards. Taking the whole group of items on the test together, in the absence of further knowledge, you must conclude that intelligence tests test what intelligence tests do test. (2) Bentham says at the beginning of his *Principles of Morals and Legislation:*

> Nature has placed mankind under the governance of two sovereign masters, *pain* and *pleasure*. It is for them alone to point out what we ought to do, as well as to determine what we shall do. On the one hand the standard of right and wrong, on the other the chain of causes and effects, are fastened to their throne.

This statement largely predetermines what follows in the book. No action can occur unless it is intended to avoid pain or procure pleasure, and all actions are justified to the degree that they succeed in doing so. Contrast with these examples the nominal circularity of Aristotle's statement that only a good man can judge what is truly good.

Professor Arrow recognizes that a formal model, taken in isolation, is what he calls a tautology; he adds, "what makes it more than that is a specification of reasonable conditions to be imposed on constitutions, and it is here that any dispute must lie." But is not his mode of formalization much closer to that of Bentham than to that of Aristotle? How does one evaluate anything so delicate, particular, and qualitatively complex as the goodness of a man or a marriage or a social policy? Here predetermined standards have at best a minimal significance. The problem is not one merely of discovering appropriate means to the achievement of a known end upon which there is prior agreement. It is one of discovering a set of operative means that will enable us to resolve more satisfactorily the complex tensions and divergent interests that constitute the elements of a highly problematic situation. The search for appropriate operative means entails a concomitant reconsideration of any previously entertained ends in view. To choose one set of operative means as against another amounts in fact to a redefinition of the objectives.

How significant to anyone who has made a careful study of the history of our intervention in Vietnam is the statement: "Our objective is and always has been a reasonable and just settlement of the conflict, with proportionate satisfaction to the interests of everyone concerned"? And would he think that the alterations of policy have been the consequence merely of influence upon the government of the shifting and conflicting currents of opinion among American citizens?

What must here be added is the active role of politicians, a major part of whose functions has aptly been called the engineering of consent. Most of the original choices of individuals and groups are determined primarily by their conception of the direct and immediate consequences that effect their own interests—largely ignoring or minimizing the derivative and secondary consequences that constitute the public interest. Public opinion at any level as an aggregate of the preferences of individuals in a group is often seriously out of alignment with what truly constitutes the welfare of a society as a whole. This is especially true where, as in the example used, the situation is a continually changing one.

The responsibility for an effective implementation of public interest devolves mainly upon the politician. It is his primary duty to find if he can a mode of dealing with social problems that will reconcile the divergent claims involved in a way that conforms so far as possible to what he conceives to be the total good of the situation.

This means that he must frequently attempt to reform public opinion. Instances (and they are always controversial) would be the calculated efforts made by Franklin Roosevelt from 1937 on to wean a large segment of the American public from the illusions of their wishful isolationism, or the way in which Mr. Wilson has recently gained the reluctant assent of business groups, the labor unions, and the British public generally to a regime of austerity necessitated by the cumulative effect of a long-standing unfavorable balance of trade.

If what I have said is approximately correct, social policies are formulated as a way of attempting to deal with situations in which there is a need both for expert information, and a point of view that transcends the particularities of conflicting opinion among individuals and groups. Choices made within a situation of this kind, one in which there is a continual ingression of novelty, if they are intelligent must of necessity be tentative and experimental in character. Decisions must be made with the reservation that they should be modified as the situation changes. Of course, the gamut of divergent and opposed public opinions is highly influential. It is a truism that the politician should respect and interpret the wishes of his constituents and, in fact, those wishes, however ambiguous and inconsistent they may be, are normally the primary forces defining the limitations within which he operates. But attempting merely to implement public opinion would almost invariably result in following the time-honored procedure of muddling through. The intelligent approach to the problem of formulating and executing social policies requires a decent respect for all the relevant facts that need be taken account of in an attempt to cope with the realities of the situation.[4]

NOTES

1. *The Public and Its Problems,* p. 27.
2. *Utilitarianism,* Ch. 4.
3. *The New Yorker,* October 8, 1966, p. 198.
4. I have attempted to make a more detailed analysis of this problem in a paper entitled "The Process of Evaluation in a Democratic Community," *The Journal of Philosophy,* LVI (1959), 253–63.

7

Policy Decisions and Value in Metaeconomics

PAUL KURTZ

State University of New York at Buffalo

AS THE PAPERS in this Symposium vividly demonstrate, there is a close relationship between economics and philosophy, or there at least should be, although economists have generally abandoned the theory of value, and philosophers have neglected economic analysis. The relationship between the two disciplines was very close at the inception of economics. It is a pity that this dialogue and communication have not been adequately sustained in the present; for there are profoundly puzzling philosophical difficulties lying at the foundations of economics, and there are several important issues in ethics that economists have dealt with which philosophers might profit by studying.

I

The problem of value is especially crucial in economics because, of all the behavioral and social sciences, economics seems to be most closely involved in policy matters. Economists are continuously requested by government and labor officials, businessmen, and private individuals to make policy recommendations; hence it is sometimes difficult to disentangle economics as a descriptive or theoretical behavioral science from economics as a policy science. Yet it would appear that this very elementary distinction needs to be made and to be made clearly. Professor Boulding's failure to do so at times leads to all sorts of difficulties. Thus I should insist that the first task of economics is the description of certain kinds of behavior and its explanation in terms of general hypotheses or causal conditions. As Professor Nagel pointed out, an account of how and why people behave the way they do is the basic foundation upon which all economic analysis rests. There are theories of market behavior, for example, the causes of business cycles, that must be tested by the range of their explanatory and predictive power. Insofar as economists engage in such objective inquiries, their value judgments presumably are *not* directly relevant and should recede into the background. It is of course the case that first-order judgments of any inquiry, whether natural science, biology, or economics, are based on value judgments—at a minimum that the inquiry is worth pursuing, or that objectivity and clarity are important. In this sense, descriptive economic science is value grounded, as are all others. But, in disagreement with Boulding, Myrdal, and others I would insist that it is surely possible to provide second-order economic principles that are relatively value free. I say this even though I suspect that many of the conclusions of descriptive economic inquiry apply only to a limited set of social conditions or an historical epoch and are not "universal" as some economists thought. And I say this recognizing that most descriptive theories, and especially classical theories of value, have been so impregnated with value judgments that it is not easy to say where one begins and the other ends. Marx's labor theory of value, for example, is not so much an account of how products are valued in a market economy as how they *ought* to be valued by reference to the amount of socially useful labor embodied. And other classical theories, in the guise of description, impute positive value to the market of exchange.

Most economists today recognize these difficulties and have given up on an explicit theory of value. Many, however, have not abandoned their value biases in descriptive economics. Thus economists, often in the very definition of key terms and concepts, imply covert value assumptions: concepts such as "stability," "growth," "inflation," "real income," etc. often involve norms and standards as a basis of classification. This reflects anew the fact that an economist's interest may simultaneously be twofold: descriptive and prescriptive. All that we should ask is that he not slip from one to the other without explicit recognition, else his science is merely a mask for his underlying interests. In this regard, I think that Professor Friedman is mistaken when he states that most disputes between economists are not about values, but about facts or consequences. I suspect that a good deal of the dispute between a Keynesian or orthodox economist, for example, is based in part at least upon value that prejudices theory. The same thing is surely true of Marxist versus non-Marxist theories. It seems apparent that the economist has need of the philosophical analyst to assist him in tidying up his conceptual framework and making the necessary distinctions.

What I have said should in no way be construed to mean that value judgments have no place in economics. On the contrary, they have an important and indeed crucial role to play. If economics is an applied or policy science, as it is, then policies involve value judgments, and it is this aspect of economics that I think is especially relevant to philosophy.

II

Contemporary philosophy on the whole is seriously deficient in its appreciation of economics, and of the behavioral and social sciences. I do not think that all the problems of philosophical ethics can be resolved by reference to ordinary language, and an investigation of the significant body of value concepts that are treated in the behavioral sciences may be instructive. The problem of decision-making is a central question for ethics, but it is also, at least in one sense, a central question for economics. For economists have asked: what constitutes a "rational" or effective decision-making procedure? I should like to examine three important areas in policy economics in which decision processes arise and value judgments function.

a) Classical economists have posited the idea of economizing or maximizing utilities within a framework of scarcities: the notion that there is a disparity between human wants, which may be unlimited and insatiable, and means and resources, which are generally limited. Many ethical philosophers have recognized that choice is a function of the means at our disposal and the consequences of our action. But the economist has explored in great detail, with the aid of powerful mathematical tools and econometric models, the problem of choice where means are limited. He has penetrated beyond the glittering generalities of philosophical discussion to an intensive inquiry of the concrete world where scarcity is a fact. It is rather surprising that the problem of scarcity has not brooked large in the philosophical literature, and especially the question of *how* to allocate resources and distribute goods in the light of it. The point is that here is a "logic of decision-making," even though it probably only applies under limited conditions.

Classical economics, climaxing in Marshall, has provided a model for "rationality"; it is the deliberate economic agent, calculating his interests and maximizing his satisfactions, who is allegedly "rational." This is reflected in the price system—which has a rationale of its own—as individual economizers enter into and exchange in a market place of supply and demand. "Rationality," however, is notoriously value-charged; and one has to be careful that it is not merely a persuasive term. Moreover, the classical framework for policy decisions was predicated upon a descriptive theory that leaves much to be desired: the development of large corporations, the administered price, the role of advertising in developing consumer preferences, oligopoly, and imperfect competition, all suggest that the classical model is deficient.

b) Welfare economics has also been concerned with questions of policy decisions. It asks: what are the conditions under which individuals may maximize the attainment of their goals by means of social mechanism? The problem of welfare economics is how far we can proceed by means of economic analysis toward defining the "best" position of any economic universe. Welfare economics as conceived by Pareto applied to both capitalist and socialist economics, for every economy has limited resources that need to be distributed efficiently in such a way as to bring about maximum results in productivity, efficiency, allocation, and satisfaction.

The key philosophical question that can be raised concerns the goals and objectives of policies. To claim that the welfare economists make no value judgments, but only take the price system or existing satisfactions as mechanisms for analysis, hardly answers the question. For the definition of optimum allocation involves the formulation of a scale of values, on the basis of which alternative uses of resources are evaluated. What we need from welfare economists is clarity about what the ends, objectives, or values of policy are, and how they propose to go about testing or verifying them.

The issue can be focused in this way: what are the criteria for warranting social decisions? There is an important difference between a theory that is based upon "consumer sovereignty," where the preferences and satisfactions of consumers as expressed in the price system are the deciding criteria, and a theory based upon the assumption that consumers do not always know what is good for them, and that a planning board may be in a better position to understand their needs. We may ask whether that which is desired is always an adequate criterion in determining what is desirable for the community as a whole. I should argue that the alternatives are not exclusive, for that which consumers desire is rarely of their own choice, but is influenced by society, and that for planning boards not to take into account consumer wants borders on dictatorship. Hence, I suspect that a combination of both criteria may be less liable to risk. In any case, what disturbs me about welfare economics is that, although it is dealing with questions of fundamental significance, the criteria or conditions in terms of which it tests its principles (e.g., the Pareto principle) seem to be based at times upon some form of vague intuition.

c) Questions of value also emerge in the area of growth economics. It is widely held that an increase in gross national product measured in constant prices is a gain in economic welfare, i.e., the economic welfare of a country is increasing if there is a rise in the real output per capita. Thus most economists today seem to be vitally interested in ways of attaining an expansion of productive resources. But intrinsic to this inquiry there emerges a whole set of values and norms. And basic questions about the comparative values of freedom, equality, justice, and material well-being, etc. are raised. The economist is sorely in need of help from the philosopher in appraising such moral values.

Whether or not a given society will attain its growth, however, depends upon a great number of factors and considerations; there is a whole constellation of cultural values that may be at work. For example, if a society is to achieve economic development, investment in capital goods must be made. But the role of economizing for this purpose is not always appreciated or recognized. The Puritan work ethic does not seem to appeal to many underdeveloped countries where leisure is prized more than capital accumulation.

What I infer from this discussion is this: most economic policy recommendations presuppose a set of value judgments that are in need of clarification. For example, economizing in terms of scarcities is a fundamental principle of economic analysis. Is economizing a condition of rational behavior, a historical condition brought into play in some societies, or a value judgment? If it is a value, can it then be questioned, as indeed Professor Boulding does when he talks of heroic sacrifice or of competing values in certain contexts? The usual argument is that some economizing is *necessary* under all human conditions, no matter what the society, individual, or household; for if we are to attain our diverse ends, then we need a "prudent" use of resources to do so. I would grant this, but only up to a point. For decision behavior entails a great number of other noneconomic values, and the scarcity factor is only one among many considerations.

III

This leads to one final point: I think that it is impossible to sustain a divorce of economics (descriptive or policy science) from the other behavioral sciences. Individual behavior has both a biopsychological and sociocultural basis; and social behavior is a function of a concrete historical and institutional framework. To separate economics from politics or sociology is to encapsulate it as a science. Policy recommendations introduced independently of political considerations or social norms deal in false abstractions. A "logic of decision" based upon scarcity then is not in itself adequate, nor is it a universal model for choice. It is *a* model for choice, a remarkably elegant one under certain social conditions. But as Professor Boulding points out, it must be seen in comparison with other values. Similar considerations apply to the decision process in welfare and growth economics.

Thus economists perhaps would do well to reexamine their basic presuppositions and to turn their attention to the question of implicit values and how to establish them. But I have one serious reservation about the virtues of metaeconomics: I would hope that economists would not get bogged down in semantic definition-mongering or epistemological bog. For, unlike the philosopher, who can enjoy the luxury of mongering and bog, economists cannot refuse to make value judgments. Public men must decide questions of policy and economists can and should assist them as best they know how, and in the light of the best evidence. I would suggest that value judgments in economics are not simply a matter of taste, they are conditioned and modified by various factors. If it is difficult to find a universal "logic" of economic choice, this does not mean that some informed value judgments cannot be made, however relative and tenuous. Indeed, there may be several different kinds of "rationality" in economics. The complex nature of economic "reason" and decision-making, however, is a problem that merits further attention by philosophers and metaeconomists.

8

The Use of Mechanical Methods for the Solution of Ethical Problems

JOHN LADD
Brown University

THE EXTRAORDINARY DEVELOPMENT of mathematical and logical techniques that has taken place as the result of the invention of game theory, decision theory, and the computer raises some provocative and novel questions about the relevance of what I shall call "mechanical methods," i.e., mathematical models and calculi, for the solution of traditional ethical problems. (I call these methods "mechanical" because, in principle at least, they can be programmed for a computer.) Arrow's paper places this general problem of the relation of these methods to ethics in the context of welfare economics, since he defines concepts like "social welfare" and "public values" in such a way that they can be calculated by means of deductions from given postulates formulated in game-theoretical and modern logical terms, that is, by "mechanical methods."

In this paper I do not intend to examine in detail any of the complicated controversies arising within the field of welfare economics, nor do I intend to discuss the ramifications of the use of economic analogies suggested by Boulding, for these subjects are quite beyond my own sphere of competence. What I propose to do is to explore some of the general ethical implications of the use of calculi, and of other mechanical methods, for the solution of practical problems, e.g., problems of social choice and problems of social policy. How can the use of these methods be ethically justified, or can they be ethically justified at all? In what contexts can they be properly used and what are the limitations of their rightful use? After discussing these questions in general I shall attempt to apply a few of my tentative conclusions to Arrow's theory.

The view that rationality consists in calculating, and that a rational ethics is a calculus, is, of course, not a new one for philosophers. Some time ago, Hobbes wrote:

> When a man *reasons,* he does nothing but conceive a sum total from addition of parcels, or conceive a remainder from subtraction of one sum from another. . . . In sum, in what matter soever there is place for addition and subtraction, there also is place for *reason;* and where these have no place, there *reason* has nothing at all to do.[1]

Bentham's calculus presupposes essentially the same conception of ethical reasoning as the one presented by Hobbes. Today, both of their ethical systems are regarded by philosophers as interesting but strange concoctions that could only arise from a consistent and thoroughgoing application of a mathematical model to ethical reasoning. The tremendous expansion, since the time of Hobbes and Bentham, of the facilities for making complicated and speedy computations has in no way removed the numerous and now classical philosophical objections to their basic view of the proper method of solving ethical problems.

Before continuing, I wish to make clear that I am not underestimating the usefulness of mathematical models (and calculi) for the purposes of explanation, description, and prediction in economics and the social sciences in general. Nevertheless, however useful a mathematical model may be for such purposes, it is fallacious to conclude that simply because it works well for such purposes, we are justified in using it for prescriptive purposes as well, i.e., as a guide for ethical decision-making. Not only is it logically impossible directly to derive a prescription from a predictive (or explanatory) model, but the criteria of a good model for prescriptive purposes are quite different from those of a good model for predictive purposes. The models belong to different categories and require different types of justification. A good deal of confusion about normative issues in the literature of the social sciences arises from the indiscriminate use of perfectly valid explanatory models for prescriptive purposes. To my knowledge, little has been done to clarify the relationship between the two uses of models.

A second qualification to what I have to say is that I shall not be concerned with the use of mechanical methods (mathematical models and calculi) for the solution of what may be called purely "strategic problems," that is, problems of determining what, under certain conditions, are the most expedient means to predetermined ends of one sort or another. Under strategic problems I would include most technical industrial and business problems, problems of military strategy, traffic-control problems, and so on. Since the end in view in such problems remains unchallenged within the terms of the inquiry itself, any possible ethical questions that they involve are deliberately put to one side, or else are begged from the start. The use of mechanical methods for the solution of strategic problems of this sort concerns only what Kant called "hypothetical imperatives." As such they may be very important, but they are ethically uninteresting.

It is unnecessary for me to repeat in detail the criticisms commonly advanced by philosophers of the exaggerated ethical claims made for welfare economics, and for the economic model, by Arrow and others. Philosophers instinctively balk at the definition of "value" and "rationality" used by economists. It is not that there is anything illegitimate about using a stipulative definition for a technical purpose. What is illegitimate is the assumption that the technical concept (e.g., "value") defined, or redefined, for a technical purpose can without further ado be exported from the technical context to other contexts and used for quite different purposes, e.g., for the solution of ethical problems. The substitution of a word with one meaning (a technical meaning) for the same word with a different meaning (an ordinary meaning) is simply an instance of the fallacy of equivocation; where ethics is concerned, it is known as the naturalistic fallacy (Moore) or a persuasive definition (Stevenson). A much simpler way of putting the philosophers' objection is that, although any definition of a term may be adopted by *fiat* if it seems to be useful for purely theoretical purposes, ethical problems cannot be solved by redefining ethical expressions in this way or by setting up postulate systems in which ethical expressions appear. In other words, ethical problems cannot be solved by *fiat*. Thus, as long as the calculi, and mathematical models, are based merely on definitions and postulates, they have no ethical import whatsoever. If they are to have any ethical import at all, the use of such models requires outside ethical justification. In sum, the relevance of any of these methods for ethics has to be demonstrated. It cannot simply be asserted.

Assuming, then, that some sort of ethical justification is required for the use of mechanical methods, e.g., calculi and mathematical models, for the solution of ethical problems, we may ask whether any such justification is possible. If the answer is yes, then we must ask what it is and under what conditions it holds. In particular, we may ask whether any ethical justification can be given for using the procedures of welfare economics outlined by Arrow.

My answer will be that under certain conditions and within certain limitations an ethical justification can be given for using these methods for solving ethical problems. The justification, as will become clear presently, rests on principles that have traditionally been included under the heading of distributive justice. I shall begin with the limitations.

The first limitation of the use of mechanical methods (e.g., calculi) for ethical purposes is that they apply only to what Arrow calls "social decision processes," i.e., decisions made for a society by public officials acting in their public rather than their private capacity. This, of course, is the context in which Bentham developed his hedonic calculus, for he intended his book to be a manual for legislators rather than individual agents. This limitation holds also, I submit, for Arrow's own theory: his calculus cannot be applied by individual agents to the making of their own choices. For it is obvious that individuals qua agents confronted with the necessity of making choices (and as subjects exhibiting preferences) cannot of themselves, in that capacity, employ Arrow's postulates of ordering, e.g., the principles of connexity and transitivity. An individual cannot deliberately choose "rationally" (in Arrow's sense), that is, he cannot make his choices (or preferences) by following the rules of a value system that itself is defined in terms of his preferences and their ordering; he can only be "rational" in the ordinary sense, that is, he can only try to structure or restructure his preferences (and choices) in the light of information available, other preferences, needs, principles and standards, etc. I cannot decide, for example, whether I prefer *Don Giovanni* to the *Magic Flute* by consulting some table of ordering, and by determining whether what I think is consistent with it or not. The very act of examining one's own preferences is creative; it changes them by clarifying, specifying, and structuring them. In other words, the concept of "value" (= preference) and of value ordering cannot be applied by the person himself to his own preferences while he is doing the preferring; it can only be applied by a third party (an observer) who wants to describe that individual's preferences or value system. But, it should be clear that when so used by a third party the concepts of "private value" and "rationality" (as defined by Arrow) operate as descriptive rather than prescriptive concepts. In this respect I go further than Brandt, who bases his criticism of Arrow's concept of private value on the distinction between intrinsic and instrumental values (understood in the prescriptive sense, of course), for I want to argue that Arrow's concept of value ordering, for reasons involving the paradoxes of self-reference, cannot be consistently applied by the individual to his own preferences.

For these reasons, and others that will be given shortly, I think that Arrow has quite properly concentrated his attention on the problem of social choice and public values as distinct from the choice and values of any particular individual. Now, it is Arrow's contention that what he calls "public value" (i.e., what, I suppose, should determine public choice and public policy) is a function of the private values of the individuals in the society. With certain qualifications, I agree with Arrow on this point, but I must hasten to point out that he is here using "value" in two quite different senses: "value" in the public context, i.e., public value, is being used prescriptively, i.e., it means what ought to determine a social decision, whereas "value" in the private context, i.e., private value, is being used descriptively, i.e., it means nothing more than that people do choose or do prefer. To translate Arrow's contentions into philosophical terminology, I think that what he is saying is that public policy (i.e., the most enlightened and desirable social choices and decisions) ought to be a function of the private choices, or preferences, of the individuals in the society. In other words, facts about people's preferences are the data from which social decisions ought to be made.

The full ethical impact of this theory is lost if we fail to note that the private choices (values) are to be taken into account no matter what they may be, for it is essential to Arrow's doctrine that the private values (choices, preferences) of the individuals be taken as they are, and not as they should be. For purposes of social decision, they are not to be challenged. The important point about this doctrine, then, is that, in the formulation of social policy, it deliberately excludes from consideration certain aspects of private choices that are commonly taken to be of fundamental ethical importance, namely, the moral quality of the choices themselves, including such considerations as whether they are enlightened or ignorant, sympathetic or loathsome, normal or abnormal, etc. Thus, what Arrow's postulates accomplish is the exclusion of certain considerations that, in a different context, might be regarded as ethically important. It is possible, however, that the exclusion itself is ethically required.

My general contention with regard to the use of mechanical methods for solving ethical problems will be that, from the ethical point of view, the distinctive value of these methods is that they provide us with a reliable way of excluding certain considerations from the determination of the particular social choice in question. This exclusion, as I shall try to show, is sometimes required by our ethical principles. In order to explain and defend the position that I have just stated, I shall examine four different types of situation in which mechanical methods might be employed for ethical reasons.

For our first situation I shall choose the familiar problem of twelve men in a lifeboat. It has been decided that one person must be tossed out of the boat in order to save the lives of the rest. Let us suppose that there is no overriding reason of expediency for saving any particular person (e.g., no one in the boat has more knowledge of navigation than anyone else), and, furthermore, let us suppose that no one volunteers to sacrifice himself (or, better still, everyone volunteers to do so). Given these conditions, the practical problem becomes: what is the fairest, most just and equitable way of deciding which person is to be sacrificed? Our lifeboat, we may assume, contains all sorts and conditions of men: old and young, male and female, educated and uneducated, intelligent and stupid, rich and poor, black and white, healthy and unhealthy, gifted and not gifted, happy and unhappy. The question is whether any of these characteristics, or combination thereof, is sufficient to justify the selection of one individual in preference to another. In the terms that we have been using, should the "social choice" be a function of any one of these characteristics?

A utilitarian would probably try to base the selection of the victim on one of the characteristics mentioned on the basis of some sort of prediction about what would, in the long run, tend to promote the greatest happiness of the greatest number. Besides the fact that such a prediction would be pure conjecture, the antiutilitarian moralist feels that it is not right to base the selection of the man to die on that kind of criterion. It is simply wrong to sacrifice a person just because he is a person of a certain sort (say, old or unhappy). One's sense of justice seems to say that the only right method of selection would to be to draw lots. The reason why drawing lots seems to be the most equitable method of selection is that this mechanical method, which is a device for assuring that the choice is random, automatically excludes the other considerations that we have mentioned. In a sense, this method treats everyone as equals, since the chances of being selected are equal for everyone, but what it amounts to is a reaffirmation of the principle that no one has a preferred status as far as his life is concerned simply by virtue of being old (or young), intelligent, white, etc.

The principle that lies behind the use of this kind of mechanical method is what I shall call the *principle of the exclusion of unethical considerations*. (I choose the term "unethical" to suggest that it would be unethical, against ethics, to allow such considerations to determine one's decision.) The mechanical method, e.g., of drawing lots, automatically excludes considerations that on ethical grounds we have antecedently ruled out as sufficient grounds for sacrificing a person. In this particular case, we are simply applying Kant's doctrine that individual human beings have dignity rather than price, that is, as far as their intrinsic value is concerned they cannot be compared or weighed against each other like commodities.

Let us now turn to a second situation. You have to cut the cake for ten children at a birthday party. How should you cut the cake? Into even pieces or not? Should one child receive more or less than another? If so, on what basis should it be decided that one receives a larger piece? Should the birthday child receive the largest? A child who has been naughty, the smallest? A child who is thin, a large piece? The host, a small piece? Here again, if the principle of equity obtains, it would seem that the cake ought to be divided into equal pieces. "Each child to count as one." In other words, the size of each piece is to be determined purely mathematically: the size of the cake divided by the number of children. A mechanical method is used.

Here again we observe the principle of exclusion operating. We use a mechanical method in order to exclude considerations such as merit, need, or even utilitarian considerations. The exclusion is justified on the ground that we consider it unethical to base the distribution of the cake on these other considerations. The principle of equity demands the exclusion of such considerations.

The two situations we have considered involve problems concerning the just distribution of both goods and evils of the indivisible (e.g., a life) and divisible type (e.g., the cake). There are, of course, many more complicated situations in which such problems of just distribution arise, e.g., with regard to taxation, income-distribution, military conscription. In all of these some kind of mechanical method of allotment seems called for, although, of course, sometimes for other reasons we have to weight some factors more heavily than others, e.g., in taxation.

More needs to be said about the ethical justification of what I have called "the principle of exclusion." A rule-utilitarian might possibly try to justify the adoption of this principle on the ground that it is a rule that has general utility. But, leaving aside well-known difficulties with rule-utilitarianism, the assertion that the exclusion principle has utility as a rule is a gratuitous empirical assumption; indeed, it is probably false. Another justification might be contractarian, that is, it might be assumed that the people in the lifeboat or the children at the party had implicitly agreed to abide by the mechanically determined outcome. (*Volenti non fit injuria!*) Such a "contract," like the contract in political theory, is not only fictitious, but also unnecessary ethically. For we want to hold that the methods employed are right regardless of whether or not everyone has consented to them. My own view is that the principle of exclusion is directly derived from some sort of principle of justice (=equality), which in turn, comes from the categorical imperative.

Let us now turn to our third example.[2] The situation I want to examine is provided by Braithwaite's interesting and entertaining application of the theory of games to the problem of allotting time for playing musical instruments between two next-door neighbors, Luke, who plays classical music on the piano, and Matthew, who improvises jazz on the trumpet. The kind of application of a mechanical model that Braithwaite proposes, i.e., the game theory model, is, I believe, highly questionable from the moral point of view; at least it raises more questions than it answers.

To begin with, Braithwaite misconstrues the problem of equitable allotment by interpreting it as a problem of obtaining "maximum production of satisfaction compatible with fair distribution." From the point of view of moral philosophy, Braithwaite's procedure, if consistent, can only be circular, for the mechanics of his solution plus his use of the probability-combination-indifference method (taken from Von Neumann and Morgenstern) makes the procedure itself definitive of the concept of "maximum satisfaction compatible with fair distribution." Since he provides us with no independent criterion of "maximum satisfaction compatible with fair distribution," these concepts are defined by the procedures themselves. Thus, either the theory is one that has no significance for the making of moral decisions, in the ordinary sense of "moral," or else all the moral questions are begged at the very outset.

From the point of view of the present discussion, however, a more significant mistake made by Braithwaite is his assumption that the moral problem of distribution is basically a problem of maximizing or, if you wish, of finding the optimum possibility. This, of course, is an assumption also made in welfare economics. Against this, I have tried to show that the methods and models provided, e.g., by game theory, are ethically useful not because they provide us with a means of finding optima, but rather because they can be used to advance equity by giving us a means of excluding unethical considerations from the solution of certain kinds of problems.

According to my analysis, we should begin our examination of Braithwaite's procedure by asking what considerations are excluded from the determination of the decision by the use of his method. Many possibly relevant considerations are, of course, excluded at the very outset by the way that he sets up the problem: e.g., whether or not third parties are listening, whether or not there is any significant relation between the man's playing his instrument and his profession, or his social life, or his marriage prospects, etc., and, last but not least, whether or not there are any prior commitments concerning the playing, such as promises, agreements between the two or with others.

Granting that such possible considerations are outside the problem as given, the principal considerations remaining on which the decision will have to be based are the two men's preferences for playing alone, for playing at the same time, for listening, and so on. In Braithwaite's solution the preferences are taken as hard data, so to speak, and are not to be tampered with. His procedure excludes any consideration of the quality of the preferences themselves, e.g., whether they are serious or fanciful, reflective or impulsive, central or peripheral, creative or imitative, enlightened or ignorant, worthwhile or frivolous. The question that we must now ask is: what possible ethical justification can be given for excluding the quality of the preferences from consideration in the solution of the problem? On what basis may we regard such considerations as "un-ethical"?

I find it difficult to answer these questions to my own satisfaction. The only possible answer that I can think of would be to suppose some sort of prior agreement on the part of Luke and Matthew to settle their differences by using Braithwaite's method. But if this is the only justification for using the procedure, the ethical basis of using the procedure is borrowed from elsewhere, namely, from the principle of promise-keeping, and has nothing intrinscially to do with the procedure itself.

Finally, we come to our fourth example, the use of mechanical methods in welfare economics as exemplified, in particular, by Arrow's four conditions on constitutions. In order to determine the moral significance of these procedures, I shall proceed as before by inquiring: what considerations does the procedure exclude? and what ethical justification, if any, can be given for excluding these considerations from the solution of the social choice problem?

As I have already pointed out, Arrow's postulates automatically exclude from the determination of social choice (public value) any consideration of the quality of the individual's preferences or of the ordering thereof. In this respect, the "hard data" for his procedure are like those in Braithwaite's example. But, unlike the latter, whose use of the principle of exclusion seems to me entirely gratuitous, I believe Arrow's use of the same principle can be given an ethical justification.

Let us begin by examining once more the underlying assumption of Arrow's theory of social choice. It is that the individual who "makes the social choice" acts in his capacity of public official and not in his capacity as a private individual with private values of his own. Furthermore, this social choice is to be made on the basis of public value, which is a function exclusively of the particular preferences of the individuals in the society. In effect, what Arrow is saying is that public officials, in formulating social policy, must not take into account the *quality* of individuals' choices, but only the *fact* of their choices. The (moral) quality of the choices themselves is none of the public official's business.

This proposal, it seems to me, is a very neat and precise, as well as satisfactory way of formulating the principle of political liberalism in the context of social welfare. The liberal principle that lies behind Arrow's procedures, and justifies them, is to be contrasted with the Platonic-Aristotelian doctrine that the purpose of the state is to make men good, rather than to fulfill their wants and to secure justice in their interpersonal relations. Welfare economics, according to the interpretation that I have presented, provides us with a theory of social welfare while at the same time providing us with a means of protection against the principles of political paternalism, i.e., it protects our individual liberties. And this, incidentally, is what classical utilitarianism fails to do. In principle, the utilitarian cannot balk at any benign interference with the preferences of individuals, for, as Brandt has shown, on utilitarian principles the choices and preferences of individuals must be critically reviewed before they can be used as the basis of social choice.

Before closing, I should point out that, although my

analysis and reconstruction of the ethical basis of the postulates of welfare economics saves this theory from the kind of criticism offered by Brandt, it does so only by severely limiting the sphere of application of its principles. As in the lifeboat example, the conditions and context of the choice-problem have to be of a very restricted sort where only a certain specific kind of social choice is required (i.e., one involving equity) before the use of mechanical methods, e.g., welfare economics, is ethically appropriate.

NOTES

1. *Leviathan*, Ch. 5.
2. See R. B. Braithwaite, *Theory of Games as a Tool for the Moral Philosopher*, Cambridge University Press, 1963.

9

The Normative Roots of Economic Value

ADOLPH LOWE
The New School

AT THIS CONFERENCE we economists are certainly not making life easy for our fellow philosophers. First, Dr. Arrow has argued that economic values, private and public, are basically nothing but preferences. Or to state it in Dr. Brandt's polemical formulation, interests and moral principles, nonmoral and moral values are all put into the same basket. And in the subsequent discussion Dr. Arrow's notion of a constitution, which is to offer the rule for society's choices among alternative social actions, was not unfairly parodied in the image of a sausage machine the handle of which the economist turns without regard to the meat it grinds. In a word, it appeared as if in Economics no objective meaning could be associated with the concept of value.

However, while still trying to get used to this proposition, the philosophers were told on the first page of Dr. Boulding's paper that, of the different concepts of value in Economics, "the most fundamental is that of the exchange ratio or terms of trade, which is the ratio of the quantities of two things exchanged." Now whatever this ratio may signify, it certainly is an objective measure. Even if subjective preferences should enter the process by which such ratios are formed, the result —a number—lies in a dimension of public demonstrability.

In the face of such a sharp contradiction one is naturally inclined to side with Dr. Nagel in treating the whole issue as a semantic problem, easily solved once we banish the ambiguous term "value" from the vocabulary of the economist and simply speak of tastes and preferences on the one hand and, on the other, of exchange ratios or prices. It is the purpose of the following remarks to contradict such a conclusion, and to demonstrate the legitimacy in Economics of the value concept when used in its original normative meaning. Moreover, I shall try to show that the exchange ratio properly interpreted is the very core of modern normative Economics. Finally, the actual norm implied in an equilibrium structure of such values or relative prices, though not itself a yardstick for the Good Life as conceived by philosophers, may well point to the material foundation on which, for most of past history, any life that befitted Man was necessarily built.

I

If this sounds strange to the modern positive economist, it is, of course, quite in accord with ancient and medieval doctrine. To Aristotle as to the Church Fathers the normative exchange ratio provided the very focus for speculation on matters economic. Neither was willing to abide with the varying ratios at which one and the same pair of goods might exchange at different times and places. It is the search for a "just" ratio that occupies Aristotle in the fifth Book of the *Nichomachean Ethics*. There, in the discussion of Reciprocity or Commutative Justice, he postulates the criteria by which, in the first Book of his *Politics*, he distinguishes the "natural" forms of household management and barter from the "unnatural" art of trade when it is devoted to unlimited acquisition of money. The source of such "unnatural" wealth is that kind of exchange which yields most profit, namely transactions with one partner holding a monopolistic position or engaging in usury. And the ultimate reason why such practices are "discredited" and "detested" lies in the fact that they violate the just principle of "equality."

Alas, Aristotle is rather vague when he tries to define the state of equality that arises from the transactions of "justly" bargaining partners. He calls it a "mean" between the extreme ratios that would confer all advantage upon either the buyer or the seller. But why, in one of his examples, the just price of a house should be five times the price of a bed, rather than than four or six times, we are never told. At the same time it is essential to realize that the just exchange ratio is for Aristotle more than an abstract moral principle. He stresses repeatedly that without adherence to it, exchange relations cannot in practice endure. Therefore we must conclude that he expects real transactions somehow to gravitate toward a just order of prices. Schumpeter has turned Aristotle's argument around by making him choose "normal competitive prices as standards of commutative justice," an interpretation that reflects his own positivistic bias.[1] But it remains true, and is important for the subsequent development of economic analysis, that Aristotle sees the just and the real subtly related.

All this is stated in much more precise terms by Aristotle's medieval followers. They explicitly introduced a value concept to define that which the just price measures, e.g., in St. Thomas's notion of a *quantitas valoris*. Above all, they give an answer to the question that Aristotle left open: what is the criterion by which the justice of a specific price is to be judged? It is that price which compensates for the necessary inputs— *expensae et labores*. And the just wage, which thus enters as a major determinant of the just price, is itself related to a fair standard of living for the producer. Again Schumpeter misses the delicate balance between positive and normative statements, when he asserts that the *quantitas valoris* "is simply normal competitive price." [2] In fact, it is the yardstick by which all prices, among them especially the planned prices imposed by the guilds, are to be judged. Nevertheless, it remains true that, like Aristotle, the Church Fathers supposed that economic reality had some affinity with the ethical norm, an affinity more easily observable in the local transactions of the smaller cities than in the distant trade of Genoa or Venice.

II

We cannot pursue here the fascinating story of how, from the fifteenth century on, theoretical emphasis slowly shifted from the normative to the positive aspects of the price order, bringing with it a gradual vindication of the price fluctuations that the rise of commercial capitalism placed into prominence. But the bipolar tradition was still alive in the classical systems of the eighteenth and early nineteenth centuries, with their linkage between the welfare goal of a "plentiful revenue or subsistence for the people" (A. Smith) and the order of "natural" prices as opposed to fluctuating market prices. There is really little difference between the determinants of the just price relations as seen by a Duns Scotus and the determinants of the natural price in Smith or Ricardo or of the "law of value" in Marx. They all represent, to quote Dr. Boulding's paper, technical transformation ratios, and can be regarded as stable unless the technology of production itself changes.

What is different and does mark a real break with the Aristotelian-Thomistic tradition is the role that Classical Economics assigns to profits in establishing natural prices and in thus promoting welfare. Unlimited acquisition, originally the ultimate source of injustice, now acquires the "dialectical" function of a private vice to be converted through the competitive mechanism into public benefit. Moreover, such "extremum" behavior oriented on maximization of receipts and minimization of expenditures is now generalized, from an exception occurring at the fringes of precapitalist markets, into a common rule. It becomes the law of economic motion from which the microprocesses and, through techniques of aggregation, even the macroprocesses of so-called free market systems can be derived.[3]

Only during the Post-Classical era, initiated by Nassau Senior and J. S. Mill, do the positive and the normative strands of inquiry begin to separate, and from then on economic theory progressively adjusts its procedures to the general scientific method prevailing. To give a famous example, for Marshall the "normal, or natural, value of a commodity is that which . . . economic forces would bring about if the general conditions of life were stationary for a run of time long enough to enable them all to work out their full effect"[4]—a good analogy to the crucial experiments undertaken in a physics laboratory. Another influence in eroding the normative tradition was the so-called marginal revolution of the 1870's, which tried to derive value in exchange from "value in use" or individual preferences. This amounted to the substitution of a highly volatile psychological relationship—transformation ratios of subjective evaluations—for a stable technical relationship—transformation ratios in production. Value in use, that is, the ultimate benefit from economic activity reaped in terms of consumption, had been a familiar concept throughout the ages, offering the rationale for the toil and trouble Man must take upon himself to acquire the means for his ends. But never before had, as it were, economic "voltage"—the force of satisfaction—been taken as the determinant of economic "ohm," that is, of the resistance that must be overcome to acquire the means yielding such satisfaction.

Recent developments in economic analysis have altered the perspective in which we now see both the marginal revolution and the ultrapositivistic trend. As Dr. Boulding has restated it, the center of gravity of economic motion has been found to lie at the point where the transformation ratios of preferences coincide with the technical transformation ratios of production. So the latter can always serve as measures, even if not as sole determinants, of value in exchange. But what is more important in our context, something of the old balance between the positive and the normative aspects was restored when the price ratios of Marshall's long-period equilibrium were shown to coincide with a state of the system at large that could be accepted—with certain reservations to which Dr. Samuelson pointed in the discussion—as a welfare optimum.

This so-called Pareto Optimum [5] is an optimum not only of consumption but also of production. It defines a state compared with which there is no second state in which one consumer can obtain higher satisfaction without at the same time lowering the satisfaction of at least one other consumer. But it also defines what is nowadays called "productive efficiency," namely, a state in which productive activity has been so organized that, within

the given limitations of resources and technology, there is no
other way of producing more of some desired commodity without reducing the output of some other desired commodity.[6] In
a word, the optimum described is a state of *maximum provision
with taste-adequate commodities,* given the prevailing order
of distribution.

III

While acknowledging the much greater analytical sophisti-
cation of modern Economics, we must give due recognition to
this shift in attention toward the early gropings of an Aristotle
or a St. Thomas. The impression of such a shift is strengthened
when we try to elucidate the precise meaning of the norm that
a Pareto Optimum embodies.

By granting to each consumer the same right of satisfaction
it stipulates a yardstick of "equality," not unlike the corresponding ancient and medieval principle, and even freed from earlier
limitations of status. Of course, so long as the distribution of
wealth and income is taken as a datum, egalitarianism is a long
way off. Still, as Mrs. Robinson has demonstrated in her discussion of a state of "economic bliss," reality can be approximated
to the idea if the mechanism of capital formation is "conceived
to work to its logical conclusion." It then gravitates to a point
where, with a constant labor force and constant technology,
capital demand is fully saturated and profit and interest converge to zero, the whole net product being absorbed by wages.[7]
Whatever may be true of historical capitalism, a radical egalitarian trend can easily be read into the constructs of modern
Economics.

But to penetrate to the normative core of a Pareto Optimum we shall have to examine more closely the meaning of
"productive efficiency." How can we justify the identification of
a welfare optimum with a *maximum* output of taste-adequate
goods? Why should such maximization be superior to Aristotle's
vision of "happy man. . . . able to act according to virtue
with moderate means" or to the medieval ideal of a traditional

standard of living or to some other "homeostatic" goal? [8] In the discussion the attempt was made to include these and, in fact, all conceivable production goals in one welfare concept, by substituting "optimum" output for "maximum" output. But such a limitless extension of the meaning of productive efficiency would deprive it of all operational significance. Moreover, it would blind us to the important role that the very maximization of output has played in past theory and practice alike.

We have only to realize that there is indeed one state of resource supply and technology in which the attainment of any life goal is conditional on maximization of production. This is a state of destitution in which the available stock of resources and the output produced from it do not rise above the threshold that assures physical survival. If we relax this extreme condition to include all societies that offer the overwhelming majority of their members a bare physiocultural minimum of existence, we describe a situation that has prevailed throughout past history and pertains to most of our contemporaries. (Even admitting the large inequalities of wealth and income that have characterized all these societies, at least up to the Industrial Revolution the most radical egalitarian reforms could not have raised per capita income noticeably above the subsistence level.)

Under these conditions the exchange ratios that define a Pareto Optimum have a very special significance for human welfare. It is not that the production and consumption relations of this economic state of affairs themselves embody any intrinsic moral, aesthetic, or "rational" principle, as these terms are used by philosophers. Economic activity, being concerned with providing means for extrinsic ends, can aspire only to intermediate goals bare of all inherent meaning. It is rather that, under the conditions described, the approximation of production and consumption to a Pareto Optimum is an *indispensable prerequisite* for the pursuit and achievement of any value to the extent to which it requires material means for its realization. One may then even accord that particular economic state a "derived" value of its own, as the only one that makes the Good Life, however understood, possible. And from there it is only a short step to entertaining the illusion that characterizes so much of neoclassical reasoning, namely, that such value is not reflected by, but is inherent in, the mechanism of perfect competition, and that it is even transhistorical.

IV

The last twenty-five years of debate on Welfare Economics and, especially, the discussion centering on Dr. Arrow's classic study of *Social Choice and Individual Values,* have thoroughly disabused us of this illusion. But in order to grasp the full implications of these abstract findings we must relate them to the concrete experience of industrial capitalism. It is one of the major lessons of the economic history of the West subsequent to the Industrial Revolution that the rigid limitations on resource supply and technology, which have controlled the past, are not laws of nature. One can agree with Dr. Boulding that we are nowhere near the Big Rock Candy Mountain, namely, an affluence utopia conceived in the image of the Garden of Eden. But our Western world is no longer one where mass destitution prevails and where maximization of output is the condition for minimum comfort, much less survival. Rather, to take this country as an example, we have succeeded in providing for two-thirds of the population a standard of living that earlier ages would have called truly prosperous. And yet even in good years we seem to produce no more than 80 percent of potential output.

In other words, technological progress has greatly reduced the traditional pressures that left room for one state of economic welfare only. It is granting us for the first time "freedom of choice," namely, a choice within ever widening limits between work and leisure, between consuming and investing today or tomorrow, between extremum behavior and homeostatic or simply routinized conduct. It is this variety of feasible alternatives that finds expression in the "empty box" character of the modern Social Welfare Function. To give it content we must explicitly introduce specific decisions on ends, for which no economic mechanism offers any criteria. The same new freedom complicates Dr. Arrow's search for "reasonable conditions . . . which every constitution [i.e., set of rules for making society's choices among alternative social actions] should obey." Again the "reasonableness" of any conditions cannot be derived from intraeconomic considerations. It is the political or social philosopher who alone can vindicate the ends. In a world of no choice his verdict could seemingly be dispensed with, though even then it was his set of intrinsic values that alone gave normative meaning to the "equilibrium exchange values" of the economist. In a society of increasing wealth, decisions on welfare become his explicit business.

Today all this is readily admitted by the writers on Welfare Economics. But the multiplicity of possible welfare goals and the profound historical changes from which this multiplicity springs have no less important consequences for the positive part of Economics that have not yet been fully realized. Neoclassical and even Keynesian theory have added very little "to the ideas of the preceding (viz. classical) period concerning what it is that happens in the economic process and how, in a general way, this process works out." [9] More specifically, it is still taken for granted that the decentralized decisions of competing marketers, certainly when supported by fiscal and monetary policy, are fully determinable *ex ante* and will converge toward a macroequilibrium of full resource utilization or, in a dynamic context, of balanced growth. Though in wealthy nations the Pareto Optimum represents only one among many possible welfare goals, it still appears as if the intraeconomic mechanism through which this optimum materializes was driven by inexorable forces. Public intervention or monopolistic practices may block their path, but their inherent tendencies, as for example symbolized in the extremum principle of economic behavior, are treated as inflexible.

These rigid premises of conventional theory, taken over also by most econometric models, contrast sharply with the information that empirical studies give us about the behavior of buyers and sellers in the markets of contemporary capitalism. They tell us about a wide spectrum of incentives and about the great volatility of expectations on the part of consumers and investors, pointing in the microsphere to the same new range of decisional freedom that, in the macrosphere, is responsible for the variety of welfare goals. As symptoms of our gradual emancipation from the compulsions of poverty and primitive social organization these changes in the behavioral substructure command our unreserved approval. But at the same time they progressively deprive the actual economic process of that pseudomechanical determinacy that the former pressures had assured, and that is so perfectly depicted in the theorems of traditional economic reasoning.

The difficulties that this transformation of our object of inquiry create for the practical application of conventional theory are well known, though rarely traced to their true source. If all the formal refinements of our methods have made our predictions hardly more accurate than were the hunches derived in the past from crude rules of thumb, it is the new facts that prove refractory to this kind of approach. Here is not the place to enter into a discussion of how Economics can be reconstructed as an explanatory and predictive science and as a guide to practical policy. Still the direction in which the solution must be sought is obvious. Once the autonomous motions of the market forces cannot assure any longer the approach to any welfare optimum, Paretonian or other, they will have to be placed under public guidance. But to be effective such public guidance must orient itself on *consciously chosen* welfare goals. These are then the stipulated ends for which economic analysis has to discover the instrumental means, in terms of suitable decentralized behavior patterns as well as of adequate measures of public control.[10]

In this approach strict division between a positive and a normative part of Economics can no longer be justified. What may have been acceptable during the brief era of near laissez-faire capitalism (but as we saw, even then with important reservations only) becomes an obstacle for the understanding of how the mixed systems of the present operate. If it is true, as has been argued here, that there has always been more continuity between modern Economics and its ancient and medieval rudiments than our textbooks give credit for, recent developments demand the conscious integration of the analytical and the normative aspects, or rather the application of analysis in the service of the realization of normative principles. For the solution of this task Economics could well use a modern Aristotle.

NOTES

1. See J. A. Schumpeter, *History of Economic Analysis*, New York, 1954, p. 61.

2. *Ibid.*, p. 93.

3. For details, see my *On Economic Knowledge*, New York, 1965, Chs. 2 and 6.

4. See A. Marshall, *Principles of Economics*, London, 1927, p. 347.

5. For a lucid exposition of the relationship between "Competitive Equilibrium and Pareto Optimality," see T. C. Koopmans, *Three Essays on the State of Economic Science*, New York, 1957, pp. 41–66.

6. For details, see *ibid.*, pp. 83–96.

7. See Joan Robinson, *The Accumulation of Capital*, London, 1956, pp. 81–83. The idea goes back to Keynes, and even to J. S. Mill.

8. See Kenneth E. Boulding, *A Reconstruction of Economics*, New York, 1950, Ch. 2.

9. See Schumpeter, *op. cit.*, p. 982.

10. My *On Economic Knowledge*, cited above, is devoted to a detailed exposition of the substance and method of such a Political Economics.

10

Normative and Analytical Welfare Economics: Arrow's Pareto Principle

ERNEST VAN DEN HAAG
New York University

I. THREE INTERPRETATIONS OF THE "PARETO PRINCIPLE"

AS ENUNCIATED by Arrow, the "Pareto Principle" either is true but trivial, or as far from being true as it is from being trivial. The principle is trivial when taken to mean: if everybody in a society prefers A to B then the aggregate preference is for A over B.[1] The principle is far from trivial however when taken to mean: if everybody in a society prefers A to B, then in that society A should be preferred to B. In this version the Pareto principle raises problems that lie on the border between philosophy and economics. They may be thrown into relief upon distinguishing two definitional and one normative interpretation of this version.[2]

1) The Pareto principle may be regarded as part of a definition of "social preference": if all individuals in a society prefer A to B then the society does; i.e., the society as such has no preferences beyond or above those of its members.[3]

2) The Pareto principle may be regarded as part of a definition of the scope of "welfare economics": as a science, welfare economics ascertains and analyzes the order of preferences in a society, to determine priorities, rankings, or preferred preferences, and thus preferred actions, in a given environment and with given knowledge of it. The preferences themselves are treated as data for this purpose and not scrutinized, evaluated, or judged morally. The weight to be given

to each and all the preferences of each person or group—equal or unequal—is another datum or postulate. Moral judgments are beyond the scope of welfare economics that is no more normative than mathematics or physics. The prescriptive (applied) uses of welfare economics are instrumental, just as engineering is, and imply no normative judgment about the preferences to be maximized or minimized; they prescribe only how this is to be done "economically," i.e., with the least impairment of anything valued. Concern with the causes and effects of preferences, and with their change and order, also is descriptive or analytical, and requires no moral judgments within the scope of welfare economics, which merely analyzes the economic implications of such moral judgments.

3) The Pareto principle may be regarded as a normative rule: "Social preference" (as described above [1]) should be followed because it is *eo ipso* a moral judgment unanimously made by society. Moral discourse about the desirable or preferable is really no more than (disguised) discourse about desires or preferences. Unanimity is a sufficient moral justification since no other justification for moral judgments is ultimately available or needed. This normative rule may also be attributed to "democracy" by interpreting the definition of "social preference" (1) normatively—*vox populi, vox dei*—or, by resorting to the "greatest happiness" of all; or, by insisting that the procedure of democracy—majority decision—is justified by the moral correctness inherent in, or achieved by, majority decision, and therefore, of course, by unanimous decision.

Which of these interpretations of the Pareto principle do welfare economists actually hold? They certainly agree on (1)—the definition of social preference—and on (2)—the definition of the scope of welfare economics—although not always aware that neither entails the other. The acceptance of (2) makes (3)—the normative interpretation—unnecessary and irrelevant to welfare economics, and equally so a normative interpretation of (1). Nonetheless, most welfare economists accept this interpretation gratuitously, and seem willing to urge the government to act according to the Pareto principle (3). Perhaps welfare economists do not distinguish sufficiently between the limited professional task of telling the client—society—how to do what he prefers, and the quite different matter of telling him to follow his preferences, i.e., of approving of them. Or, perhaps welfare economists identify the preferred with the preferable because of undisclosed and questionable philosophical convictions.

II. SOME CAUSES OF NORMATIVE BIAS IN WELFARE ECONOMICS

The implicit emphases of economics, and even more of welfare economics, may be the intellectual cause of the confusion. Economics generally stresses the importance of alloplastic action, and of wish fulfillment thereby. Logically, this need not be a moral judgment against asceticism and endoplastic action, and certainly not in favor of the wishes to be fulfilled. The apparatus of economics could be used almost as well in an ascetic or Zen Buddhist society. But historically, economics has stressed production for the sake of accumulation and ultimately of consumer satisfaction by means of external goods and services, leaving evaluation thereof to consumers (the market). One assumes the desirability of consumer satisfaction for reasons listed under (2) above—but easily treats what started as a definition of scope as though it were a norm not requiring justification. The customary historical emphasis causes us to grow insensitive to the normative bias inherent not so much in economics as in its customary use.

In welfare economics the normative bias is even harder to separate from the analysis. Welfare economics necessarily works within an exclusive range of normative assumptions that produces the problems to be solved. Thus, unless one assumes a plurality of individual orderings of preferences, each counting for something, no "social ordering"—which is the problem of welfare economics—need be constructed. In this sense, Arrow's "non-dictatorship" rule is an analytically necessary normative assumption. The analytic indispensability of such normative assumptions may appear deceptively to lend them unquestionable normative force, to make their ethical justification redundant. And, the logical leap from "each ordering must count for something" to "each ordering must count equally," psychologically may become a small step; so may the *salto mortale* that identifies the actual (or assumed) rank of each preference qua preference with an ethical justification thereof, or, that assumes that a preference not held by anybody, and therefore correctly ignored by the welfare economist, cannot be preferable from a normative viewpoint, or, that one held by everybody *ipso facto* is.

Whatever the cause of the intellectual confusion, the possible effect of normative advice not clearly separate from logical analysis or empirical findings is momentous and maleficent social confusion. Let me turn from the possible causes of the acceptance of the normative interpretation (3) by welfare economists to the arguments available to defend it.[4]

III. ARGUMENTS JUSTIFYING THE NORMATIVE INTERPRETATION (3) OF ARROW'S PARETO PRINCIPLE

A

One may argue that it would be idle to think of a unanimous preference as less than morally preferable to all others since, by definition, nobody in the society would so think. Thus, the unanimously preferred could not be distinguished from the preferable, and therefore must be regarded as identical to it.

Such an argument confuses fact (or prediction)—actual preference and ignorance of alternatives—with justification, and perception with its object. Unanimity, while relevant to the preference as fact, is irrelevant to its justification. Unawareness of preferable alternatives may explain, but does not justify (make preferable) an actual preference. Lack of objection does not indicate lack of objectionability. Indiscernibility may possibly, but lack of actual discernment certainly does not establish identity.

The argument also illuminates a methodological point: moral scrutiny by definition comes from the outside. The preferences of a unanimous unit—an isolated person, a group, a society, a universe—are scrutinized by the—more or less ideal —outside observer; else they could only be expressed or carried out. If they wish to treat any economic rule, such as the Pareto principle, as a normative one, economists must accept this methodological rule of ethics; if they do, the argument that there is not, and there cannot be an objection to the preference of a unanimous society is irrelevant; if they don't, ethics is irrelevant to economic rules, and Arrow's Pareto principle cannot be interpreted as normative.

Empirically, the argument might compel us to accept as morally right preferences we feel intuitively to be morally wrong. Thus, the members of the society might unanimously and freely decide to have a social order including slavery, mutual torture, or purposeless torture of consenting victims.[5] But most moralists would feel it to be immoral to harm people even when they consent to the harm—unless there is a justification other than preference.

More important, we must question how inclusive the unanimity of the Pareto principle is to be. Are we to include future generations? children? the insane? alien societies? animals? If so, the Pareto principle is empirically irrelevant, for it is impossible to carry out; possible unanimity at most refers to a group of mentally competent living humans. But if we make the Pareto principle relevant by such a definition of "unanimity," once more it would authorize actions that everybody, including welfare economists, would intuitively regard as morally wrong, even when unanimously preferred. Thus, the living generation may intentionally by wanton destruction deprive future generations of the ability to live; alien societies may be destroyed or enslaved; the insane, infants, and animals may be tortured for the sake of a psychic gratification their suffering may yield. Unless these preferences can be justified, the Pareto rule cannot be.[6]

B

One may argue that the moral judgment of individuals is validated by that of others; unanimity thence is the best available validation, and, therefore, sufficient: unanimity makes right;[7] and, one may add, this principle is basic to democracy, or, even, needed to justify it.

Social validation certainly affects belief, but not its object, be it empirical or analytical "truth." In moral matters, belief would have to be shown to be, or become, necessarily correct when it is socially validated. But even though it may be ruled out in any particular case by the unanimity assumption, the possibility that mutually exclusive normative beliefs may be held in a society must be conceded; and this rules out any general equivalence of "moral belief" and "morally correct belief." Correctness will have to be demonstrated independently of belief, however widely the belief is shared (even if it is shared by all), once it is conceded that belief is not by itself sufficient to demonstrate correctness, that there can be wrong belief; and that much is shown by showing that contradictory moral beliefs can be held.

One may argue, however, that normative rules are commendations designed to influence conduct without asserting facts or inferring conclusions; unlike propositions, and like imperatives or emotional expressions or definitions, they would be neither true nor false. Therefore, conflict among normative rules would not show any to be wrong. If this argument be accepted, it would not entail that beliefs about normative rules, and about what may be inferred from them, might not be mutually exclusive, and at least some therefore incorrect. The unanimous preference of the Pareto principle may rest on such a belief. Even if one assumes prefect knowledge and excludes inconsistencies in preferences in a specific society (although that exclusion is not assumed in the welfare rules proposed subsequently by Arrow), inconsistency of beliefs about norms is not *generally* excludable; therefore we cannot exclude the possible falseness of such beliefs, which therefore cannot be identified *ipso facto* with their object, the correct norm, or the correct inference from it.

Nor, if the nondemonstration or even the nondemonstrability of the correctness of normative rules be conceded, does it follow that all beliefs about them—all preferences—are equally right. It follows only that none can be shown to be right, wherefore none can be shown to be more, less, or equally correct compared to any other (even if we know, as shown above, that some cannot be right if others are). Wherefore unanimous preference would be no better justification than unanimous rejection. Unanimity may be accepted by a society as normative of course. But to point out as much is either to state a prediction, or a tautology, and not a justification of the acceptance. Yet the Pareto rule must be justified if it is to be interpreted normatively; at the least it must be shown that no preference other than the one unanimously accepted could have been preferable. The arguments so far considered do not justify; and the argument from undemonstrability actually precludes the required exclusion of an alternative preferable to the preferred one.

Generally the argument from unanimity of belief confuses social with ethical justification.[8] The social fact that individual moral belief is socially validated by the moral belief of others is irrelevant to the ethical justification of the belief. However, social validation is relevant to awareness of the correctness of moral beliefs; to be unaware of the wrongness of an act is to commit it without *mens rea;* the wrongness of the actor (guilt) is affected, though not the wrongness of the act.

The foregoing argument may be restated by asserting that moral preferences do not differ from taste preferences. Tastes cannot be right or wrong; they only can be accepted or rejected. A unanimous preference by definition is accepted by all and therefore sanctioned as right as much as any taste or moral judgment can be. This argument may even concede that moral judgments differ from tastes in some respects; moral judgments affect the rights of others; and they must be as applicable to others in identical circumstances as they are to the proponent. These differences, however significant, would not affect the argument that moral preferences do not relevantly differ from taste preferences here, for unanimity means that all find the moral judgment as applicable to themselves as to others; and that all feel that their rights are unimpaired by the actions contemplated by the normative preference. Hence these differences between preferences as tastes, and as moral judgments, would not rule out the relevant equivalence on which this defense of the normative force of the Pareto principle is based.

However, if we grant that moral preferences are like taste preferences, it certainly does not follow that a moral preference shared by all is, thereby, justified. It only follows that it is shared by all—which may have social effects but is irrelevant to normative justification, which has become impossible. One cannot deny the possibility of ethical justification, and then let it in by the backdoor.[9]

Further, if moral preferences are taste preferences, it does not follow that taste preferences are moral preferences. The moral judgment is distinguished from a taste preference by usually being contrary to the desires of the one who makes it. One feels morally obligated to do what one would rather not do if one's taste were consulted. What is regarded as morally desirable is often not what is desired. Morality is concerned not with the desiredness of desires, but with their desirability, with our obligations. This is not the place to further analyze the nature of moral judgments and the kind of scrutiny to which they can be subjected. It is enough to demonstrate that they are not automatically correct when unanimously preferred, that they are not expressions of desire but of a feeling of obligation that requires a justification other than being shared unanimously, and is capable of being mistaken.

C

Does the justification of democracy rest on the moral correctness of the results of its decision procedures? I don't think so. The normative interpretation of the Pareto principle is not relevant to democratic theory; democracy does not imply or require that unanimous decisions lead to morally correct results. If one were to justify democracy by the morality of its results, it would be enough if democracy makes ethically correct results more, or at least not less, likely than other political systems—that the ethical beliefs of the majority are no less often correct than those of the decision-makers in others forms of government. But note that this justification assumes some standard of moral correctness other than the belief to be judged, or the number of voters sharing it. If we deny the possibility of, or need for, such a standard, as the argument at issue basically does, then this justification of democracy amounts to no more than saying that in a democracy the voters believe in the ethical correctness of their decisions, which outside observers therefore ought to believe to be ethically correct. This *non sequitur* once more confuses the fact of widely shared belief with its object—the morality of what is believed to be moral. It seems more reasonable to justify democracy by the assertion that majorities (and unanimous decisions, too) can be morally wrong. Wherefore the possibility of change should remain open, while it still may be a social advantage that the decisions are believed to be correct when taken: it makes for easier acceptance.

Democracy also can be justified by arguments relying not on the likelihood of the ethical correctness of results, but of procedures. Apart from economy and peacefulness, government by consent may be preferable to any other even when leading to ethically worse results: voters have the satisfaction of committing their own sins, i.e., of being morally responsible. Further, if it be conceded that democratic procedure may not lead to the right decisions one may still argue that for various reasons no way of assuring the "right" decisions with greater certainty than doing so by majority vote is available. Error, however, is as possible as it is when the preferences of a king are followed—in both cases the decision-makers may believe themselves to make the correct decision, but their belief need not be correct. In a democracy, however, open dissent is permitted, as is persuasion, which need not be the case in other systems of government.

CONCLUSION

It must be concluded that the techniques and results of welfare economics are irrelevant to any evaluation of the desirability of choices made within or by a society.[10] Any appearance to the contrary springs from normative judgments made by the welfare economist without justification. This is so, even though these techniques can throw light on the implications, the consistency, and the effects of normative judgments.

NOTES

1. There are important analytical problems when there are several preferences, and the initial tautology may serve to lead to them. Arrow has ably dealt with these problems; my argument is irrelevant to his analytical results, but concerned with his normative interpretation of these results.

2. I am confining myself here to Arrow's version of the Pareto principle. The principle is more usually regarded as a principle of optimality, or dominance, asserting that one should prefer the alternative that satisfies one's original desires, and yields a welcome and costless increment, over the one that fails to do either. This, of course, follows from one's wish to satisfy more rather than fewer of one's desires at the same cost. There are problems with this version of the principle too, hidden by the word "cost." But they are different from those raised by Arrow's version, and I see no need to discuss them here. Further, it seems likely that Pareto thought in

terms of the definitional interpretation rather than of Arrow's normative one.

3. For the sake of expediency, I shall neglect sociophilosophical objections to the view embodied in this definition. They are well known to philosophers, and rejected by most economists. I doubt that I have objections more persuasive than those rejected. Further, this definition need not actually commit the welfare economist to any philosophical view of society; the definition may be selected only because suitable for the logical problems he wishes to call attention to. For, technically, it would be possible to redefine "social preference" so as to avoid objections to an aggregative view (from, say, an organismic, traditionalistic, natural law, or religious viewpoint) by inserting God's (or any other) preference in place of some of the individual preferences aggregated. This might impair Arrow's "non-dictatorship rule," but not his Pareto principle that concerns us here. (Brandt's objections based on the imperfection of human foresight and the changeability of human desires are ruled out of the discussion—though not out of reality—by the assumption of perfect foresight and constancy that for Arrow's purposes is legitimate. It seems technically feasible anyway to replace these assumptions with realistic ones, without altering the structure of the argument.)

However, my own avoidance of general objections here and elsewhere should not be mistaken for an unreserved assent to any or all premises of welfare economics. I am taking the widely accepted framework of welfare economics for granted so as to be able to scrutinize the interpretation of a principle that occurs within it.

4. Without attempting to be exhaustive or to avoid all overlapping, I have tried to select the most typical defenses of the normative interpretation.

5. Note that ancient Rome in its *circenses* enjoyed the torture, injury, and death of animals and men for the sake of psychic gratification alone; and that, although most gladiators were slaves, some free men volunteered.

6. The difficulty is not overcome by assuming a perfect (or perfectly rational or sane, in a sense that includes ethics) society. This amounts to no more than a *petitio principii:* sanity (or rationality) is what makes ethical disagreement possible, not impossible.

7. The argument appears to repeat the previous argument (A)

or the proposition (3) it is to defend; but it requires a different refutation.

8. It should be clear now that we are dealing largely, though not exclusively, with varieties of G. E. Moore's naturalistic fallacy.

9. Again, a confusion between desires felt and desirability justified may be involved.

10. If a unanimous choice has no normative bearing, no others will.

11

Axiomatic Choice Theory and Values

V. C. WALSH
University of Montreal

I AM SURE we all share with Professor Samuelson the very highest regard for the work of Kenneth Arrow, in *Social Choice and Individual Values,* and the belief that this path-breaking analysis is significant beyond any narrow technical boundaries. I doubt if there are many who read this book in its first edition and have followed the literature that has developed from it who would think its importance even open to question.

I was therefore startled as I listened to Professor Brandt's comments on Professor Arrow's paper. Their pervasive tone is perhaps most strongly to be felt where Brandt is taking Arrow to task for saying that the "rational" choice is the "preferred" one, a view that leads, he feels, to consequences false "for any ordinary sense of the word 'rational.'" I shall not spend time here commenting on Brandt's handling of the appeal to ordinary usage. This is partly because at many points in his paper I felt it was unclear whether a particular passage concerned certain members of the family of uses of certain words in English, or whether he was concerned rather with certain constructioned concepts that had been built by philosophers by the expedient of tailoring or extending the families of uses of such English words. Secondly, I feel that at least the philosophical members of the group, having seen the analysis of ordinary usage conducted now for many, many years with everything, from the exquisite classical bullfighting of the late John Austin to the lamentable results of its sloppy adoption, must by now be well past the satiation point.

To some extent, however, I am forced to become involved in comparison between certain elements in a constructed language and certain words in English. This is simply because one of the things Arrow offered in his paper was a series of remarks about an axiomatic system—the system known to the world through *Social Choice and Individual Values.* It is a nice question in what language or languages these remarks are written. Many of them wouldn't stand a snowball's chance in hell of getting by John Austin's ghost. In *that* (perhaps rather puritan) sense they are not in "English." On the other hand, neither are they themselves formally derived from his axiom set. They seem to me to be best described as in an informal metalanguage designed for the discussion of his formal system, and conducted by a series of rapid racing changes between English, bits of his formal structure with, as it were, their jackets off, and some constructed concepts of philosophy. To take such a paper and proceed to submit it to a run-of-the-mill ordinary language criticism would surely be to exhibit a striking logical innocence.

In fairness, it has to be admitted that Arrow must bear a little blame for misleading innocent hearers. He inflicts none of the notation of his formal system on his hearers. Now, everybody is probably in sympathy with the avoidance of unnecessary symbolism, but after all philosophers have been messing around some of the problems raised by mathematical logic (and have thus had to live with its notation) ever since *Principia Mathematica* came out, which was long before economic-choice theorists made that scene. But, what is worse, even in the informal account of his axiomatic system that Arrow gives in his paper he lays no heavy stress on its structure, and the logical necessities that follow from that structure.

I therefore feel it necessary to follow Samuelson in going back to the formal structure in *Social Choice and Individual Values* in order to say anything pertinent to our discussion.

If you looked again at that wonderful book when the second edition appeared, you may have found something a little startling if you are used to the way decision theorists write today. Certainly there is a formal structure, properly axiomatized with proofs of theorems properly shown. But there is also much informal writing, and this is not clearly separated—not set in a different type, for instance—and the status of different bits of it is not always clear. Some of it is concerned with showing possible interpretations of the formal system, some simply with giving examples that help to make the force of a bit of notation clear to the reader, some is definitely philosophical speculation.[1]

I think that if anyone who has doubts about any of Arrow's system will set up a still, and distill out the purely formal structure, he will admit its complete purity. But I admit that philosophers—and logicians—may have qualms about some of the informal passages.

This assertion cannot be fully justified here, but I shall now try to clear up some of the puzzles that apparently bothered Brandt and others at the meeting. Brandt objects that Arrow's conception of value seems to omit "the distinction between moral and nonmoral values." His way of making this distinction is to say that "any feature of a world which is my ground for choice because I want or like it, we may call a nonmoral value." One recalls this constructed concept from Kant, though even he admitted that a perfectly good will would choose the good from love of it and not under the constraint of duty, in which case the distinction cannot in principle be universal even in his system.[2] To take some of Brandt's own examples, the companionship of friends, the capacity to enjoy music and respond to sex, could surely be correctly spoken of in English as both intensely enjoyable and morally valuable.

Surely there is much justification for Arrow's remark, after distinguishing explicitly between "tastes" and "values," that the "distinction between the two is by no means clear cut. An individual with aesthetic feeling certainly derives pleasure from his neighbor's having a well tended lawn." [3]

The whole passage that follows offers what is clearly an interpretation of the ordering relations in his formal system, if the latter is to be used for welfare analysis. He could hardly have been more explicit: "It is the ordering according to values which takes into account all the desires of the individual, including the highly important socializing desires, and which is primarily relevant for the achievement of the social maximum. The market mechanism, however, takes into account only the ordering according to 'tastes.'" [4]

We are thus clearly told that for some x and some y such that xRy in Arrow's system, this x and y may be thus ordered on account of "tastes"; on the other hand, it may be thus ordered on account of "values"—if the two be distinct. Indeed the latter are most important. Do not forget however that there is nothing in the formal system *as such* that requires us to interpret it in this way.

Brandt suggests that the distinctions on which he insists may not matter "from the economist's point of view." Now if the economist's purposes were those of pure choice theory, the issue over "tastes" and "values" could be ignored. But if the purposes are those of analyzing the possibility of a social welfare function, surely "values" are highly relevant, and Arrow rightly insists on this.

Let us next consider the concept of "rationality." From the formal point of view moves are "rational," within an axiom system, if and only if they obey the axioms. To claim that Arrow's concept of "rationality" is inadequate, if one is speaking of his formal system, thus amounts to an objection to the adequacy of his axiom set. Yet nothing was said about this at the meeting by his critics. Arrow himself, as long ago as the first edition of *Social Choice and Individual Values*, has some interesting remarks to make about the model of rationality in the system there, built as it is out of pair-wise comparisons. He even admits, in drawing attention to this structure "it is at least a possibility to which attention should be drawn, that the paradox to be discussed below might be resolved by such a broader concept of rationality." [5]

Now in ordinary English the word "rational" is used in many ways that have little or nothing to do with the properties of axiomatic systems of Choice Theory. For instance, "irrational" is sometimes used of someone who is confused, and is making mistaken judgments as a result: "Arrow says that the 'rational' choice for a person is the preferred one, in terms of his system of values in Arrow's sense, for the situation he is in. This view seems to imply that if a man gives away all his goods, because a chain of confused reasoning has led him to think this is an absolute moral obligation, his action is a rational one. This consequence of Arrow's suggestion seems to me obviously false, for any ordinary sense of the word 'rational.'"

How true, but how irrelevant. Unless, of course, someone confuses satisfying the axioms of decision theory with being fully "rational" in all the senses this word can have in English.

Now consider a situation that got some attention in the discussion. I pick an extreme case. Imagine a society containing two groups: masters and slaves. The masters group has a simple ordering, with sadistic activities as the maximal set. The slaves are extreme masochists and rank masochistic submissions as their maximal set. The ranking of other activities is unanimously agreed to. Manifestly, on Arrow's system, a social welfare function is no problem. Is this a damaging criticism of the system in *Social Choice and Individual Values*?

Only, I submit, if one misunderstands what the axiomatic system was designed to do (and does, very well). It was designed to discover, formally, the possibilities of passing from individual to social orderings. It cannot *simply by virtue of its character* insure that either the individual values or the social orderings will be noble or good. Trained moral philosophers *at least* should not expect it to—they ought to remember from the problems of Kant the pointlessness of trying to extract concrete moral judgments from an analysis of the form of rationality.

Unfortunately, however, in certain passages of informal speculation and discussion Arrow makes remarks that could encourage this mistake in the unwary. For instance where he says "the hedonist psychology finds its expression here in the assumption that individuals' behavior is expressed by individual ordering relations R." [6]

And again in his paper he says "For the single isolated in-

dividual there can be no other standard than his own values."
Whatever the philosophical merits of this view, it is not en-
tailed by and does not entail his formal model. For philosophers I may put my point vividly by saying that you could be
an old-fashioned Oxford deontologist and fully accept Arrow's
formal model.

I now want to draw attention to one or two points that did
not come up in the meeting, but which strike me as puzzling
and interesting, and have to do with the interpretation of the
formal system in *Social Choice and Individual Values*. Consider
first the interpretation of the "P" relation. In some axiomatic
choice theories the "P" relation is taken as primitive, in others
(of which Arrow and Peter Newman are instances), it is definable in terms of the relation "R" (usually read informally as
"at least as good as"). Thus, if x and y are actions, or choices,

$$1)\ \ xPy \leftrightarrows xRy, \wedge \sim yRx.$$

The relation "R" may however itself be defined in the following way. Consider the relation "Ind" (which may be read
informally as "indifferent to"). It may be defined as follows: [7]

$$2)\ \ xIndy \leftrightarrows \underset{z}{\wedge} [(zPx \leftrightarrows zPy) \wedge (xPy \leftrightarrows yPz)]$$

One may then notice that:

$$3)\ \ xRy \leftrightarrows xPy \text{ v } xIndy$$

However, even if the "P" relation be taken as primitive and
undefined it certainly cannot be identified with the word
"Preference" nor its uses be identified with the family of uses
of phrases like "is preferred to" in English.

Let us consider the noun "preference," the verb "to prefer,"
and the adjective "preferable" for a moment.

In English we can be said to prefer things even if on a
particular occasion we do not choose them, even if we seldom—
perhaps even if we never—choose them. On the other hand, the
fact that in a *particular* situation we *do* choose something

would not usually be said to entitle the claim that whatever we had chosen was thus and finally established as one of our preferences. The verb "to choose" belongs to a different logical category from the verb "to prefer." Choices are made once and for all and the language reflects this; "I made ten choices this morning" is perfectly good English, whereas "I made ten preferences" is not. The verb "to prefer" is what used to be called "dispositional"; it is not an "occurrence" verb (to use the language Ryle introduced many years ago). Talking about "preferences" is speaking about dispositions of mind, which may or may not reveal themselves in choices on a particular occasion. We find out about preferences—our own and other people's—gradually, and if we do see one suddenly the verb we use for this is not "make" as of a choice but *"discover"*—"I discovered her real preference as I saw how she reacted." [8]

Now, I have never heard of an axiomatic choice theory—Arrow's or anyone else's—that had a formal relation—call it "C"—that behaved in the family of ways in which the verb "to choose" behaves in English, and at the same time another relation, "P," that behaved in just the ways in which the verb "to prefer" does in English. I don't even begin to claim to know what it would look like, how "C" and "P" would be formally related.

As far as existing choice theory goes, if one must try to translate the "P" relation by an English word, "chosen" would be better than "preferred." Say you read "xPy" as "x is chosen over y." At least one thus avoids the suggestion that the whole delicate subtle structure and varied powers and uses of a dispositional verb in a natural language have somehow, by waving a wand, been brought into the properties of the "P" relation.

A choice theory is possible if, for any given attainable set of choices, the choosing agent has an ordering. The existence of members of this attainable set among whom he is indifferent need not complicate the ordering since we can treat the indifferent elements as sets, and thus get an induced simple ordering of the indifference sets. But none of the formal structures that may be or so far have been elaborated out of this simple core take account of the dispositional properties of the English word "prefer." These considerations have considerable bearing on attempts to use axiomatic choice theory to study the possibilities of social agreement. It is a matter of observation that a set of people may be able to agree on their "preferences" —in the dispositional sense this word can have in English— even where they find themselves choosing differently on particular occasions. Lovers, ocean-racing skippers, politicians and department chairmen all know this. Now, an analysis of the possible cases of social agreement that runs solely in terms of choices cannot show the possibilities of any such understanding. If one stays on the "choice" level only, then one will not be able to understand "preference" behavior.[9]

NOTES

1. See pp. 81–86 for instance.
2. I discussed this at length in *Scarcity and Evil, passim.*
3. *Social Choice and Individual Values,* p. 18.
4. *Ibid.,* p. 18.
5. Pp. 20–21.
6. *Op. cit.,* p. 22. The whole discussion on pp. 22–23 suggests an underlying utilitarianism that in fact has nothing to do with Arrow's formal system.
7. The definition comes from a forthcoming paper "On the Necessity for a Change in the Axioms of Choice Theory" by H. Putnam and the present author.
8. I am at last trying to do justice to the suggestion made in a letter to me over ten years ago by Professor James Buchanan: that an argument in an old article of mine bore on Arrow's concept of "preference." The paper in question appeared in *Economica* in 1954 and was called "On Descriptions of Consumer's Behavior."
9. "Preferences" being dispositions, I am glad to note interest on the part of some of my colleagues in psychology in the possibility of constructing mathematical models of behavior that would embody structures designed to relate the empirical observable, namely choices, to the psychological construct of "preference." I am interested to find psychologists unimpressed by any such hangover from

old-fashioned logical positivism as the suggestion that "preferences" are simply choices or sets of choices. I have been helped by personal communication with Professors Scott Gardener and George Marshall, both of the Psychology Department of Sir George Williams University, Montreal, Canada.

12

The Economics of Economists

PAUL WEISS
Yale University

THE TITLE of this paper can be read in two ways. It refers to the economics that is studied by economists, as well as to the economy exhibited in their accounts. The two meanings, though related, are distinct and ought not to be confused. An understanding of them will, I think, make evident why some of the things economists say seem not to be relevant to economic practice, and are not able to withstand the usual critical scrutiny to which the fundamental ideas of a discipline should be subjected. The title could therefore be paraphrased as: the economists' account of the nature of the common wealth; or alternatively, a philosophic approach to the discipline of economics and its bearing on economic practice.

Economic practice involves an actual and prospective distribution of resources. Production and consumption, though often treated as coordinate parts of economics, alongside distribution, are in fact both instances of it. Production relates to the distribution of materials, work force, machines, and capital, with a consequent promotion of certain operations and results rather than others. Consumption relates to the distribution of goods that are to be removed from the economic situation, usually partially and for a limited time, but sometimes completely and permanently. It obviously includes waste, inefficiency, and materials utilized in the making of something else. So far as economists treat all these types of distribution as though they were on a footing their studies will be repetitious, economically inefficient. The opposite fault however has usually been the fault characteristic of economists' accounts. It is to be found in the papers and in much of the discussion in the present symposium, with the consequence that some vital economic factors are ignored and others misconstrued.

Economics is a *social* science seeking to understand the nature of distribution. It has a distinctive descriptive, and a distinctive explanatory, dimension. The descriptive reports the actual working out of economic practice. It attends to the differences that scarcity, advertising, war, the stock market, and so on have on the course of economic practice. What is done here by one economist cannot be faulted except by another, since it depends on the collection and understanding of data not within the provenance of any other enterprise. The explanatory dimension is occupied with the principles and laws that explain and perhaps govern the operation of distribution. It teaches us how and why resources are and can be distributed. Here hypotheses are framed, rules suggested, and interpretations produced. These are all to be judged in terms of their relevance to economic practice, and the clarification they provide for our understanding of a world in which men interplay with one another intermediated by the goods they receive, usually though not necessarily as the result of an exchange.

It is tempting to develop explanatory economics along the lines followed by mathematics. An account is then constructed by forging a set of axioms or postulates. But then one confuses mathematics as presented in textbooks with a genuine, creative, exploratory mathematics. This does not hang precariously from a set of axioms or postulates. And one will forget that the function of the explanatory side of economics is to enable us to follow the contours of the descriptive dimension with fidelity and understanding.

Others are tempted to try to repeat the enviable successes of theoretical physics; they therefore entertain theories that pivot about the supposed behavior of unobservable entities, expressed in highly abstract, nonempirical terms. But this is to overlook the fact that economics is a social science—which is to say that it must approach the problem of the distribution of resources armed with an understanding of actual men, in actual societies, living through real time.

There are some who say that a man is nothing or little more than the locus of stimuli and responses; others speak of him as though he were only a tissue of preferences or habits. Those who take these lines too often forget that man cannot then be spoken of as though he were entirely public. A merely public man merely interacts with others. We must take account of his private side if we are to do justice to the fact that he has intentions and purposes; desires, fears, and hopes; knowledge, beliefs, prejudices, and passions. He is a commonsense being, a partly conventionalized reality living in a partly conventionalized world in which what is known and done is largely determined by what had been known and had been done. Attempts to deal with him as though he were a unit exchanging unit goods for unit goods may yield interesting numerical results, but will nevertheless move at a tangent to economic realities.

Because of man's limited size and powers, he cannot do all that he would like to do, and usually cannot get all that he would like to have. As a consequence he must make decisions. These are either in the form of preferences or choices. The one has to do with the acceptance of this instead of that as a means for reaching some goal accepted consciously or unconsciously, willingly or unwillingly, rightly or wrongly. The other, choice, has to do with the acceptance of a desirable end together with an appropriate means. Since most goals are at least in part dictated by what had been done, by authorities and by tradition, most of our decisions are in the form of preferences. What we prefer are not values or valuable things, but better or worse agencies for arriving at what might be for us indifferent or even undesirable goals. But we sometimes do choose. It is then and then only that economic decision deals with goods that have values, in the sense of worth, of what ought to be preserved, of that which has some degree of excellence.

If we can be said to elect being in a democratic society,

we can be said to exercise choice, for we then, while taking this means rather than that, also accept the kind of peace and prosperity that is integral to the democratic ideal.

Because economics is a social science it must take society seriously. This means that it must find room for the presence and operation of such subsocieties as families and unions, such organizations as businesses, corporations, and monopolies, and for such qualified societies as nations, states, and blocs. Each one of these is distinct from the men within it. Not only do some of these societal unities have a longer temporal span than any of their members, but all of them have structures, foci, rhythms, and powers that the individuals do not have. All of them are caught in a web of customs, traditions, and practices of a distinctive kind. Together with individual men they determine the nature and rate of distributions.

The open and free market is a societal unit. It represents an ideal that perhaps never was or could be realized. We can of course treat it as an ideal that the actual market should approximate or in terms of which we can at least understand the more complex working of the actual market. Though the actual market is an important economic institution, because quick judgments have to be made in it, because of the limitations and prejudices that characterize groups of men, and because of man's failure to exchange everything in it, it can be only one of a number of important factors determining distribution.

Our basic resources are human knowledge and skills geared to the course and fecundity of nature. The fundamental mode in which we make use of these resources is through our involvement with time. Time, however, has two basic forms: calendral and vital. In calendral time equal units follow monotonously one upon another; it is to this we turn when we seek to quantify the distributions of rents, interests, and promises. In vital time the units of calendral time are bunched together in various ways through activities that have distinctive beginnings relevant to distinctive endings. Combined with technical knowledge and skill, vital time becomes service; combined with raw material, it has the shape of goods. No one who is content only with calendral time can therefore grasp the nature of economic services and goods.

We can quantify economics the way we can quantify music. But then we ought, as we do with music, attend to phrases rather than to notes, to spanned intervals rather than to points, and leave room therefore for the idea of relevance and for a distinctive economic causality. We will then not be so readily tempted to follow Mr. Boulding and look at economics solely in terms of the idea of scarcity. Neither goods nor services need be scarce for economics to be a possible and significant enterprise. Even plentiful material may be distributed in economically interesting ways to bring about various concentrations, opportunities, and habits. But if what I have said about man, society, and time has any validity, it becomes evident that some economists have been operating with an unnecessary scarcity of ideas and distinctions. They should add to their present goods ideas of a more robust man, a commonsense world, an actual society, and a lived-through time.

PART III

The Role of the Corporation
in American Life

A

The Business Corporation as
a Creator of Values

CARL KAYSEN
Institute for Advanced Study, Princeton

IN THEIR PURSUIT of the ordinary business of economics, economists take values—in their own language, the structure of preferences—as given, rather than as a subject of inquiry. Formally, they are assumed to inhere in individuals or households as consumers and as factor suppliers; in plain language, people have preferences in respect to what kinds of goods they buy; where they live and work, what kinds of occupations they pursue, what kinds of bank accounts, stocks, bonds, insurance policies they own; what kinds of mortgages, automobile loans, bank loans they owe. The working of the market, provided that it is competitive, makes the best possible reconciliation of these preferences with the technical possibilities of production, which in combination with these preferences (and, to be complete, whatever "institutional" limitations on production or consumption are accepted as given; e.g., the definition of illegal commodities, such as narcotic drugs, or the limitation of child labor, or the requirement by law of education up to some age or level of attainment) determine what jobs, goods, services, are available. Divison of labor makes for greater productivity in intellectual work as well as in pin-making; such specialization is therefore inevitable. Further, the economists' specialization has paid off, both in terms of abstract understanding of how an economic system works, and in socially vital applications of this understanding to public policy. In this respect, economics has clearly been the most successful of the social sciences.

Yet this specialization has a price. The very success of the analytic structure in its own terms tends to confirm the unexamined acceptance of its assumptions. Economists, with a few scattered exceptions, have not studied the sources of household preferences, and little has been done by other social scientists to fill the gap.[1] The comments on the process of value creation that follow are thus more speculative than scholarly, more suggestive than conclusive. But the problem appears significant enough to warrant such an approach.

The large business corporation is in many ways the characteristic institution of American society. The combination of ingredients that is typical for these corporations is: large absolute size, tens or hundreds of thousands of employees, tens or hundreds of thousands of stockholders, hundreds of millions or billions of dollars of annual sales; a hierarchical, bureaucratic structure of "professional" management not necessarily connected with substantial ownership holdings, recruited at the lower levels in large part from colleges and professional schools and promoted from within; command over a wide range of technologies and production of a wide range of products and services; operation at a large number of locations spread over the whole country, and increasingly, over the whole world, and a correlative mobility of managerial personnel during the course of their ascent up the corporate hierarchy; reliance on mass marketing, including heavy use of advertising in the mass media. Not every large corporation shares in all these characteristics to an equal degree, of course, but they are typical of the group as a whole. They, in turn, reflect three underlying features of our society: its open, egalitarian character; the rationalization and transformation of production technologies through the application of science; and the growth of aggregate and per-capita income, which, together, have created a mass middle class over the last generation. But changes in the character of the market and methods of marketing are in general far more determinative of the characteristic structure of the large corporation and its relative importance in our economy than changes in the technology of production in the narrow sense. It is the dominance of the national market and the need for the national media in selling to it, rather than economies of production at a large scale, that are often decisive for the structure of industry. When the Brand Names Foundation points out in an advertisement that an American family moving to a new city, though surrounded by strangers, its head in an unfamiliar job, its children in new schools, nonetheless has the comfort of seeing "old friends" in the shape of familiar brands of merchandise—TIDE and LIFE, SPRY and FORD are all there—it is pointing to an important truth about our society, as well as making a statement of embarrassing bathos. In turn, it is these aspects of the market that give the process of value-creation by the corporation salient features to which I wish to call attention.

To speak of "value creation" may sound pretentious; labeling the same processes with the appellation "taste formation" may appear more appropriate. But to the extent that these two labels do carry different connotations, I would suggest that the more serious sound of "value formation" is appropriate, because of the wide reach of what we describe over our whole society.

The contributions of the business corporation to value formation can be viewed under three rubrics: the shaping of the material environment of our society; the shaping of its symbolic environment, verbal, visual, and, perhaps to a much lesser extent, auditory; and the definition of "work," and in particular, worthy achievement in work. This last, in turn, has a significant impact on the definition of a worthy or ideal person for the society, especially for its male members.

Criticism on both esthetic and technical-functional grounds of the material outputs of our market system are not new. Neither is the standard response of the businessman to these criticisms: he merely gives the consumer what he wants, and indeed, his success depends on his effectiveness in so doing. The economist, by and large, accepts the businessman's answer, with certain qualifications in respect to markets that depart substantially from competition, but with little disposition to believe the exceptions important in the aggregate. Yet, in the face of the combined effects of producers' initiative in designing and offering goods, the rapidity of introduction of new products, and the role of advertising and consumer followership in determining what is bought, this answer, *simpliciter*, is unconvincing to the critics, and not much more so to the economist. But, because one of the key features of a market system—its capacity to achieve an efficient allocation of resources under certain circumstances—depends on accepting this answer, the economist has been disinclined, on the whole, to look further.

A more elaborate, more sophisticated version of the proposition that the market gives the consumer what he wants can be made. A sketch of it would suggest that the stabilities or invariances with which the businessmen and advertisers work are not fixed consumer preferences or tastes, as such, but rather fixed learning capacities in respect to taste-formation: it is easier to learn to like some things than others. The objective of the designer and marketer is then to discover, to the extent that he can, what consumers will, in the event, readily learn to like. But, of course, what they will learn to like will depend to some extent on the past history of what they have learned to like; thus the order of experiments, so to speak, affects the outcome. But once we admit this description of the process, or something like it, the case for believing the underlying proposition of the rationale for the market, that consumers *ought* to get what they want, becomes much less clear. It is one thing to accept the rule of given consumer preferences; it is quite another to admit that preferences are shaped within some broad constraints, but not to inquire into the process by which they are shaped.

Substantively, products have been criticized for being, on the whole, uglier than they need to be, and shoddier than they need to be. Typical is the comment that has focused on automobiles, but it is applicable to a wide range of products. Again, a more sophisticated version of these criticisms points to the increasingly large resource expenditures that are made for the continuous modification of products, especially consumer durables, when the changes are dubiously worthwhile in either functional or esthetic terms, and novelty becomes an end in itself.

The mass media, newspapers, magazines, television, radio, are the great teachers in our society, far more pervasive in their reach and far more persistent in their influence than school and church. A major part of their content, verbal and pictorial, is explicitly "sales talk"; the whole of it is shaped by the sales purpose that is their essential aim. The words, slogans, pictures, symbols, jingles have one major message: consumption is happiness. Consumption, especially the consumption of new and (therefore) better goods is identified, more or less explicitly, more or less strongly, with familial love, sexual satisfaction, youth, health, social status, whatever primary good the advertiser can plausibly or implausibly connect with his product. There are subsidiary messages as well; perhaps the most important one is the description of the economic, political, social system that provides all the pleasurable goods as the best of all possible ones, and its encapsulation in the slogan of "free enterprise." The language and images of the media, which match their content in blatancy and crudeness, have become, for all except a small minority, the language and images of our culture.[2]

It is worth making explicit that the elite who shape the market—corporation managers, executives of advertising firms, the press, television, and radio—are not catering to mass tastes they themselves scorn. On the contrary, what is infinitely sadder is that, for the most part, they share these tastes, and are in this sense honestly expressing their own values in what they say and sell. Cadillacs are only larger and more expensive than Chevrolets, not less vulgar.

Freud observed that work was the chief link that bound the human psyche to the world of reality. Indeed, we can go further, and say that the idea of "work" is one of the central defining ideas of human society, and humanity, and, throughout history, man's definition of himself has been heavily in terms of his work. What has become of this idea in the world of the modern mass market? One writer answers our question as follows:

> We . . . suggest a threefold division of work in terms of its human significance. First, there is the work that still provides an occasion for primary self-identification and self-commitment of the individual—for his "fulfillment" if one prefers. *Thirdly*, there is work that is apprehended as a direct threat to self-identification, an indignity, an oppression. And secondly, between these two poles, is work that is *neither* fulfillment *nor* oppression, a sort of gray, neutral region in which one neither rejoices nor suffers, but with which one puts up with more or less grace for the sake of other things that are supposed to be more important—these other things being typically connected with one's private life. . . . For better or for worse (and, by most possible criteria, probably for better), the first and third category have shrunk in favor of the second. This would seem to be an inevitable consequence of ongoing industrialization. Rationalization of work, bureaucratization of the administrative machinery, mass organization for mass production and mass consumption—these functional necessities of the industrial system must inevitably lead to a shrinkage of the first category of work. Only at the top and in certain special positions elsewhere is there much room for work that involves the totality of the person. More commonly the entrepreneur is replaced by the bureaucrat, the individualistic professional by a team, and the craftsman by a machine. But at the same time the demand for masters shrinks, so does the demand for slaves. Work becomes safer and cleaner, its administration more humane, its demands in time and energy more lenient. If some people have less joy in work, most have less pain. . . . The expanding area in the middle will generate its own problems, . . . among (which) that of the 'meaning' of work is central.[3]

We can put the same point even more succinctly by observing that in our society the twelve-hour day and the six- or even seven-day week are known only to those at the very bottom and the very top of the occupational distribution, the harvest laborers and nonunionized service trades at one extreme and the managerial chiefs of business and government and the more successful practitioners of the liberal professions and the arts at the other; forced on the one, chosen by the other.

The fragmentation of work by the continued division of labor, and the growth of assembly-line technique and other similar techniques of work organization that view man as an organic machine are now old occasions of complaint, dating back to the origins of the industrial system. True, the growth of mass production for mass markets, the continued rationalization of the techniques of work, and the application of these rationalizing methods to a wide variety of tasks outside the factory proper may widen the sphere to which this complaint applies. In addition, however, the large corporation in its typical context has added a new element: the trivializing of the substantive content of work at higher and higher levels of the corporate hierarchy. This is chiefly the consequence of the dominance of marketing over production and other technical problems in most large businesses. There is a deep and genuine human difference between endeavoring to discover how to make more and better steel out of a ton of iron ore, and endeavoring to discover more dimensions along which to differentiate one synthetic detergent from another; yet it is the latter kind of activity that is likely to be the more valuable to the firm. The man who excels in the strategies of selling, the man who can see a new market, is more likely to rise to the top of the corporate hierarchy than the one whose excellence lies in seeing a new technology. There, of course, he is not only significant for what he does within the enterprise, he also serves as a model of excellence for society as a whole.

It has been suggested that the routinization and trivialization of work has the idealization of increasing and ever-novel consumption as its psychological complement: the two form a necessary pair, but this is a proposition that goes beyond our present argument.[4]

Yet to the extent that the top members of the corporate

hierarchy represent one of the important, probably even the dominant, exemplars of successful achievement in our society, it is noteworthy that the symbol of their achievement is purely abstract: the size of their earnings. This is because it is impossible to assign to them the kind of concrete, comprehensible accomplishment that a successful baseball player, brain surgeon, or popular novelist displays. Achievement does therefore tend to translate into the universal terms of potential consumption, rather than the more variegated specifics of personal accomplishment.

Even from the prespective that would prefer to term the preceding list disvalues rather than values, there are items to be entered on the other side of the corporate account. First is the promotion of efficiency and rationality in production. Archetypically, every process, every input, is scrutinized under the criteria of economic efficiency, seeking out how more can be done with less. Again, to the extent that competition slackens, this process may fall short of being pushed to its limit, but the tendency in this direction is a powerful one; and the large corporation builds this drive into its organizational arrangements so that it is to some extent independent of competitive pressures. Second is the increasing universalism of its internal organization, and the opening of careers to merit. This is still more promise than accomplishment, but the logic of efficiency pushes in this direction, and as access to college education becomes more democratized, so does recruitment and promotion in the large corporation. Third, the very mass market to whose pressures we attributed so much that is negative in business performance does represent a democratization of consumption that diminishes the sharpness of differences in class and status, and makes its own contribution to the openness and egalitarianism of our society.

The balance of the account, as set forth so far, may well appear different to different readers, though it is clearly negative to the writer. But rather than strike it in these terms, it may be more appropriate to ask how the large corporation and its economic context are changing or could change to achieve a balance. The first relevant change is the increase in the productive power of our society. This has been a more or less steady process for as long as we can measure it, with perhaps some acceleration in the last two decades; its cumulative effect has been enormous. Marx saw the historic social task of the market economy as increasing the productive powers of society; if he could look around him today, he would conclude the task was accomplished. Or to put the matter in less grandiose terms, our society has become so rich that the marginal utility of a further increment of productivity, used in the way it is now being used, is small. We can afford a price in efficiency to achieve other goals, if that price must be paid. The second change is in the nature of what we consume, and especially, the nature of how we perceive what we consume. Goods that are not produced and sold in conventional markets—education and health, for example—are becoming more important in our consumption budget, another reflection of our increasing wealth. Further, we are recognizing increasingly the "public good" or external interdependency elements in much of our consumption, so that simple acceptance of the view that the market gives the consumers what they want is no longer fully persuasive even in its own terms. We can see this in housing and neighborhood and city planning, or the purchase of automobiles, the building of freeways, and the generation of smog.

Both these changes point in the direction of making it more appropriate to ask the question: could the large corporation typically become directly concerned with the broader values it was creating, and correspondingly less oriented to increasing its profits in the context of market rivalry? "Could" here has two senses: what change in the institution and its environment would be needed to make such a shift in purpose possible? what price in other values would such a change entail?

Preliminary to answering the first of this pair of questions is the observation that the typical large corporation is already seeking a structure of goals too complex to be described simply as profit maximization, and that the competitive constraints of the markets in which it operates are not so narrow as to preclude a variation in the mix.[5] However, this is not to say either that these constraints are so loose that every change in the mixture of goals is possible, or that, if they were, or were to become so, changes of the sort we view as desirable would automatically take place.[6] Both the large corporation and its environment would have to alter substantially to allow these changes to take place. An attempt to provide a blueprint for these alterations is beyond the scope of this brief paper, whose purpose is essentially critical, but some suggestions as to what shape they might take are in order. First, positive value goals would have to be built into the organizational structure of the corporation. This could be done primarily in two ways. Professionals, asking professional rather than business questions, could be given more responsibility and scope within the corporation than they now have. Thus, for instance, instead of the research and medical staff of a pharmaceutical house asking of a possible new drug only can we sell it? will it pass the FDA standards? they might ask in addition, will it do something for medicine that existing drugs do not do? enough to be worth the effort of development and marketing? The first pair of questions would continue to be relevant; the second would simply place a more severe constraint on what a firm would be willing to introduce in the way of new drugs. Similarly, when a new model of an automobile, refrigerator, washer, etc. was considered, the additional standards over the economic one— will it sell enough to make it pay?—might well be: is it sufficiently more efficient, safer, more durable, more beautiful (!) to justify adding it to the market or seeking to substitute it for the present product? To back up and enforce these professional judgments, some institutions of public, professional criticism would have to be developed. Professional societies, independent testing organizations, supported by some combination of subscription and subsidization, all would need to make a contribution to the discussion. Perhaps analogues of the Food and Drug Administration with a wider scope might also be useful. But this in itself would not suffice, if the relation between the audibility of sales talk and that of critical evaluation remained at all what it now is. Radical change in the institutions of advertising, and the relation of advertising to the media, would also be necessary.

These changes are all directed to the relations of enterprise with the markets in which it sells. Equally great changes would be needed in relation to its internal functioning, especially in the way work was organized, and people recruited and promoted. These are less easy to sketch, because we are much less able even to speculate on what they should be.

In order for these changes to take place, it may well be necessary to allow further relaxation of the constraints of competitive rivalry in the market. More reliance on professionalization implies some softening of competition. Again, without trying to specify in detail what changes might be made, there might be much more tolerance of the growth of large firms, including growth by merger, than there has been in the recent past. Nonetheless, sheer monopoly as such need not be encouraged, where it is not dictated by the facts of technology and the market. Public discussion and informed criticism could play a wider role in supplementing the constraints of the market in both limiting excessive profits and enforcing efficiency, but the rivalry of autonomous organizations would remain as a central feature of the new arrangements we envision.

The analogy that naturally suggests itself to the academic is the university. In our society, universities are many, they compete for funds, for students, for faculty. This competition forces them, in some respects, to pay attention to what their "markets" want, but they, and their markets as well, act within the boundaries of a strongly felt code of professional standards. Students may avoid hard courses and important, but dull, subjects, but it is the faculty that decides what courses should be offered and what their content should be. Nor are individual professors simply free to please themselves; they operate under the critical eyes of a guild of colleagues, whose standards they have to a greater or lesser extent internalized in the course of their own graduate training. Each individual university must balance income and outgo, and in so doing feels itself pressed by all three "markets" in which it deals—students; trustees, donors, and legislatures; professors—but it can meet these pressures only within the broader standards of what the academic profession considers proper. There is no use trying to trace a point-by-point correspondence between the situation of the university and the situation of the kind of enterprise we envision; the usefulness of the parallel is simply to point out that it is not merely fanciful to suggest that it is possible to combine competition amongst autonomous organizations, each operating under the constraint of balancing its outgo with its income in the absence of taxing power, and each forced to "sell" its output to customers who are not without alternatives, with strong professional standards operating to define both what the output should be and under what conditions it may be produced.

The reader who is an economist—if there are any left at this point—will naturally ask two questions. First, what will the relation be between the "new" enterprises of the type here sketched, assuming that all giant corporations are so transformed, and the more traditional small- and medium-size firms that will continue to provide a very substantial share of output and account for a large volume of employment? Second, admitting the validity and importance of the criticisms made—which many economists would—would it not be more desirable to move toward more rather than less competitive markets, because it is really the limitations and obstacles to competition that make possible much of the behavior described above?

To deal with the second question first; it is not at all clear that the traditional economists' answer to poor functioning of markets, more competition, is indeed relevant to our problems. Competitive markets function well to satisfy *given* tastes; our concern is how tastes are shaped. Further, the very features of our economy in terms of the scale of marketing, and the institutions of advertising and distribution that are central to this taste-shaping process, are exactly those that work most strongly against competitive markets. What is more, the changes in these institutions, and in the nature of large enterprises that would be required to eliminate or drastically reduce the significance of these elements would be at least as radical as the ones proposed above, but they would have to go against the tide of events rather than with it. Even if successful, they would deal with only a superficial part of the problems posed, missing especially the questions of the content of work and the nature of standards of taste.

On the first question, our answer is exactly the traditional one: leave these relations to the market. To the extent that the "new corporation" was less efficient in meeting the test (of the revised and newly informed) marketplace, the area of economic activity of small and medium enterprises would expand; conversely, if the "new corporation" produced more attractive products, became a better place to work, and an even more efficient producer.

We raised above the question of what cost in other values the attempt to pursue the values we here seek might impose. This is obviously a deeper and more difficult question. In one sense, we have already answered that the values of productive efficiency and technical rationality should be given lower weight in our already highly productive society; thus, if the diminution of competitive pressures and the intrusion of guild standards on the standards of the marketplace lessen the rationalizing forces making for productive efficiency with the corporation, this is simply a price worth paying. But we value the market for more than its economic efficiency. Its impersonality, its decentralization of decision and dispersion of power, are all far more important virtues in the broader political and social evaluation of institutions. It is of course hard to predict how the balance of social forces between "private" and "public" spheres, and the balance of decision-making between explicitly "political" and market forces, would change if the evolution of the business corporation were pushed hard along the lines suggested. Such inevitable ignorance is a most convincing part of the argument for conservatism and caution. But it may be that the alternatives are rather a choice between much more explicit centralized regulation of the business firm, and some change in the direction suggested, than a choice between the status quo and the results of an unpredictable process of reform. However, if this prediction proves correct, in that we see an accelerating trend toward centralized regulation, it will probably reflect in large part a response to problems and complaints other than those we have listed, especially those arising from the search for economic stability and steady growth without substantial inflation. One possible set of solutions to these problems points in the direction of "indicative planning," which in turn involves some weakening of the reliance on pure market forces and some tempering of the rigors of competition. However, some problems more directly connected with the questions we have raised, including car and drug safety, racial discrimination in employment, retraining of labor for new jobs as technologies change, geographic distribution of new investment are also becoming concrete and urgent enough to generate public discussion and political pressure. Whatever the pressures, the importance of the choice is clear, and the arguments we have presented for one choice should have their weight in the balance.

In considering these suggestions, it is well to bear in mind that we have already used the envelope of the private business firm for contents of quite novel kinds. The large defense supplier—General Dynamics, North American Aviation, Raytheon —has the appearance and legal form of a private, profit-making corporation; its working substance, however, differs radically from that of the ordinary large business serving the civilian market. The more recent developments of nonprofit corporations, or limited-profit, quasipublic-quasiprivate corporations like Comsat, are also suggestive of the possibilities of variation. There is much current discussion of the possibility of using similar forms in dealing with the problems of urban development, or educational television. Essentially, what we have here proposed is a much broader and more general exploration of these possibilities in all those important sectors of the economy in which the large corporation is characteristic and dominant, believing that there is a common set of less immediately obvious but ultimately more important problems that their operation has created.

NOTES

1. Thorstein Veblen's *The Theory of the Leisure Class* is of course the most striking exception. A more recent one more within the framework of neoclassic economic analysis is J. S. Duesenberry's *Income, Saving, and the Theory of Consumer Behavior* (1951). Also noteworthy is Talcott Parson's analysis of Marshall's views, "Wants and Activities in Marshall," *Quarterly Journal of Economics* (1924).

2. A vivid analysis of the language and images of advertising is contained in Marshall MacLuhan, *The Mechanical Bride* (1951).

3. P. L. Berger, "Some General Observations on the Problems of Work," in P. L. Berger (ed.), *The Human Shape of Work* (1965), pp. 218–20.

4. See Hannah Arendt, *The Human Condition* (1958), for a full exposition of this view.

5. See the writer's essay, "The Corporation: How Much Power? What Scope?" in E. S. Mason (ed.), *The Corporation in Modern Society* (1959).

6. A. A. Berle has been the leading exponent of the opposite view, that indeed the desirable changes are already in train. See his *Twentieth Century Capitalist Revolution* (1954) and *Power without Property* (1959).

B

Skepticism of Wants, and Certain Subversive Effects of Corporations on American Values

DAVID BRAYBROOKE
Dalhousie University

1) THE OBSERVATIONS found in the paper that Professor Kaysen contributed to the Mason volume on *The Corporation in Modern Society* [1] remain topical. I am inclined to agree very nearly completely with what he said then. I am also persuaded by the suggestions of waste that he joined in raising against the annual model changes of the automobile corporations [2]— though I am more skeptical about the changes being what the consumers wanted, even at the time. Unsportingly exploiting the automobile giants as conveniently familiar examples, though already much-vexed ones, I shall fling some further darts at them.

2) I propose to amplify Professor Kaysen's point about the "irresponsibility of business power." [3] I shall touch upon the effects, which Kaysen likewise mentioned, of business power on the tone of the mass media [4] and on the tastes and styles of American life. [5] I shall also, like Kaysen, call attention to the discretion that corporation managements exercise regarding innovation in products. [6]

3) Professor Friedman, relying like Adam Smith on market controls to check the predatory tendencies of business, has scornfully repudiated the claims of businessmen and their public-relations experts that corporations have lately taken on public responsibilities in broad social spheres. [7] Who authorized them to do that? Let them stick to their trade, while we see to it that their trade continues to be competitive. Kaysen has been equally doubtful: "It is not sufficient for the business

leaders to announce that they are thinking hard and wrestling earnestly with their wide responsibilities, if, in fact, the power of unreviewed and unchecked decision remains with them, and they remain a small, self-selecting group." [8] Like Friedman, he has been inclined to ask for more vigorous antitrust policy, regardless of business protestations about their self-imposed responsibilities.[9]

4) The charge of irresponsibility does not therefore necessarily entrain an exhortation to corporation management to take larger views and assume wider responsibilities. What is being charged is not neglect of responsibilities duly assigned—they have not been assigned in advance, and Taylor has indicated, among other things, that the law as it stands makes assigning them *post hoc*, in the way of remedy, problematic.[10] What is being charged is the creation of untoward effects in fields where there are insufficient external controls, whether these are controls established by new legal assignments of responsibility or other sorts of controls (such as more vigorous competition). The point about irresponsibility is thus, in fact, not really a charge at all, but an index designating a problem. The charges against corporation leaders are, properly speaking, that some of them, some of the time, pretend no problem exists, and that (by this and other means) they obstruct efforts to deal with the problem.

5) I wish to focus my comments on one particular—familiar and deplorably effective—device used by corporation management, their public-relations experts, and other apologists to keep up the pretense that no problem exists. This is the device of saying, "We only give the public what it wants." In the manner of ordinary language philosophy, I want to examine this statement very literally and deliberately. This examination, though it will begin with what may seem to be petty details, will fairly quickly bring us to matters of deep concern about economic judgments. It will also, by the way, justify at least in part the provocative suggestion contained in my title. Corporations do subvert American values, very extensively, in important ways, though I do not mean to suggest

that everything any corporation does amounts to such subversion, or that all corporations do so all of the time. Corporations also, no doubt, do much good; but since they spend night and day singing their own praises, the praises need not be repeated here.

6) At first sight, the statement, made on behalf of the corporations, "We only give the public what it wants," may be taken for an excuse. But I think no one—especially not those putting the statement forward—would want to hold that it is an excuse when they take a second look at it. For to be an excuse, the statement would have to be relevant in a certain way to the actions or policies being excused. It is a necessary condition of its being relevant in this way that there be something objectionable about those actions or policies—else why do they need an excuse? I think spokesmen for the corporations would be unwilling to grant that (barring occasional imperfections) there is something objectionable about what they produce and sell. But suppose it is insisted that there is. Then the statement, "We only give the public what it wants," would fulfill one condition of being an excuse; but it would immediately fail others. For by its very meaning, the statement could not be accepted as an excuse; we in fact clearly rule it out as a way of excusing people from supplying objectionable commodities. It is no excuse for the drug-peddler to say that his customers wanted the drugs; for the mail-order antitank merchant to say that he only gave the safecrackers what they wanted; for the manufacturer of defective automobiles to say that the public wanted them. One does not excuse oneself from contributing to evil by saying that other people wanted the contribution.

7) If it is not an excuse, the statement, "We only give the public what it wants," may still be regarded as a device for escaping blame, now not as a device for diminishing it or transferring it to someone else, but as one for preventing questions about blame or praise from arising.[11] I think it does this by, on this interpretation, presupposing that the transactions at issue fall within the free moral competence of the customers to choose what they want; and by implying that the goods that

the customers receive are those that they have, within this competence, expressed themselves as wanting.

8) So interpreted, the statement is a very effective one. It calls into play not only our generalized feelings in favor of personal liberty and against interfering with other people's choices, even trivial ones, but also the refined scruples of economists about respecting other people's preferences, and the theory of market optima in which these scruples are assumed. It is no drawback to the effectiveness of the statement, furthermore, that so interpreted it seems to be substantially true. Most things bought in the United States are chosen within the free moral competence of the customers to choose; and the customers do receive what within that competence they express themselves as wanting.

9) Moreover, are not the customers who express these wants the ultimate authorities on what those wants are? If a person, N, says, given a choice of x, y, or z, "I want z," it follows that he does want z (in the sense of "want" that corresponds to the philosophical term "desire") provided that, knowing the language, he speaks sincerely and provided that the name or description represented by "z" accurately designates what N intends it to designate. Philosophers have thought that these provisos suffice to guarantee the truth of certain first-person statements; indeed, they have thought that the first proviso, about speaking sincerely, knowing the language, suffices; [12] and they have called such statements "logically incorrigible." Thus "I am in pain" is regarded as logically incorrigible; and "I want," taken as expressing an inner experience or feeling, may be thought to be on somewhat the same footing.[13]

10) There may seem to be nothing more to be said. Very likely, the spokesmen for the corporations would gratefully join us in believing that there is nothing more to be said; our ideas (and their ideas) about personal liberty and consumer sovereignty, as well perhaps as some awareness of the philosophical point just made, cooperate in silencing us. But we all know lots more to say, of which we need only be reminded. N's state-

ment, "I want z," made under the provisos mentioned, and given a suitable time coordinate, will properly be recorded as true, and the record will stand; but this doesn't mean that his statement is very happily called "incorrigible." By its very use of the concept of want, it invites criticism; and it is corrigible, as first-person statements about pain and (in suitable circumstances) about seeing afterimages are not. It is corrigible by being superseded, as N revises his view of what he wants. Without implying that he did not want z at the time, N will now, on revision, say that he was *mistaken* in wanting it. Thus "I want z" assimilates to "I believe p" rather than to "I am in pain." [14]

11) The dimensions of criticism that might lead to revisions of want-statements support six reasons for thinking that the claim made by the corporations, "We only give the public what it wants," is in respect to one or another of its implications much less than fully warranted. I shall now canvass these reasons.

12) In the first place, the evidence about consumers getting what they want may be indeterminate; the evidence to decide crucial questions of economic policy all too often is. The automobile companies have said that car-buyers did not want safety, when safety features were offered them. But, I wonder, how conclusive was their evidence on this point? Does it rule out what in the eyes of the consumers themselves would have been misjudgments of what they wanted? Was the information about safety as widely distributed, and as effectively communicated, as other information about the cars being offered? If N did not know of the presence of all three alternatives, x, y, and z, or did not know of certain properties of these alternatives, or failed to apply certain principles to which he himself subscribes, but whose relevance then escaped him, N's statement, "I want z," is ripe for revision. Now, this consideration would be effective even if all consumers had been unanimous in expressing themselves as wanting cars other than those with the safety features; but it is of interest to inquire whether there was not in fact a sizable proportion of con-

sumers who did then want the cars with the safety features,
perhaps a proportion large enough to cover the costs of producing such cars, if the consumers making it up had been
reached with information and offers. One might note, furthermore, that there are other ways in which the evidence about
consumers not wanting safety features may be defective. How
did the cars with these new features compare with other cars
on other points? Was there agreement between companies and
the public on what features of cars are most important for
safety?

13) Rather than branch out, however, into such general
skeptical considerations, healthy as they are, let us return to
the particular subject of wants. The second reason for distrusting the statement by the corporations, "We only give the public what it wants," is that the corporations have had a good
deal to do with instilling these wants in the public; they have
done enough, one would think, to destroy any implication depending on those wants being spontaneously the consumers'
own. The automobile companies have shaped the public's ideas
about safety, and hence the wants related to safety: negatively,
by suppressing information about the dangers of the cars that
they produce; and positively, by extolling speed, and selling
cars on the basis of power. Half a century of dilation on speed,
power, and thrills have fostered and intensified wants that now
seem questionable to many; and those who have the wants,
without now questioning them, might be brought to revise
them by perceiving the interested part that the automobile
companies have played in instilling them.[15] When N discovers
that he was more under someone else's influence than he
thought, he has a good reason for reconsidering his statement,
"I want z."

14) The automobile companies and the advertising that
they have paid for have operated to subvert the American
value of safety. A third reason for refusing to agree to all the
implications of the statement, "We only give the public what
it wants," consists in the extent to which this subversion has
been carried through the whole field of American values. The

subversion affects not only safety—which we profess to cherish, and mean to, but which the automobile companies connive with us in undermining—but all sorts of other values, in many insidious ways. American business spends a great deal of time and energy confusing the public about values, and thus deliberately produces the sort of misjudgment about x, y, and z that will lead N to revise his expression when he detects his mistake. I shall mention just two further illustrations. There is, specifically, the systematic abuse of sexual interests, so that people have their wants for automobiles and all sorts of other things seriously mixed up with their sexual desires. The automobile companies (though certainly not these alone) have strenuously assisted in mixing us up about sex, making it more urgent, but also more diffuse, and commonly misdirected. More generally, I might mention the besetting clamor about goods and gadgets, which all the corporations join in generating. How often do members of the public get a chance to think quietly in a sustained way about what they might want out of life? Do they ever have time to reflect that perhaps they want too many things already and could well do without wanting still more? [16]

15) In the fourth place, the claim "We only give the public what it wants" is suspect because the corporations not only assist in confusing the public about what it might want; they also obstruct institutional remedies for the lack of information that leads N and his fellow consumers into misjudgments about wants. A simpleminded man might ask, if the corporations were devoted to the public interest (as they so continually and profusely profess), would they not press for greatly enlarged facilities, public or private, but at any rate disinterested (and known to be so), for consumers' research? For public standards of quality? For trade fairs giving prizes for honest workmanship? Perhaps the corporations have objections to the relevance and thoroughness of the particular tests used by going consumers' research organizations; but such objections do not explain why the corporations resist disinterested tests of any kind, by any institutions with the capacity to do more thorough research than consumers can do

for themselves. How shameful to find, besides the automobile companies dragging their feet about safety standards, the tire companies doing the same thing; the grocers and packagers objecting to truth-in-packaging; the credit firms protesting against truth-in-lending. If corporations wonder why they do not attract idealistic young men fresh from college, they need only consider the impression that such conduct makes on people outside the corporations.

16) One must remark, fifth, carrying forward an observation of Professor Kaysen's, that corporations often have a considerable amount of discretion respecting innovation,[17] and hence respecting the variety of products that they offer the public. In the automobile industry, with its high concentration and high barriers to entry, the variety of products is especially subject to arbitrary limitation on the producers' side. But from the fact that given a choice between x, y, and z, N expresses himself as wanting z, nothing can be inferred about his wants for u, v, w, goods that were not offered him. Many consumers might prefer very different cars—if they are never produced, so that consumers never have a chance to see them or to try them out, how can it be known that they are not wanted? It is true, one could say of *any* industry that there might be some other products that the industry is not now offering the public, but that the public would prefer to anything that is being offered. But I do not believe the fact that this could always be said makes it sometimes entirely trivial to say it. Saying it is not trivial as a reminder of the limitations on what can be inferred about wants from the wants expressed in the face of some limited set of alternatives. In the case of the automobiles offered the public, moreover, it is not nature, or even the market, that determines what shall figure in the set of alternatives. They very corporations that affect to be doing no more than responding to the wants of the public determine what range of wants shall be expressed. Furthermore, the alternative products that have not been introduced can be significantly specified—for example, the various backward-seating safety cars.

17) The sixth and last reason that I shall mention for dis-

trusting the statement by the corporations, "We only give the public what it wants," lies in the existence, or possible existence, of wants that consumers may have but can satisfy only by concerted action, not in the market. Historic cases in point are legislation for safety in factories or legislation against child labor (in which consumers have been joined by conscientious producers, unable to risk independent self-restraint). I do not think that the allowances economists make for third-party costs or neighborhood effects suffice for wants respecting concerted action. For such wants may range even beyond the examples just given, to wants regarding the overall structure and development of the economy. One might well think, because of the resources that it uses up, and the pressures that it creates, ranging from conspicuous consumption to the destruction of urban amenities, the automobile industry is much too large for the country to keep going, much less continue expanding. Rising to another sort of choice, between R, S, and T, N may express himself as wanting an alternative that would either entail not choosing z or preclude choosing between x, y, and z at all. So many people might, confronted with such a choice, want to have the automobile industry reduced in size; but such a choice could hardly be effective unless it were not a market choice, but a political one, offering the possibility of concerted action.

18) My six reasons are (I think) so obvious, once stated, and so compelling, that it might well be asked, how could any of them be overlooked? Now, if they are overlooked in some connections, they are of course frequently mentioned in others, though not perhaps all at once. All of them, I am sure, have often been mentioned by economists. Indeed, what is correct in the way that I have stated the reasons may depend on the teaching of economists; the mistakes are my own contribution. Yet I believe, for all the familiarity with which economists will greet the six reasons, one of the effects of economic teaching has been to divert attention from them, and so to open the way for general unthinking acquiescence in the corporations' contention, "We only give the public what it wants." The trouble

is that the core of economic teaching is the fascinating idea of the free, self-regulating market—which I join Professors Arrow and Boulding and Friedman in admiring as one of the most beautiful thoughts ever to occur to man. The six reasons are all distressing qualifications to the application of the market idea. I conjecture that economists are happier refining the idea by expressing it in elegant models than entangling themselves with the qualifications that must be entered to it. Moreover, the qualifications that economists do elaborate are mainly qualifications on the supply side of the market—monopoly in its various degrees. Finally, economists have backed steadily away from the criticism of wants, first, by renouncing Benthamite utility, which was both intersubjective and normative; next by discarding the notion of subjective satisfaction—the pleasure, however perverse, that the consumer might realize from the goods that he bought; and lately, I gather, by abandoning in favor of "revealed preference" even subjective expectations of satisfaction.

19) These tendencies on the part of economists, combined with the incautious simplifications of their students, lead to the statement, "We only give the public what it wants," frequently, I think, being taken at face value. Dare I suggest that sometimes even economists let it slip by without protesting? The wants at issue are identified with the wants *assumed* by the economist as expressed within his models, defining the demand side of the market. But one of the most important observations to make about wants actually observed is that they are not to be taken for granted; they require examination and invite criticism. What people want is even in their own eyes always contingent on the circumstances in which their expressions of wants have been called for.[18]

APPENDIX: CRITICISM OF "WANT"
(IN ONE SENSE)

THE VERB "want" subdivides into roughly two main senses, one that corresponds to "lack" or "need," and one to which "desire" has been made to correspond by a philosophical extension of ordinary usage. (The ordinary use of the verb "desire" is very limited by comparison.) [19] It is the second sense of "want"— "want" as "desire"—that is at issue in the present paper and in this appendix, not the sense in which a plant may want watering or a man want agility.

Given a choice between x, y, and z, N expresses himself as wanting z. He may say, "I want z." Then it follows that "N wants z" is true, if N has spoken sincerely and knows the language; and if "z" accurately designates what N intends it to designate (he has not, for example, misidentified x as "z"). The second proviso rules out possible grounds for saying, "N thought he wanted z, but he didn't." [20]

From N's truly wanting z, it does not follow that N's wanting z is beyond criticism, or that the only criticism that can be levied against it would raise doubts about N's sincerity. (N may say that he wants z because he thinks that it is expected of him, or because he wishes to please someone else by conforming to this other person's expectations.)

"N wants z" may be discredited by discrediting the expression "I want z" in N's own eyes. Then though "N wants z at time t" is not falsified (if the corresponding statement was made sincerely in the first person), N will himself regard his wanting z as having been mistaken, and will wish to revise it if there is still time to do so.

In the long run, N's structure of wants may be so modified that he would not on similar occasions with similar information, choosing between x, y, and z, any longer express himself as wanting z.

But the discrediting that is most important for my purposes occurs *in the short run,* by exposing one of the following sorts of limitations on the occasion on which N says, "I want z," and predictably, on like occasions with similar limitations, would say the same thing:

1) Misjudgment occurred: N did not know of the presence of all three alternatives, x, y, and z; or did not know certain

properties of x, y, or z; or failed to apply certain principles to which he himself subscribes, relevant to choices such as that between x, y, and z.

2) Alternatives u, v, w, etc. were not presented to N; if they had been, N would have expressed himself as wanting one of them rather than z. (Possible complication, x or y would have been chosen rather than z, violates independence of irrelevant alternatives.)

3) Another sort of choice, between alternatives R, S, and T might have been made, which would supersede the choice between x, y, and z, either by leaving none of them available for choice, or by entailing that N would not express himself as wanting z (unless confusion as in [1] occurred).

Furthermore, so far as N's expressing himself as wanting z has been determined by the persuasion of another agent, M, this other agent cannot argue that N's expression was spontaneous, and infer that he has nothing to answer for if N's expression is inconsistent with N's interests, needs, principles, or long-run desires, or is otherwise objectionable. (But being responsible in this sense must be distinguished from failing in an assigned responsibility to safeguard N against these disadvantages; such an assigned responsibility may not exist.)

The six reasons for distrusting "We only give the public what it wants" relate to the above outline in the following ways:

i) refers to the indeterminacy of the evidence, given the possibilities of (1), misjudgment;

ii) refers to the instilling of wants by the corporations, hence the failure of any inference hanging upon the expression of want being in that relationship spontaneous;

iii) refers to the subversion of values, the deliberate production of confusion, including confusion about applicability of principles (included under [1]);

iv) refers to the failure to support remedies for (1);

v) refers to failure in innovation to provide possibly preferable alternatives, hence to (2);

vi) refers to a particular way in which choices may be restructured, i.e., between market choices and concerted action, with the effect of (3).[21]

NOTES

1. Edward S. Mason, ed., Cambridge, Mass.: Harvard University Press, 1959. Kaysen's contribution was entitled "The Corporation: How Much Power? What Scope?"

2. F. M. Fisher, Z. Griliches, and C. Kaysen, "The Costs of Automobile Changes since 1949," abstract in *Papers and Proceedings of the 74th Annual Meeting of the American Economic Association, American Economic Review,* LII (May 1962), 259–61; article with same title, *Journal of Political Economy,* LXX (October 1962), 433–51.

3. Mason, pp. 102–03.

4. Mason, p. 100.

5. *Ibid.,* p. 101.

6. *Ibid.,* p. 93.

7. *Capitalism and Freedom* (Chicago: University of Chicago Press, 1962), pp. 133 ff.

8. Mason, p. 104.

9. *Ibid.,* p. 103.

10. See the *Harvard Business Review,* XLIII (March–April 1965), especially pp. 127–28.

11. In its main lines the treatment of excuses adumbrated in paragraphs 6 and 7 seems to accord with the main lines on which Austin approached the subject in his "A Plea for Excuses"—J. L. Austin, *Philosophical Papers* (Oxford: The Clarendon Press, 1961), pp. 123–52. Though not consciously anticipated, the accord may well reflect reading the article some time ago and attending Austin's seminar on excuses even earlier.

12. Against such views, see the remarks of Austin, in the second section (i.e., pp. 161–69) of his "Other Minds," *Proceedings of the Aristotelian Society, Supplementary Volume XX* (1946), 148–87.

13. Cf. the interesting discussion, with which I agree only in part, by F. E. Sparshott, in his *Enquiry into Goodness* (Toronto: University of Toronto Press, 1958), pp. 139–41.

14. In the articles on automobile-model changes (cited above),

Kaysen and his coauthors suggest, on the one hand, that consumers did not fully understand how much they were paying for annual model changes, estimated by the authors to cost as much as $5 billion a year. They say, on the other hand, that since new cars without the more significant changes continued to be available in the period under study, while consumers turned to buying models with the changes, "it is difficult not to conclude that car owners thought the costs worth incurring at the time" (abstract). The subject seems to me to be much more complex than the subject of safety features, and I do not want to get entangled with it; but I might point out, in the light of my own argument, that accepting wants as being accurately expressed at some given time does not make them incorrigible even in the view of the people expressing them. They may in fact be drastically corrigible, and deserve a very skeptical reception. Compare the concession of my paragraph 8—in which I concur with Kaysen and his coauthors—with the six countervailing reasons of paragraphs 12 to 17—which give the concession some much-needed skeptical ventilation.

15. "Je dirai qu'il y a aussi mauvaise foi si je choisis de déclarer que certaines valeurs existent avant moi; je suis en contradiction avec moi-meme si, à la fois, je les veux et déclare qu'elles s'imposent à moi." Jean-Paul Sartre, *L'Existentialisme est un humanisme* (Paris: Les Editions Nagel, 1946), p. 81.

16. Cf. remarks by Sir Geoffrey Vickers on "the metabolic criterion"—that a high rate of exchange with the environment is good *per se*—and "the criterion of material expansion"—that it is good for this rate to increase without limit, both of which he ascribes to Western culture, especially in North America. *The Undirected Society* (Toronto: University of Toronto Press, 1959), pp. 73–75.

17. Mason, p. 93.

18. This study was written while I enjoyed a research appointment in the Department of Philosophy, University of Pittsburgh, to work on the values-study project supported by the Carnegie Corporation of New York and IBM. My aims in the study will perhaps be fully appreciated only if I publicly recall that the comment was prepared for delivery a few weeks after *The New York Times Magazine* had published an attack on contemporary American philosophy for discussing trivial questions of language rather than offering religious inspiration (or some robust substitute for inspira-

tion). I set out to demonstrate that minute questions about language may quickly lead to important questions of social policy, and that answers to the one may crucially affect answers to the other.

19. A point brought home to me by Professor J. B. Schneewind and others, discussing a paper of mine on need and desire. Cf. Sparshott, *op. cit.*, p. 134; and recall the use of "desire" as a comprehensive term by Hobbes and in translations of Aristotle and Spinoza.

20. I am not quite sure that it rules out all possible grounds. The form of words, "N thought he wanted z, but he didn't," may be regarded as an alternative form of correction, available in ordinary language, for wants as initially expressed; and it may be that, though we have the option of using this form rather than the form of saying, "N was mistaken in what he wanted," if we do use it, we are somehow committed to inferring that "N wanted z" is untrue. But is there really a free option? If misidentification has occurred, we cannot in fact say that N was mistaken in what he wanted; he was instead mistaken in what he *said* he wanted. But if there was no misidentification, we can say "N was mistaken in what he wanted"; then has not the option of saying anything that implies he did not want z disappeared? The form of words, "N thought he wanted z, but he didn't," was brought up by Professor Hugh Chandler in a discussion at the University of Illinois, Urbana, of the paper on need and desire; and, independently, after reading the penultimate version of the present paper and appendix, by Professor Richard Gale. Gale finds in this alternative form of correction a suggestion that "I want z" is even more extensively corrigible, and hence open to skepticism, than I have allowed in a paper already very skeptical. Gale has also referred me to a short paper by Gertrude Ezorsky, "Wishing Won't—But Wanting Will," which appeared as Chapter 28 of an earlier New York University Institute symposium, edited by Sidney Hook, *Dimensions of Mind* (New York: New York University Press, 1960); and to the symposium paper by Stephen Toulmin, "Concept-Formation in Philosophy and Psychology," *ibid.*, Chapter 22. Miss Ezorsky makes a number of good points against Toulmin, but I think that her principle that wants (as contrasted with wishes) must be backed up by behavior does not allow sufficiently for a basic datum in economics—namely, the great variation in urgency of wants. N may want something, but want it so little that his behavior never shows it, apart from (at most) his so ex-

pressing himself. Is it then not a "real want"? Or only a wish? I think it may be a want, really and truly, but with vanishing marginal urgency attached to it. However, Miss Ezorsky's principle is satisfied in my model situation; given the choice between x, y, and z, N's expressing himself as wanting z is not only an indication of his wanting it, but constitutes as well behavior designed to obtain it.

21. After hearing the six reasons presented during the New York University discussions, Professor Friedman remarked that there would be no merit in any of them, except the sixth, were it not for monopoly. I would say in rebuttal that the fifth gains very significantly in force with increases in the degree of concentration in an industry; the first four, and the fifth to some degree, will continue to have force so long as there is extensive product differentiation, advertising designed to create tastes, and for these and other reasons a grossly imperfect distribution of information. Only, I believe, by diverting oneself with fantasies about an ideally perfect market can one fail to feel the weight of all six reasons.

C

The Role of the Corporation in American Life

ROBERT R. NATHAN
Washington, D.C.

THE CHANGING CHARACTER and improved functioning of our economy in recent decades have encompassed fundamental revolutions in economic policy. It is only within the context of such policy changes that we can evaluate the role of the corporation now and in the foreseeable future.

Perhaps most basic of all impacts on corporations has been the moderating influence on business risks resulting largely from government policies. When America's history of the twentieth century is recorded at some distant future date, the taming of the business cycle and the setting of minimum standards of welfare for all our people will quite sharply distinguish what occurred in the second third of the century from the whole of America's previous economic history.

Certainly the grave risks of recurring losses and of widespread bankruptcies among corporations have been greatly diminished with the end of major booms and busts. The short durations and mild severities of the recessions that have occurred since the end of World War II are generally viewed among economists as indicative of the likely pattern of future fluctuations in the economy. In fact, very few economists today expect that we will ever again suffer mass unemployment. Far more are confident that America's economic performance in the future will improve far beyond the relative stability that has been achieved in the past twenty years. Also, many expect that the rate of growth is likely to increase in the years ahead.

However, it should not be concluded that the change in

the business cycle has largely eliminated risk for the American corporation. The pace of technological change has increased risks in some geographic areas, for certain industries, for many types of capital equipment, and for specific commodities and services. Though risks seem to have lessened, profit levels and patterns seem to reveal greater rewards relative to investment than in the past, especially when we look at averages over years rather than set our sights only on previous transient boom periods.

The role of the corporation has been significantly altered and broadened by our changing attitudes toward worker and family welfare. The setting of minimum wages, the positive protection of the rights of workers to organize and bargain collectively, the introduction of a nationwide system of un-employment compensation, the adoption of social-security pension and welfare provisions, the recent medicare program, Federal aid to education, housing mortgage insurance pro-grams, and a host of other governmental efforts have by no means served to reduce the responsibility of corporations for the welfare of their employees.

Greater public activities in the welfare and personal se-curity areas have been paralleled by greater corporation activ-ity in these fields. Private arrangements by corporations for pensions, medical benefits, supplementary unemployment com-pensation, and the like are now commonplace. There is every indication that the scope of private welfare systems will be expanded. Also, corporations can be expected to contribute increasingly to nongovernmental educational, health, and other welfare programs.

The role of the corporation has also been materially changed by the growing scale of enterprise resulting from our rapidly expanding economy and the quickened pace of tech-nological progress. Concern over gaint corporations has been with us for a long time and properly will be the continuing subject of scrutiny and policy considerations. Of particular significance is the matter of competition and the related as-pects of restricted entry of new businesses, degree of concentration, mergers, administered pricing, and various other practices of a more or less monopolistic nature.

A distillation of past and recent actions and attitudes seems to indicate a declining militance against monopoly and a growing reliance on overall economic policies of the government to assure sustained prosperity and economic growth. From time to time there emerges a resurgence of actions to slow the pace of mergers or to prosecute antitrust suits. But, over time, there does seem to be less vigorous effort devoted to the fight against "corporate power" and more vigorous effort devoted to public policies designed to make the economy more productive and more equitable. Thus the threat of concentrated economic power among corporations might be as great or greater than ever, but the focus of public attention increasingly is on other economic problems.

The ongoing role of the corporation in American life will continue to depend on its dynamism and vigor in the processes of production relative to the dangers arising out of the emergence of more and more giant corporations. The stifling influences of monopolistic practices, administered pricing, and political power exerted by some of these giants might be brought under greater control by more specifically focused regulations. But the effectiveness of such regulations to date has hardly been an unqualified success. Yet they, in conjunction with overall expansive economic policies and particular policies and programs such as assistance to small business, have helped preserve the reasonably competitive nature of our enterprise system. This kind of mixture of general and specific approaches is likely to be the best hope for the future.

Recently some of my associates undertook a comprehensive study of the factors affecting the future of small business in the United States. This undertaking was started with real misgivings about the future of small business. After intensive research and careful study, the conclusion was reached that the quickening technological pace contributed more to opening the doors of entry for new enterprises than to bringing greater concentration in many sectors of the economy.

When it comes to certain problems such as price increases in periods of relatively full employment or near full employment, the nation properly becomes concerned about administered pricing, the lack of vigorous competition, discrimination in employment, barriers to labor mobility, and other obstacles to reaching low levels of unemployment without inflation. Special efforts will be needed to ferret out and attack administered pricing, but the approach will have to be custom-made rather than through broad and general policies.

On balance, it is difficult to arrive at any conclusion other than that our economy continues to be a vigorous and dynamic one in growth and innovation. There is a lack of evidence that the changing role of the American corporation in our changing economic environment has had an atrophying influence on competition. Abuses are ever present and imminent, but the benefits of corporations still far outweigh the costs. The challenge is always that of enlarging the benefits and reducing the costs.

A continuing fear arises out of the intensive efforts of corporation executives to influence public policies that have significant impacts on the performance and profitability of their corporations. The solution is certainly not to prevent corporate management from exerting its influence in appropriate areas, but rather one of assuring that the tremendous economic power of huge corporations will not be used by hired management or even by a few large shareholders to dictate or unduly influence important political decisions.

Executives of corporations may generally de depended upon to serve the economic interests of the shareholders in managing the business activities of the corporation. But when it comes to broader policy measures these executives cannot be equally relied upon to reflect accurately the diverse interests of the shareholders as shareholders or as citizens. Top officers of large corporations do, however, speak out on wide ranges of issues in a manner to convey the impression that all the shareholders and all the members of the management team are unanimously in support of their views. No one can spend

many years in Washington without being aware of the powerful influence of corporations in the formulation and implementation of economic policy. Individual entrepreneurs and
business partners also seek to influence public policies, but
their individual or aggregate power is far different from that of
larger corporations.

No government policy on tariffs is ever established without a monumental struggle in which the interests of corporations are strongly asserted. It certainly is necessary and
desirable to take into account the impact of tariff policies on
industries and companies. Diverse interests ought to be heard
and fully understood. But the efforts of large corporations and
trade associations that they dominate do not stop with eluci-
dation. The pressure associated with their financial power is
more often than not so great that they are successful in secur-
ing special interest legislation.

Of course, all policy is the product of conflicting interests
being reconciled in one manner or another. The role of unions
in our society is also powerful and fruitful. They, too, can use
their power for good or bad. There are exceptions, but union
leaders probably reflect the varied views of their members
more than corporation executives reflect the divergent attitudes of shareholders. Sometimes, as in tariff matters, labor
and management get together in support of principles that
are in their immediate interest and contrary to the public
interest. Even when it comes to seeking price stability the
self-interest of different segments of our society serves to generate inflationary pressures far more than to support stabiliza-
tion policies and programs.

We cannot and should not seek to render corporations
and their executives innocuous in the policy arena. Rather we
should seek both to maximize the democratic process within
corporations so that shareholders are as fully represented as
possible and also to set rules of the game so as to avoid abuses
and minimize excessive power exertion.

Inevitably, the government will need to play a larger
and larger role in our economic life and this can be done with-

out diminishing the strength of the competitive free enterprise economy. The tussle will be one of balancing the degree of public participation and regulation with the continuation of incentives and responsibilities for corporations and other economic entities to play their full role in expanding our production and increasing our efficiency.

There are endless internal determinations that corporation executives must and do make that affect the well-being of the total economy. For instance, there continues to be a growing need for better training and upgrading of our less skilled workers. Much of this must be on-the-job training. There must be less discrimination in hiring on the basis of race, age, and sex. We require more and more internal policy decisions by corporate executives compatible with public interests. There continue to be problems of health standards and safety standards and for quality control for goods and services, fair trade practices, pure air and water conservation, and other functions that affect the public welfare and in which corporate executives will be influential, by design or by default.

Business corporations are and properly should be motivated by the desire to maximize profits. Dollars cannot be expected to possess philanthropic motivations. Corporations cannot be and should not be relied upon as channels for altruistic motivations. On the other hand, as our affluence grows and as our economic life becomes more complex and interdependent, standards of conduct and ethical practices in corporations will need to be heightened. Some progress will be achieved through public policies and public regulation, but more will have to be achieved through the exercise of restraints and positive efforts by corporate executives both to take some account of public interest and to recognize that longer-term corporation interest may be more rewarding profit-wise than total emphasis on short-term rewards.

1

Basic Values and Economic Policy

SIDNEY HOOK
New York University

ONE OF the curious aspects of the discussion of the papers presented at the Institute sessions was the failure to mention and adequately consider what specific human values were to be taken as guides to desirable programs of economic change, and what the difficulties were of realizing such values under the existing economic system. Some of the participants, in their peripheral observations on values, implied that they were shared in common (all of us wanted the same "ultimate" things) and that the only relevant question was whether specific economic policies advocated to further them did in fact lead to the anticipated consequences. Combined with the view also expressed in the discussion that all competent, i.e., scientific, economists agreed on purely economic issues of importance, the disagreement among them on how to maximize human welfare is hard to understand. After all, the testimony of economists in the past on what is sound economic policy, although not so discordant as that of psychiatrists on how to achieve sound mental health, has certainly not been one of near uniformity.

In the past, questions about the desirability of one or another economic proposal have often been approached with antecedent commitments to the validity of the market economy. Anything that involved interference with the free market, except for purposes of defense and some areas of international trade, was considered suspect, presumptively nonrational. This judgment was often made prior to an independent showing that the proposal in question, in the light of the economic possibilities, could not achieve its ends, or that if economically feasible, its consequences would be morally worse than the evils it aimed at removing.

If human values are defined in terms merely of choice, the strength of which is quantitatively measured by price, then to assert that the equilibrium established in the uncontrolled market maximizes human welfare is to utter a stupendous tautology. One must reflect on the consequences of the equilibrium achieved—requiring so to speak a second-order judgment—in order to determine whether they adequately fulfill, in the light of the possible alternatives, whatever human needs we reflectively conclude are essential to a good life in a good society. The choices we make on a first-order level are not ultimate data. They have a history behind them that depends on the way the market economy has functioned in the past. A whole library of social criticism has called attention to the manifold ways—subtle and blatant—in which first-order choices have been influenced by the operation of the market. A judgment about the way in which the resources of a society *should* be organized cannot be rationally evaluated by criteria that presuppose antecedent acceptance of the market system.

Such judgments are not always implicit but sometimes explicit. For example, Professor George Stigler, in an interesting and amusing essay on "The Politics of Political Economists," argues that most professional economists tend to be politically conservative not because of external pressures or extrinsic reasons, but in virtue of the rules of rationality imposed by their subject matter. He defines a conservative in economic matters "as a person who wishes most economic activity to be conducted by private enterprise, and who believes that abuses of private power will usually be checked, and incitements to efficiency and progress usually provided the forces of competition." [1] (A political conservative today apparently is yesterday's economic liberal!) He asserts this, insisting at the same time that most economists are interested in social reform, and more aware than noneconomists of the deficiency of existing economic institutions. The main reason for the economist's conservatism, he contends, is his scientific training. Presumably this training has shown him that "the problems of *all* economic systems" can be solved by "the methods by which a price system solves these problems." [2] This system is, so to speak, the paradigm of rational behavior. But such a conception of rationality obviously cannot enable one to make a rational choice between systems in which prices and the distribution of goods and services are left to the operation of a free market and one in which they are controlled, or between systems in which the extent and nature of the controls are greatly varied. Presumably choices or decisions concerning the scope and sway of this criterion of rationality itself can have only the allegedly "subjective" warrant of ultimate judgments of value.

We do not have to settle questions of "ultimate" value to make warranted judgments about the validity of economic policies if they are related to economic *problems* and to the penultimate values that in any historic period constitute the norms of human welfare. Economic policies, and even an economic system as a whole, can be evaluated in terms of their consequences for the quality and significance of human life in the same manner as we evaluate modifications in the marriage system, or political system, or challenges to the systems entire. That something—a mechanism, a machine, a system—does *not* work may constitute a powerful reason against perpetuating it; the fact that it does work is, by itself, not a sufficient reason for perpetuating it. We must know what it works *for*, what ends-in-view are to be realized.

I understand by a welfare state or society one whose economic institutions and practices are responsively and responsibly oriented to the production and equitable distribution of the goods and services necessary to realize the cluster of values that are the objects of reflective choice, and constitute our synoptic conception of the good life. The explicit premise of some defenders of the open market or free-enterprise system is that it provides the best chance of accomplishing or approaching this goal without risking the evils of tyranny and permanent terror. Little effort is made to show with respect to specific values that this is empirically true. The upholders of the welfare state or society have not found it difficult to document the extent to which it is untrue not only in the relatively free enterprise systems of the past but in the still rudimentary welfare societies of the present.

The very efforts of American corporations to prove that their profits depend upon their service to the community, that production for profit is impossible except as it is production for use, betrays uneasiness. There is awareness that within the memory perspective of our generation too many consequences of the market economy have resulted in widespread human misery rather than human welfare. Such consequences cannot be laid at the door of state intervention in the economy, for most of these interventions took place only after these evils developed.

What I wish to do briefly is to state four basic values that seem to me central to the present conception of a welfare society, and to raise the question whether their realization can be better furthered by an economic system in which the principles or practices of the free market prevail or one in which there is a variety of social controls, not excluding social ownership of certain strategic industries. I select these four values— material values rather than formal values like justice or equality—not only because we can assume antecedent agreement on their validity independently of our initial commitment to one set of economic arrangement or another but because they are easier to identify and define.

The first and most obvious is the preservation of life. On this all men in modern society seem to agree whatever their other differences, at least to the extent of holding that *all* members of the community have a right to the protection of life against physical violence—a right valid against anyone. And this independently of their capacity to pay for such protection.[3] Wealth enables an individual to hire additional protection, but this does not affect the responsibility of the community for the physical safety of all its members. It is true that this protection sometimes breaks down because of the unavailability of resources in personnel and material. But no one contests the reasonableness of utilizing existing resources of police protection for all members of the community on a non-preferential basis, as a general rule, i.e., the degree of protection is to be commensurate with the degree of danger.

On the same grounds I believe a persuasive case can be made for extending the existing right of protection against human agents who threaten men's existence to the right of protection against the natural, nonhuman agents that threaten their health and ultimately their life. There are some who assert that adequate medical protection should be a function of a person's ability to pay. But they usually modify their position when asked whether they believed that the children of poor families have less right to protection against crippling diseases than the children of the well-to-do, especially where the remedies have been discovered in consequence of community-financed research. Actually, many of our social practices are already based on a recognition of this principle. We take it for granted that all available resources of the community will be commandeered to rescue a man in distress at sea or when he is the victim of a natural catastrophe.

Whether a person is receiving adequate medical care is not a matter of subjective opinion but of scientifically grounded judgment. And as I read the evidence that has been adduced, the medical profession itself is convinced that, by and large, in the light of the technological possibilities of modern medicine, the people of the United States on the whole are not receiving adequate comprehensive medical care. This shows up most sharply in surveys of groups that have not had the benefit of diagnostic and preventive services.

It seems to me a natural extension of the argument to make the provision for decent housing, the elimination of slums, and the reconstruction of our cities, the primary responsibility of the community. The effect of substandard housing and metropolitan slum conditions on the physical and mental health of their denizens may be difficult to assess directly but there are indirect quantitative indices of the toll they take. A free-market economy may maximize rationality of economic behavior but the equilibriums it establishes cannot be relied upon to maximize human health in its major dimensions, for the "price" placed upon proper medical treatment reflects the intensity of one's choice not the magnitude of one's needs. The choice made by a head of the family between alternative uses of the family income may bear no relation to the objective medical and dental needs of the children. Whatever makes for better health, makes for better human welfare. An uncontrolled market economy can at best establish only how important those who have money to spend consider their health, and that of their family, to be with respect to other uses of their money. It does not make medical facilities available to those who need it. Here is one sector of the economy, an ever widening one as the results of scientific research accumulate, in which the responsibility for initiating programs, founding new medical schools, introducing the elaborate network of facilities required for diagnostic and preventive medicine, removing slums and reconstructing our cities must rest with Federal and local state authorities working in coordination with each other.

The second basic value is vocation or calling. Professional economists are themselves in disagreement concerning the extent to which the technological revolution is leading in erosion of job opportunities, and the rate at which the process of displacement is going on. I do not know enough to make a well-founded judgment on the phenomenon, but there does seem to be considerable evidence that, in a manner which neither Marx, nor Veblen, nor Dewey anticipated, large numbers of workers, without any decline in total productivity, have lost their vocational viability without being prepared for the performance of more skillful tasks or for the creative use of their leisure. I have argued elsewhere [4] that the difference between work or toil and vocation or calling is that the latter can serve as a center around which to organize one's experience. To be sure, it is not the only center, for love and the family provide their own integrating bonds. Leaving this aside for the moment, it is not an exaggeration to say that without a vocation or calling very few human beings can achieve a sense that they are living a significant life, one of abiding satisfactions.

Among the perennial tasks of education is preparing human beings for vocations in which they can find adequate personal fulfillment. But this is not enough. The community must also accept the responsibility for making vocations accessible to those qualified to fill them. This calls for vast outlays for a type of education that will individualize instruction in order to give each child an opportunity to develop to his farthest intellectual and emotional reach. It calls for a social and economic policy that will not subordinate individuals to the needs of production so much as subordinate production to the needs of the individual.

This approach to education, although gradual, can have a profound, even revolutionary, effect upon society. It is implied in John Dewey's philosophy of education. Were we to lay down, as he suggests, as the educational guide lines for the community that "it must want for all its children what the best and wisest parent wants for his own child," it would open up a perspective of vast social transformation.

It may very well be true that in the future the computer revolution, the growth of automation, and the harnessing of nuclear energy for peaceful purposes will, by making obsolescent almost all but managerial skills, undercut Dewey's noble ideal of eliminating the dualism between "earning one's living" and "living one's life." Even so this would not reduce the importance or need for educational reconstruction—not only of the physical educational plant and of the neighboring environment but of the curricular school programs. The true vocation for the vast majority of men would then become active citizenship.

On either option of development the responsibility of the community is heavy. It cannot be fulfilled without far more extensive and systematic planning of the economy than has hitherto been accepted. Whether this planning is exercised through indirect controls or through shifts in the form of ownership is not important. It need not abandon all the mechanisms of a market economy. Public agencies must remain on the alert to intervene vigorously in behalf of the scheme of central priorities required to expand and improve the educational process.

The third basic value is responsibility or shared power in determining the conditions, tenure, and rewards of employment so long as technological unemployment has not made employment an anachronism. It seems banal to say it, but despite countervailing forces and the shift of effective control from owners to managers, property is still power, and property in the means of production gives power over the lives of those dependent upon their use. This power, of course, has been limited by public law and trade-union strength; but the ultimate decision to continue in production or shut down, to expand or contract operations, to move to another region or stay put rests largely with those who own, not those who work. Anyone who has observed the effect of a shutdown of a large plant on a town economically dependent upon it knows what hardship, dislocations, and even tragedy may result. To be sure, even if the ownership were social, hard economic decisions may produce distress. When the English coal mines were socialized, the decision to shut down those that were unprofitable led to similar hardships. But there are two key differences. In the latter case, those who make these decisions are answerable to some kind of public control that rests on democratic authority. Secondly, the decision in such cases is not necessarily guided by the sole criterion of production efficiency. There are other justifying considerations that may override the issue of profitability. But those who make the crucial decisions in the gigantic economic enterprises that function like private collectivisms are not responsible to those affected by their decisions in anything like the same way as those who make political decisions in a democracy. Some of these economic decisions have consequences as fateful for the public weal or woe as some political decisions. And when they are made, the Law and the Prophets are considerations of profit.

Even at the cost of some economic efficiency, it would be desirable to introduce some methods, especially in large industrial enterprises, private and public, that would liberate workers from their fear of job insecurity, of managerial tyranny and arbitrariness, and consequent sense of frustration. Through processes of consultation, they could get a sense of participating in the large decisions that affect their lives and destinies.

The fourth basic value is best expressed in an awkward phrase, "beautifying the natural and social environment." What Churchill said about our public buildings—"We shape our buildings, and then they shape us"—is true for our neighborhoods, our cities, our roads, our countryside. We can afford to do much more than we have done. What should be done cannot be left to the vagaries of private philanthropy, which in any case cannot undo the ugliness that is the by-product of an uncontrolled market economy. In times of scarcity we may have to choose between bread and roses. But where the means exist to enjoy both, in a market economy there is no provision for roses in public places except through the uncertain expressions of private philanthropy. Those who command wealth go to great lengths to control the areas in which they live from the strident and ugly intrusions of communal activity. Yet the source of their wealth may be derived from enterprises that have transformed large sections of our cities and towns, and some of our most wondrous natural landscapes, into esthetic abominations.

These four values involve each other. The means by which any one of them can be properly realized will further the realization of the others. Political economy, as I understand it, is the art of devising economic policies to further these and any other human values that recommend themselves to us after reflection. There is nothing in the proposal to redirect and reconstruct our economic system in order to give institutional embodiment to these values that threatens the preservation of democratic society.

Let the professional economist tell us what the costs are of allocating resources to implement this or that program. The order of our wants still remains a political and basically ethical question. This means that we cannot accept the choices that are reflected in the uncontrolled market economy as authoritative of what we really want. Nor is it guaranteed that when the political decision is made, it will favor these values rather than others. Whether the community accepts or rejects them, depends upon the outcome of the political education that all groups provide. So long as the processes of political decision remain free, the Cassandra-like warnings that the decline of a free-enterprise system necessarily spells the end of an open society are unwarranted.

NOTES

1. *Quarterly Journal of Economics,* LXXIII (November 1959), 524.

2. *Loc. cit.,* p. 528.

3. Cf. R. Brandt, *Ethical Theory,* New York, 1959, p. 450. I have developed this argument at length in the *Proceedings of the Group Health Symposium* reprinted in the "Health Care Issues of the 1960's," Group Health Insurance, N. Y. (1963), pp. 179–99.

4. S. Hook, *Education for Modern Man,* 2nd ed., New York, 1963, *passim.*

2

The Role of the Corporation in American Life

HENRY C. WALLICH
Yale University

AT A MEETING convened to study the role of the corporation in American life, it may not be a welcome contribution to say that this role seems to have been slight. A broad view of the evidence suggests, however, that while the rise of the corporation has run parallel to major changes in American life, the corporation has not been the cause.

PER CAPITA INCOME

The great change in American life has been the rise in per capita income. This has determined standards as well as patterns of living, including the great shift from rural to urban life. These changes cannot be visualized as taking place in the absence of growing technology and a growing capital stock. They can quite well be visualized, however, in the absence of the corporate form of business. It is quite conceivable, for instance, that businesses might have become very large without going public—witness the Ford Motor Company. In some countries now enjoying rapid economic growth family concerns are still the rule, e.g., in Latin America. The public corporation is a form of organization almost certainly superior to the family firm but it is not essential to economic development.

Alternatively, the same phenomena of capital accumulation, growth of technology and large-scale production can occur under conditions of government ownership. What is unlikely is that they should occur in an economy consisting exclusively of very small units.

STABILITY OF GROWTH

The rate of growth of productivity, and hence of per capita income, has been extraordinarily stable in the United States. For a good part of the nineteenth century gains in output per capita averaged (disregarding business cycles) a little below 2 percent per year. During the twentieth century and particularly since World War II they seem to have moved a little above 2 percent. These hundred years of productivity gains span the life of the industrial corporation. The stability of the productivity trend shows that the corporation's impact on economic growth has been slight at best.

The same argument applies to the ratio of gross savings to the gross national product. It has been remarkably stable, at full employment levels, over many decades. During this period, the corporation with its very large gross savings (depreciation plus retained profits) has become an important factor in the total supply of savings. Yet the savings rate has not changed. I would reject the interpretation that the rise of the corporation has accidentally offset a declining tendency in personal saving. Much more likely, some broader propensity has led Americans as consumers and producers to hold the national savings rate constant regardless of the channels through which savings flow.

LIVING HABITS

The belief that the corporation has significantly shaped our living habits is an illusion, analogous to the European illusion that Europe is being "Americanized." All that the United States has experienced, and Europe after it, are the manifestations of rising per capita income. At high per capita income, food consumption represents a small part of expenditure. Hence the farm sector shrinks relatively and the economy becomes largely urban. The manifestations of urban life, including the rise of services, are largely technologically determined, as even the Communist countries are now discovering.

If the corporation has not greatly influenced per capita income, it cannot have greatly influenced the principal aspects of American living habits. Some minor aspects no doubt have been affected. First, the corporation may have helped to broaden the ownership of the capital stock. Nevertheless, with only some 20 million stockholders we are still very far from "Peoples' Capitalism." Small-scale capitalism manifested by over 3 million farms and about 5 million business firms, the vast majority of them owner-operated, seems a more important indicator of moderately widespread distribution of ownership than holdings of corporate stock in often minute amounts.

Second, corporate advertising has influenced consumer behavior. Probably, however, this influence has been greatly exaggerated. In evidence may be cited the experience of countries where owing to import difficulties sellers find it useless to advertise their small supply of automobiles and other consumer durables. The demand for these goods is nevertheless very strong, as indicated by the high premium that, in countries like Argentina and Brazil, raises used Chevrolets to the price of new Cadillacs in the U.S. Furthermore, advertising is an activity not reserved to the corporation. Large family firms would find it equally profitable.

EVIDENCE FROM TAX SHIFTING

The corporate income tax has become a major source of government revenues in the U.S., 27.3 percent of budget and 21.3 percent of the total revenues of the Federal Government being derived from this tax in fiscal year 1965. With respect to this great revenue, it is a peculiar fact that economists have been unable to reach reliable conclusions as to who pays it— the stockholder who may have to absorb it, the consumer to whom it might be shifted forward in terms of higher prices, or the worker to whom it might be shifted backwards in terms of lower wages. Such as it is, the evidence suggests that corporate owners are more successful in shifting the tax in the long run than in the short run. Long-run shifting implies a shrinkage of the corporate sector and of corporate output relative to the unincorporated sector and output. This would be a phenomenon of some economic, social, and political importance. That on matters of such potential magnitude we possess so little knowledge strongly suggests that the phenomena that supposedly would occasion them, the corporation and its behavior, are not of great importance.

THE CORPORATION AND COMPETITION

The rise of large firms may have reduced competition, in the sense that competition conceivably could be much more nearly perfect if the vacuum into which corporations expanded had instead been filled by small units. Nevertheless, the outcome depends quite strongly on legislation and social practices governing competition. In many European countries, for instance, a particular industry may contain a larger number of firms, many of them family owned. Because of the weakness or absence of antitrust legislation, however, competition has frequently been restrained by agreement among these smaller firms. In the end result, the probably more concentrated industries of America may be more competitive than their European counterparts.

POLITICAL STRUCTURE

The corporation is a political instrument of the wealthy, much as the labor union is a political instrument of the lower income groups. In contrast to the labor union, the corporation nevertheless seems to have influenced the balance of power in the U.S. very little. The upper income groups were politically powerful before and after the rise of the corporation. They lost a good deal of this power when the labor union came into its own in the 1930's.

SOCIAL RESPONSIBILITY

An important role may be ahead for the corporation as a center of social responsibility. Some managements view themselves as arbitrating the respective interests of owners, workers, and consumers. Because of the separation of ownership and control in large corporations, these "managerial" corporations seem more susceptible to social and political pressures than are family firms. Nevertheless, it can reasonably be argued that in the absence of public corporations the owners of large family firms, following the tradition of *noblesse oblige,* would assume similar responsibilities. The transfer to foundations of many great fortunes suggests such a propensity on the part of some of the most successful industrialists. It is not evident, therefore, that up till now the corporate form has greatly altered the willingness of the owners and controllers of property to accept social responsibility.

CONTINUITY

As contrasted with family firms, corporations offer the possibility of greater continuity. Up till now this potential has not been realized very fully. Many once great corporations have declined owing to competition or shifting demand. Nevertheless, corporate management does seem to aim increasingly at continuity and can do so more successfully than a family firm. In this respect, the future may see a stable role for corporations with a flexible product range, such as General Electric and General Motors, which seems difficult to achieve for family firms and even for corporations dependent upon products of possibly temporary usefulness such as steel or coal.

If this view is meaningful, the corporation's chief contribution to American life may still lie ahead.

Index